Epitaph for American Labor

How Union Leaders Lost Touch with America

Max Green

The AEI Press

Publisher for the American Enterprise Institute
WASHINGTON, D.C.

1996

Available in the United States from the AEI Press, c/o Publisher Resources Inc., 1224 Heil Quaker Blvd., P.O. Box 7001, La Vergne, TN 37086-7001. Distributed outside the United States by arrangement with Eurospan, 3 Henrietta Street, London WC2E 8LU England.

Library of Congress Cataloging-in-Publication Data

Green, Max.
    Epitaph for American labor : how union leaders lost touch with America / Max Green.
        p.   cm.
    Includes bibliographical references and index.
    ISBN 0-8447-3996-0 (cloth : alk. paper). — ISBN 0-8447-3997-9 (paper : alk. paper)
    1. Trade-unions—United States—Political activity.   2. Labor movement—United States.   3. Radicalism—United States.   4. Right and left (Political science)   I. Title.
HD6510.G74   1996
322'.2'0973—dc20   96-17916
                                                                          CIP

THE AEI PRESS
Publisher for the American Enterprise Institute
1150 17th Street, N.W., Washington, D.C. 20036

Printed in the United States of America

In memory of my father and mother, Sol and Clara Green, and of my sister, Marge Green Pausman

Contents

Foreword

For any American coming of age in the 1940s, 1950s, and 1960s, it was taken for granted that one major institution in any decent society was organized labor. Just as you had business corporations and government agencies, charitable institutions and churches, so you had labor unions: America would not have seemed like America without them. To be sure, unions as major national institutions were relatively new, the product of the 1930s; yet quickly they sunk deep roots in American soil. Big government, big business, and big labor—sometimes adversaries, but ultimately working in tandem— helped Americans recover from the depression, win World War II, and build the prosperous postwar economy which its children would come to take for granted. Organized labor could plausibly claim to have played a significant role in all these happy and, if one can recover the expectations of Americans who lived through these times, by no means inevitable events. Organized labor was as American as apple pie.

Not so today. For Americans coming of age in the 1980s and 1990s, it is hard to imagine how large organized labor bulked in American society three and four decades ago. By the mid-1950s, more than one in three private-sector workers were union members. Unions represented workers in the most visible manufacturing industries—autos, steel, coal—and their negotiations with management made national headlines and were assumed to set wage levels for the entire economy. It was true that some industries—textiles— were mostly not organized by unions and that the union movement had made little headway in the South or in the sparsely populated states of the Great Plains and the Rocky Mountains. But it was assumed that, in time, these backward areas would follow the pattern of those Northeastern and Midwestern states which for more than a century had led the growth of the American economy. Unionization was the norm in most places and would become the norm everywhere.

Instead, the union movement has come close to disappearing. It is not the only big institution to have encountered trouble over the past thirty years. Big government is now less respected than disdained—to the point where in 1996 a Democratic president felt compelled to say, "The era of big government is over." Big business no longer has the command over markets John Kenneth Galbraith thought it had: each of the Big Three auto companies has come close to bankruptcy, while behemoths like IBM have been shunted aside by recent startups like Microsoft. But big labor has declined the most. By the mid-1990s, not much more than 10 percent of private-sector workers were union members, and about half of union members were government employees—in an antigovernment era. Statistically, organized labor is no larger a part of American society than it was a century ago, in the years after Samuel Gompers created the AFL. Spiritually, it is arguably worse off, with far less reason to believe it is the wave of the future.

It is the contention of Max Green that the decline of organized labor is a good thing, partly because the union movement has abandoned the pro-American ideals of Samuel Gompers, but partly, and even more importantly, because Gompers's enterprise was fundamentally flawed, based on a misunderstanding of economics. Gompers oriented the American labor movement against socialism at home (he thought politicians would be no more proworker than capitalists) and communism abroad (he saw that free institutions could not survive under totalitarianism). Today, the election of John Sweeney as president of the AFL-CIO completes a move left, toward support of an ever-bigger public sector at home and of disengagement from the world beyond.

Remaining is a distaste for economic competition and free markets. Gompers welcomed the formation of trusts and relished bargaining with monopolistic employers: he realized they would not have market incentives to hold down wages. Sweeney prefers to deal with the ultimate in monopolistic employers, the government, which can send people to jail if they do not hand over their money. The problem is that the trusts' monopolies did not prove eternal (U.S. Steel's market share plummeted as soon as it was founded) and big government cannot forever survive voters' determination to make it smaller. Sooner or later, unless there is a war or an economic collapse like that of the 1930s, markets rule.

What remains to be said in organized labor's behalf is that unions, like the big city political machines they replaced in the Democratic Party, served a constructive function in a democratic society. At their best, they were mediating institutions, cushioning the effects of the market on individuals and channeling the potential for violence of the huge urban masses. For, of course, there is an implied violence in unions' classic tactics: picket lines, strikes, boycotts are all intended to intimidate with threats of physical force, only partly modulated by legal rules forbidding violent acts. But instead of the French Revolution or the Bolshevik coup d'etat, America had the Ludlow Massacre and sitdown strikes. Labor unions, like political machines and churches, were voluntary associations providing services and fellowship, discipline and guidance for urban masses which might otherwise have become revolutionary mobs. They fostered good habits and raised expectations. "The labor movement," Green quotes Walter Reuther as boasting, "is developing a whole new middle class."

In retrospect, there was nothing inevitable about the American labor movement. Its huge size from the 1930s to the 1970s, the vast influence it had over the economy and even on foreign policy: these were as much the result of accidents of history—happy accidents, many would still say today—and the extraordinary efforts of specific individuals as of any economic trend or historical necessity. More typical, growing more naturally out of the soil of the society, is organized labor today, with union representation primarily with monopoly employers, which in practice increasingly means only governments. Over the past thirty years, market economics has seen a great resurgence, in the academy and in the political arena. This has put at grave disadvantage the American labor movement, which since Gompers has never believed in market economics. Those who would disagree with Max Green's conclusion that it is time write an epitaph for American organized labor need to show a reason to believe that unions will learn to embrace markets or that general belief in market economics will wane.

Michael Barone
Senior writer, *U.S. News & World Report*

Acknowledgments

My first thanks go to Arch Puddington, my nearly lifelong friend, with whom I discussed on more than one occasion every idea that appears in these pages. Of course, he should not be blamed for the final outcome.

I am also thankful to those who read the manuscript in earlier stages and offered good suggestions for improvements and much needed encouragement. They include Linda Chavez, Naomi Munson, Rachel Abrams, and Myron Lieberman.

I received generous financial support from the Bradley and Smith Richardson Foundations, for which I am very grateful. Irving Kristol, who has been a help in many ways, secured funding to finish the book.

Finally, I want to express my appreciation to the American Enterprise Institute for publishing this book. Particular thanks are due to Chris DeMuth, AEI's president, and to Ann Petty, who did the final editing.

1
Introduction

No institution in America has changed more since the late 1960s than the American labor movement. From its founding in 1884, supporters and detractors alike noted how distinctively American the movement was. In contrast to its counterparts in Western Europe, the American movement rejected socialism and explicitly accepted the private enterprise system, seeking to improve the living and working conditions of workers, not through political change, but rather by collective bargaining. That concept was the core of the decidedly nonrevolutionary, indeed antirevolutionary, trade unionism that it practiced and preached. To establish its bona fides as a truly American institution, the union movement studiously rejected not only political radicalism but cultural radicalism as well. The movement claimed to embody American values as much as, if not more than, any other institution in the country.

Finally, but certainly not least important in its own eyes and those of its many critics, the labor movement counted itself among the staunchest supporters of America's foreign policy from the advent of World War I through the long decades of the cold war. A strong case can be made that it was the most consistently anti-Communist institution in the country.

As recently as twenty-five years ago, those who called themselves traditional liberals (as against New Politics liberals) saw organized labor as perhaps the only hope for resisting the onslaught

1

of the Left against the nation's economic system, social culture, and foreign policy. Leaders of the Left agreed: the New Left and then the McGovernite wing of the Democratic Party took aim at the union movement, regularly denouncing labor leaders as defenders of America's capitalist, racist, and imperialist establishment.

But, to the surprise of supporters and critics, labor put up little resistance to the Left. For all intents and purposes, the movement capitulated to it in less than a decade; by the early 1980s, labor had changed sides. Increasingly disaffected from American capitalism, it relinquished any serious claim to a distinctive character and for the first time became an integral part of the American Left. Organized labor came to mirror the Left in its criticism of capitalism; in its commitment to statist economic policies; in its abandonment of the traditional American value of individualism in favor of the race- and gender-based policies of the civil rights, feminist, and gay rights movements; and in its strong penchant for challenging the pursuit of U.S. interests abroad, particularly but not exclusively its opposition to the now bipartisan policy of promoting free market economies through free trade and other means.

Although the fundamental transformation was nearly complete by the mid-1980s, few observers on either the Left or the Right seemed to notice, primarily because labor was never captured by the Left. Ironically, the transformation was presided over, first, by George Meany, the *bête noire* of the Left in the 1960s, and, then, by Lane Kirkland, the candidate of labor's right-wing and Meany's chosen successor. The transformation during the Meany-Kirkland years was so total that it no longer makes any sense to speak of left and right wings of the labor movement. Whatever slight differences remain are fast disappearing. Unions such as the International Ladies Garment Workers Union and the United Steelworkers, which not so long ago were denounced for their "right-wing" politics, are now merging with unions that represented the Left (the Amalgamated Clothing Workers and the United Automobile Workers, respectively).

Another indicator of the new situation was the 1995 contest for the presidency of the American Federation of Labor–Congress of Industrial Organizations (AFL-CIO). Kirkland had been forced to resign because he seemed to have no idea how to stem the decline of the labor movement. The candidates were Thomas Donahue, who had served as an aide to George Meany and then as Kirkland's secretary-treasurer, and John Sweeney, a former Donahue protégé who had become president of the Service Employees International Union. Although Donahue was the candidate of the right wing of the AFL-CIO, and Sweeney of its Left, no discernible ideology differentiated between the two, as Donahue himself indicated on National Public Radio in September 1995: "We need to be—just as John [Sweeney] has said—the force that drives the Democratic Party to the left." Sweeney won the election and has perhaps moved the direction of the organization a degree or two to the left. But then so would have Donahue. The organization had been drifting, sometimes lurching, left for more than two decades and under the leadership of either would have continued moving in that direction.

Early Inclinations

A close reading of American labor's history reveals that the potential for a leftward turn had been there from the start. The founders of the American Federation of Labor (AFL), including its first president, Samuel Gompers (1850–1924), understood the tenets of socialism; the young Gompers, for instance, devoted much of his free time from his job in a cigar factory to learning German so that he could read Marx in the original. Others may have belonged to socialist organizations. But Gompers and his colleagues prided themselves on being what one of Gompers's mentors called practical men rather than ideologues.

The goal of these practical men was to build a trade union movement in a country that lacked what every socialist movement of the time took for granted: a distinct, self-conscious, and relatively united working class. The AFL thus opted for what Gompers and his associates called "trade unionism pure and simple," the collective-bargaining strategy on which workers of every political stripe could agree.

According to Gompers, the unions merited the support, not merely from workers, but from the great mass of Americans. By raising the wages of the workers they represented, unions served the larger purpose of preventing an otherwise inevitable Marxist revolution as capitalists in their pursuit of profit drove down wages to the point where workers could not buy the products they produced.

But Gompers was not so naive as to believe that sweet reason would convince capitalists that trade unions were in the country's best interest. Unions would have to organize and battle the owners of industry for ever-higher wages. For this collective-bargaining strategy to succeed, trade unions would have to take wages out of competition by organizing virtually every firm in an industry. Otherwise, nonunionized producers would undercut unionized competitors whose labor costs were higher. Accordingly, the trade unions succeeded first where an industry was limited to a single geographical area and, conversely, failed for decades to organize national industries.

By Gompers's reckoning, union prospects promised to improve in time. He believed that the U.S. economy was exiting the era of competitive capitalism—or cut-throat capitalism in union parlance—and was entering a phase, which he welcomed, in which trusts and oligarchies would predominate. In this new environment, employers would be rewarded for cooperating (with higher profit margins) and penalized for competing against each other, and unions would come into their own. At Gompers's death in 1924, the trade union movement had still not made the breakthrough he expected. Within a decade of his death, however, he was vindicated by the organization of the great industrial unions. As he would have predicted, the first and strongest of the new unions were in industries dominated by a few huge firms.

Yet, contrary to Gompers's hopes, the industrial unions did not go from strength to strength. The movement for industrial unionism that arose in the 1930s was only a stopgap. Support for trade unionism in the United States was always weak, with even workers themselves showing surprising resistance to the union appeal. Confidence in business had fallen precipitously in the Great Depression, however, and waned still further as many corporations engaged in an apparent class war against their own workers. As a result, Congress passed labor legislation in the early 1930s that for the first time put the government on the side of workers. But by 1937, Franklin Roosevelt declared himself a disgusted neutral between management and labor. In a matter of a few years the industrial unions had largely worn out their welcome with the American public.

The representative of the new industrial unions, the Congress of Industrial Organizations (CIO) peaked in 1937, barely three years after its creation and less than a year after its formal split from the AFL. In less than two decades, the AFL and CIO merged, mainly because both were stagnating. Leaders of the AFL and CIO attributed organizing difficulties largely to the tremendous resources flowing into jurisdictional battles between AFL unions and CIO unions. They assumed that once they joined forces and focused their organizing efforts on the remaining unorganized workers, growth would resume. But the merger hardly made a difference.

Setbacks in Growth

The inherently competitive nature of the American free enterprise system had put a brake on the growth of the industrial unions. In later decades, the intensification of competition started eroding the strength of craft and industrial unions alike. Even as the leaders of labor (along with leaders of middle-class liberalism) were bemoaning the ever-increasing influence and power of big business, the economy was moving into the early stages of a new era of heightened competition, the full dimensions of which have begun to become apparent only within the past several years.

Manufacturing firms began moving south to lower their costs, primarily labor costs. The preeminence of manufacturing industries ended, with the far more competitive service sector taking its place. These changes shook the accepted system of industrial relations but were modest when compared with the consequences of increased business competition—domestic and international—that began in the late 1960s and continues.

These shifts have traumatized the American labor movement. The private-sector unionization rate sank precipitously from a high of 35 percent in 1956 to less than 11 percent today. Only the rise of the public-employee unions, which organized public monopolies, has kept the absolute number of organized workers from shrinking. Moreover, union negotiating clout has dwindled, in some cases to the vanishing point, as evidenced most dramatically and embarrassingly by the concessionary bargaining that marked the early 1980s. Even after that crisis passed, decreasing geographic density combined with increasing competition has dramatically reduced the unions' power to raise wages above market rates.

For decades, the liberal economists who dominated the field argued that the largest and most advanced industries were increasingly dominated by oligopolies that choked off most competition and therefore did not have to compete over the price of inputs, such as the cost of labor. In that way liberal economists of the period, such as John Kenneth Galbraith, explained the fat contracts struck between big labor and big business. Hindsight reveals doubts that the process worked in that way. Nonetheless, the common view held was that labor unions had a large effect on wages, a belief that worked to the unions' advantage. Once that perception was shattered, the unions' prospects dimmed. After all, if unions could not deliver the goods to workers, there was no reason to belong and pay dues.

Changes in Philosophy

Some knowledgeable observers denied that the unions' setbacks had any effect on the movement's basic philosophy. Harvard professor John Dunlop (who served as secretary of labor in the Ford administration and whom President Bill Clinton appointed to head a commission on labor-law reform) acknowledged in the mid-1970s that international trade had become a sore spot with the trade union movement. But he asserted that labor was more committed to the private enterprise system than it had been in the 1920s.[1] Yet, at least a decade before, in response to the new, more competitive economic environment, the labor movement had begun moving leftward on virtually every issue.

First, consider labor's attitude toward state intervention in the economy. Gompers believed the state to be the executive arm of the dominant economic class (as had Marx), and, therefore, saw nothing to be gained by bringing government into the equation between business and labor. To the contrary, labor's top political priority during the Gompers era was the passage of legislation to keep government *out* of labor-management disputes. Conversely, Gompers did see a positive role for government during recessions and depressions. At those times, government could, and should, prime the pump by adopting expansionary monetary and fiscal policies. During the Great Depression, unions, even those in the Gompersite tradition, sought government assistance for their efforts. And they became more committed to government pump priming.

Over the past several decades, the labor movement has moved far beyond the advocacy of such measures—and out of the mainstream of economic thought. In direct response to intensified competition in the private sector, labor began arguing for far more government spending, which it called investment, and for more government control of the economy generally. Concurrently, labor launched its most severe ideological attack on business. During the same period, most economists were moving in precisely the opposite direction, arguing that future economic growth most required more savings and more freedom for the private sector.

The new competitive economic environment has also had a profound influence on labor's foreign policy. Gompers was an anti-Communist from the outset, knowing full well even as the Bolshevik coup unfolded in 1917 that no Leninist state would ever accept free unions. Indeed, he took the view that trade unionism was the antidote to communism overseas just as it was the alternative to socialism in the United States. Had there been an AFL in Russia in 1917, Gompers argued, the Bolsheviks could not have seized power. Free trade unions would have an increasingly important role to play in promoting U.S. interests and values abroad, and labor would be advancing not just the national interest but its own self-interest as well. The organization and strengthening of trade unions abroad would reduce the possibility that U.S. businessmen would move their production overseas to avoid paying union wage rates.

At the outset of the cold war, labor promoted Gompers's argument—made in the immediate aftermath of World War I and the Bolshevik Revolution—that the fight against communism and for democracy and economic recovery in Western Europe required most of all the establishment of strong and free trade union movements. The cold war, as U.S. labor leaders pointed out, was worldwide; with communism everywhere striving to bend working-class movements to its own purposes, it was in the best interests of the United States to support free trade unionism wherever possible.

Under the leadership of David Dubinsky, president of the International Ladies Garment Workers Union, and Jay Lovestone, one-time official and theoretician of the American Communist Party (CPUSA), the AFL intensified its struggle against communism once the war against fascism had been won. Because of its toleration of Communists, the CIO was slow in coming to this view. But after its expulsion of the Communists in 1948, it too became a reliably anti-Communist institution. During the height of the cold war, no American institution dedicated itself more to the anti-Communist cause than the AFL-CIO.

Not that its anti-Communist efforts had been effective: just as labor's ability to raise wages was more apparent than real, so was the part it played in the West's victory in the cold war more myth than fact. Its intentions were praiseworthy. But, more often than not, the particular policies it supported were counterproductive. The stress on building trade unions abroad was a mistake of the first order. In not a single country did unions play the kind of role that American labor predicted. And, for the most part, foreign unions promoted statist policies that prevented or impeded economic growth and, in so doing, contributed to the creation of economic and social conditions that Communist Parties and other left-wing anti-American movements exploited.

In labor's defense, its thinking was consistent with that of most policy makers. Both groups believed that the struggle against communism was primarily political and that the decisive political battles would be waged on the left wing of the political spectrum, between the Communists and democratic leftists who therefore deserved American support. It followed that the United States should not attempt to promote the development of free market economics.

In retrospect, this view was mistaken. Free market policies worked wonders where they were applied consistently, while socialist policies failed nearly everywhere. But this evidence did not affect conventional wisdom until the dramatic success of the economic policies of East Asia's Four Dragons: Hong Kong, Singapore, South Korea, and Taiwan. Since the Four Dragons' stunning achievement, the thinking on development has changed dramatically. Now, for the first time ever, there is a bipartisan consensus that the United States best serves both its own interests and those of developing countries by actively promoting the development of market economies throughout the world.

But this consensus does not include the labor movement. In every one of the Four Dragons, wages lagged behind productivity increases. According to Gompers's economic reasoning, which is essentially that of labor's current leaders, economic decline should have resulted from the inability of workers to purchase the products of their labor. But the wage lag had the opposite consequence, in part because much of the new production was exported to the developed world, especially the United States. The developing countries have benefited along with U.S. consumers, but the labor movement has suffered. The exports have only increased the competitive pressures that are undermining the effectiveness of American unions.

Lacking arguments that have general appeal, the labor movement simply denies that the East Asian miracle ever happened and argues strongly against other developing countries' adopting the economic policies that produced it. For exactly the same reasons, labor has opposed shock therapy for the sick economies of the post-Communist nations. If anything, the movement has aimed ever more strident criticism at what it calls neoliberalism abroad, as it has at competitive capitalism at home.

The same logic has driven labor to reverse its position on free trade. From the end of World War II through the 1960s, it supported the lowering of trade barriers to spur the economic development of countries in Europe and elsewhere that were or might come under Communist threat. But when the industrial unions started to lose members, the AFL-CIO flip-flopped. Blaming many of its losses on the foreign investment of American corporations to secure cheaper labor, the AFL-CIO launched an all-out attack on multinational corporations and sought to make it far more difficult for American-based corporations to invest abroad and for foreign-based corporations to invest in the United States. Second, labor turned against free trade and became the country's most powerful advocate of protectionism, as it demonstrated in its no-holds-barred opposition to the North American Free Trade Agreement (NAFTA) in 1993 and in its effort to defeat other free trade agreements.

As labor's views on economic issues, domestic and international, have become absolutely and relatively more radical, the movement has been forced to find new political allies on the Left and has paid an ideological price for that support. The dramatic reversal of labor's stance on civil rights and other social issues is a case in point. Despite its claims, labor never fully embodied America's ideal value system. In principle, unions in the Gompers tradition sought a working class undivided by color or nationality. But no such unity existed. To keep this mostly white constituency intact, the unions of the AFL generally discriminated against blacks. To advance the interests of the same membership, they also lobbied for restricting the immigration of East European and especially Asian workers. The CIO, conversely, had always supported equal treatment for blacks and had never supported anti-immigration legislation. The merged organization adopted the CIO position on both matters. Within a few years, the AFL-CIO had become a significant force in the effort to pass civil rights legislation.

In the late 1960s and early 1970s, the civil rights movement abandoned its traditional advocacy of colorblind policies in favor of race-conscious measures. For a short while, the labor movement resisted the new direction. Then, quite unexpectedly, it capitulated and became an ardent supporter of race-based policies, even though union members and their families often suffered the most from policies enforcing racial balance and, therefore, strongly opposed them.

But, by this time, the views of union members were not as important to union leaders as were the policies of the civil rights organizations. Political calculation was at work. Union members were an increasingly unreliable source of support for the unions' political programs, whereas the civil rights leaders were the most reliable. Hence the interests of the former were abandoned in favor of the latter. The same political imperative drove labor within a few years to accommodate its policies to new groups of victims such as women and homosexuals. The labor movement today lends its full official support to a wide array of groups that seek special treatment by society at large on the basis of allegations of past injustices.

This desperate search for political allies also goes a long way toward explaining why American labor's support for defense spending and military action began to flag toward the end of the cold war. A growing left wing that had established political and organizational relationships with the Left strongly opposed the Reagan administration's defense buildup and its support of anti-Communist insurgencies. In response, the leadership tempered its support of defense spending and also its support of the administration's policies in Angola, Nicaragua, and El Salvador. That internal left wing has since become the new leadership of the federation. As a result, American labor, for the first time since before World War I, cannot be counted on to support the active pursuit of the national interest in the world.

Is there any chance of a reversal, of a return to the time when labor was a proud member of American civil society—before it degenerated into a left-wing interest group? That seems highly unlikely. It would require an accommodation with competitive capitalism, which labor has rejected since its founding. It is far more likely, then, that labor will continue along the path of the past three decades. In so doing, it will condemn itself to a life on the leftward fringe, exactly the fate that Samuel Gompers feared and tried so hard to avoid.

Today's Movement

The existence of this book testifies to a reversal of my own thinking. I began my adult life as a dedicated democratic socialist and a firm believer in the AFL-CIO and spent ten years working for the teachers' union in New York City. Yet, as the labor movement veered left, I found my own political thinking moving to the right. Finally, I could no longer believe that American labor, as currently constituted and led, served the public or national interest. I continue to respect the dedication and the idealism of my friends who remain in the movement. But whatever was true of yesterday's movement, today's movement practices a variety of reactionary leftism that opposes America's values and interests. Too few Americans are aware of American labor's left turn or of the reasons for it. My hope is that this book will make some contribution to understanding this lamentable phenomenon.

2
The Philosophy of the American Labor Movement

T hrough its first century, the American trade union movement was distinguished by its rejection of socialism. Unlike its European counterparts, American labor never called for the nationalization of major industries. It accepted the private ownership of the major means of production. Conversely, it never subscribed to the basic tenets of competitive capitalism. Market economics in all its variants, increases in the compensation paid to workers are a function of growth in the productivity of labor. Marxist theory predicts the opposite outcome. Marx argued that capitalism's capacity to produce tended regularly to outstrip its capacity to consume, causing crises of overproduction or underconsumption.

Gompers and his successors agreed with critics of the market economy that capitalists, if left to their own devices, would seek to raise profits by lowering wages. Gompers asked, "What would be the condition of the working men in our country in our day by acting as individuals with as great a concentrated wealth and industry on every hand?" His answer: "It is horrifying even to permit the imagination full swing. Think what would be possible. Slavery! Slavery! Demoralized, degraded slavery. Nothing better."[1] In the absence of a countervailing power, the workers in a capitalist society would be reduced to a "much worse condition than the slaves in ante-bellum days."[2] (Decades later, George Meany would aver that, without unions, the world would be "one big sweatshop.")[3] Gompers scarcely needed to add that such a situation would spell an economic crisis severe enough to provoke the socialist revolution predicted by Marx.

Therefore, Gompers concluded, the "great question that agitates the civilized world is—how much shall the wage worker receive for his labor and how much shall the capitalist receive for his profits."[4] For him and the socialists, then, redistribution of income from capitalists to workers was the first priority. The difference between them—and it was a huge one—was that in Gompers's scheme the means of redistribution would be the trade unions. The higher wages that they negotiated would enable workers to buy the products that they produced, thereby preventing economic depression and political unrest. Not only that, higher wages would result in increased output:

> As wages are raised, new and better machinery with the highest developed propelling forces are introduced and applied. New tools are brought into existence, division and subdivision and specialization of trades and industries follow, making production far greater and at a lesser cost than ever before, despite—yes, because of—the increase in wages.[5]

Thus wages—the dependent variable in free market economics—become the independent variable in Gompers's conception, making the trade union movement the savior of the private enterprise system.

Free Labor

But the difference between Gompers and free market thinking does not end there. By all accounts, an essential characteristic of capitalism is the principle of free labor, a principle that Marx decried because he thought that it reduced workers to commodities. In his book *The Spirit of Capitalism*, Michael Novak offers a rejoinder:

> The precise quality which Marx sees as so inhuman—that labor is treated as a commodity—. . . [is] the condition of its liberty. If men are to choose their work, they must have multiple possibilities of employment and reward, under conditions of mobility. Thus free men will necessarily trade their labor so as to obtain what they deserve.[6]

Novak considers himself a friend of the American labor movement, but the principle that he upholds is inconsistent with labor's view since its beginning.

Gompers considered the Clayton Anti-Trust Act of 1914 labor's Magna Carta precisely because, at his initiative, it included the following language: "The labor of a human being is not a commodity or article of commerce." A generation later, Philip Murray, then president of the CIO, explained that if labor were treated as a commodity, then employers would compete "as to which can establish the lowest wages, which can establish the worst sweatshop conditions, and thereby achieve an advantage over the other in the sale of products."[7] The job of the labor movement, therefore, was to "take wages out of competition."

But taking wages out of competition in a profit-seeking, competitive economy is no mean feat. Indeed, socialists thought it impossible: hence their desire to build a new society around what they saw as the opposing and higher principle of cooperation. Socialists viewed the increasing concentration of industry as a progressive development, a necessary stage on the way to the socialization of production.

American Progressives, who believed strongly in the virtues of competition, viewed the rise of the trusts with trepidation. But Gompers found the trusts "an inevitable economic development before which the law was completely helpless" and was not disturbed by them.[8] Indeed, he called the trust system "the most perfect yet attained" and looked on the increasing concentration of industry and the consequent diminution of competition as reasons for believing that unions could thrive in an advanced capitalist society. The trade union, he wrote, "finds its greatest development under the same economic conditions which produce the trusts; that is the introduction of machines, the subdivision of industry, the adoption of vast and complicated systems of production which obliterate the individuality of the worker thus forcing him in to association . . . with his fellows."[9]

The Rise of the Industrial Unions

The economic and social philosophy of industrial unionism is often portrayed as a rejection of Gompersism. One is hard-pressed, however, to find a single significant difference between Gompers's thinking on economic issues and that of John L. Lewis, the first president of the CIO. Like Gompers, Lewis argued that holding wages down reduced purchasing power and caused economic downturns—and vice versa. Lewis also repeated Gompers's argument about the productivity-enhancing effect of raising wages above the market rate. High wages would drive out of business less productive, marginal producers who depended on low wage rates to survive. Additionally, high wages would force the surviving companies to invest more in capital than otherwise to save on labor costs.

For the same reason that Gompers welcomed the development of the trust, Lewis favored what he called cooperative capitalism. Lewis's own United Mine Workers (UMW) had suffered greatly in the late 1920s because of intense competition within the coal industry and from other fuels. Naturally, there was downward pressure on wages in the unionized sector. To prevent wage slashing, Lewis and Secretary of Commerce Herbert Hoover got the operators of unionized mines in several states to agree to hold the wage line. But the agreement broke down, with devastating effects on the UMW. The experience convinced Lewis that competitive capitalism was inimical to strong trade unions.

Lewis—and the AFL—strongly supported the New Deal's National Industrial Recovery Act (NIRA) because section 7a guaranteed unions the rights to organize and to bargain collectively and also authorized business to divide markets and fix prices. When the Supreme Court ruled the NIRA unconstitutional in 1937, Lewis supported the Guffey-Vinson Act, which provided for product allocation and price fixing among coal operators. When this law too was ruled unconstitutional, the UMW took action of its own to accomplish the same end by strikes or work stoppages whenever supply threatened lower prices.

Attitudes toward the State

Initially, the industrial unions differed widely from craft unions in their attitude toward the state. With good reason, Gompers feared that a welfare state providing unemployment insurance, health benefits, and the like would displace unions. But industrial unions, which charged little or nothing for dues, acted in accordance with a different logic altogether when it came to government programs. It made sense for them to support programs such as unemployment insurance, which the AFL opposed during Gompers's reign and for years thereafter.

The New Deal precipitated a radical and permanent change in the AFL's attitude toward the state. Matthew Woll, Gompers's heir-apparent, wrote as early as 1930 that "we have rejected laissez-faire individualism, absolutely, both in economics and in politics. . . . Our political program in most respects, is very similar to the political programs of the labor unions of Great Britain and Germany."[10] Gompers's actual successor, William Green, took the same line. High among his accomplishments as president of the AFL he listed his support of laws providing for "unemployment compensation, old-age benefits and public assistance for maternal and child welfare . . . public assistance into the field of medical care in the form of a national health insurance plan . . . a long-range program of permanent public works . . . ," and so on.[11] Without overtly rejecting the principle of trade unionism pure and simple, the AFL was increasingly honoring it in the breach.

Yet, labor, whether the craft unions or their industrial cousins, had little to do with shaping the New Deal. New Dealers, according to Arthur M. Schlesinger, Jr., did not "have much expectation in 1934 of creative contribution from labor. In FDR Secretary of Labor Francis Perkins' experience, the unions never had any ideas of their own; most labor and welfare legislation in her time had been brought about by middle-class reformers in face of labor indifference."[12] Moreover, chief industrial unionist John L. Lewis was not all that different: "Essentially he wanted to increase labor's power, not to alter the system. . . . The difference between Lewis and the A F of L mandarins was that where they remained faithful to the letter of the Strasser-Gompers doctrine, Lewis sought to transpose its spirit to a new age."[13]

Whether labor should be criticized for not supporting New Deal legislation more vigorously is open to question, but it is a fact that it did not. For labor, the most important pieces of legislation of the 1930s were those, like the NIRA and then the National Labor Relations Act of 1935 (NLRA), that gave government sanction to trade unionism and collective bargaining. Second in importance were measures like the Davis-Bacon Act and the Walsh-Healy Act, which mandated that federal contractors pay prevailing, that is, union, wage rates, thereby depriving nonunion firms of their one advantage. No doubt Gompers would have supported the NIRA and the NLRA, as well as Davis-Bacon and Walsh-Healy.

During the 1930s, labor did support public works programs such as the Works Progress Administration (WPA), as Gompers would have. During the recession of 1893, Gompers called for "work on public enterprises" in New York State: deepening the Erie Canal, building and improving parks, constructing a subway system in New York City, erecting schools, and extending the sewage system. He supported such measures because a high rate of unemployment weakened the labor movement. In a tight labor market, unions could negotiate higher wages and better benefits. But in the presence of what Gompers—following the socialists—called a "reserve army of the unemployed" that was ready to take jobs at less than the prevailing rate, unions were hard-pressed to hold on to what they had already won.

The motivation of depression-era union leaders in supporting public works was the same. Reducing unemployment, in and of itself, was a secondary concern. Hence, as leader of the New York Central Trades and Labor Council in the 1930s, George Meany took the position that "under no circumstances are any of our organizations to permit their members to work on relief at less than the prevailing rate."[14] He won that battle, at the obvious cost of reducing the total number of workers that the WPA could employ.

Labor leaders split over the Fair Labor Standards Act of 1938, which set minimum wages and maximum hours. Trade unionists in the Gompers tradition opposed it out of fear that if government could impose a minimum wage, it could also impose a maximum wage. John L. Lewis did not unequivocally support the legislation. Conversely, most leaders of the new industrial unions had no such reservations. The Steel Workers' Organizing Committee "sought to use the Fair Labor Standards Act of 1938 to raise the wage rate paid by Bethlehem and Republic—the most important Little Steel holdout—on government work, thereby improving the competitive position of the unionized sector of the industry."[15] But this deviation from Gompersite dogma based itself on a traditional collective-bargaining rationale.

Considering the heavy influence of Communists and socialists in the early CIO, the industrial wing of labor placed surprisingly little emphasis on supporting collectivist measures. Even proposals that sounded socialistic were not much more than calls for full-employment policies that labor had always supported in one form or another.

There were exceptions. As the country started preparing for World War II, Walter Reuther of the United Auto Workers proposed converting idle automobile factories into aircraft plants that would build 500 planes a day. As the war wound down, he then suggested reconverting aircraft plants into automobile factories and the like so that defense workers would not be laid off during the transition to a peacetime economy. When Philip Murray succeeded Lewis at the CIO, he pushed a proposal that was even more reminiscent of social democracy. At the beginning and then again at the end of the war, he called for the establishment of tripartite (industry, organized labor, and government) industry councils that would be authorized to increase employment and output. As collective bargaining was reinstated, the proposals for the council and Reuther's reconversion were dropped; fear of a return of massive unemployment receded quickly after the war.

The Continuing Importance of Collective Bargaining

Labor still emphasized collective bargaining during this period. Even Reuther acted for the most part in the Gompers tradition, with its strong emphasis on collective bargaining. Following World War II, for example, he demanded that General Motors open its books for UAW inspection to refute his claim that the corporation could afford to grant a substantial wage increase without raising prices. "Labor," says a 1946 UAW pamphlet, "contends that the economic facts of life prove that wages can be increased without increasing prices. Increased production must be supported through increased consumption and increased consumption will be possible only through increased wages."[16]

Excited by this rhetoric, some socialists made too much of it. Trotskyist Max Shachtman, for instance, argued that here was an implicit "demand for direct intervention by labor in the running of the economy as a whole. . . . From this demand to the demand for a government which will control wages, prices and profits, in the interests of labor is only one step."[17] But that was hardly the purpose of the demand, to which General Motors refused to accede anyway, despite a long strike. Both the AFL and the CIO still believed that they would make their major gains at the bargaining table, not in the halls of Congress. "For the industrial worker between 1945 and 1960, the union contract was becoming the passport to a better life. 'The labor movement,' exulted Walter Reuther, 'is developing a whole new middle class.' "[18]

3

The Radicalization of Labor's Economic Policy

E ven though the labor movement was failing to grow as expected after the AFL-CIO merger, labor leaders in the mid-1950s expressed the general contentment of the decade. During this period, Meany was most enthusiastic about the virtues of the free enterprise system.

But automation was looming. Because it improved the productivity of American industry and therefore increased national wealth, automation was good for most Americans. But labor was beginning to have doubts. Meany told the 1963 AFL-CIO convention that automation had been more a curse than blessing, threatening to thin the ranks of the great industrial unions. As one AFL-CIO pamphlet reported, "In 1965, there were fewer production jobs in manufacturing than there were in 1953."[1]

Even as labor claimed credit for productivity increases, it had expressed concern from the beginning about the consequences: hence Gompers's proposal for an eight-hour workday. At the beginning of the Great Depression, labor supported a proposal by then-Senator Hugo Black (Democrat, Alabama) that sought to relieve unemployment by mandating a thirty-hour workweek. Three decades later, labor once again called for a shorter workweek to counter the effects of automation. The AFL-CIO argued that a reduction of hours was essential for full employment under accelerating technological change.

Labor's leadership did not press the issue, probably because it knew that it was unlikely to prevail. Instead, labor pushed hard for government pump priming to increase consumer demand, on the theory that higher consumer demand would spur a rise in the demand for labor, particularly in the larger industries. This position was as consistent with labor's own past policy and philosophy as its call for a shorter workweek.

Moving Out of the Economic Mainstream

The kind of economic thinking manifested by labor's call for expansionary demand management had been in the mainstream during the depression, when the reduction of mass unemployment was the problem. After the war, the control of inflation came to be generally recognized—outside labor precincts—as equally important. This reassessment was reflected in the Full Employment Act of 1946, which was a major defeat and disappointment for labor and its allies.

By the 1960s, labor's economic thinking was leaving the mainstream. Consider, for example, the night-and-day contrast between its own views and those of President John Kennedy's liberal Council of Economic Advisers (CEA). The Kennedy economists "thought of a continuous relation between unemployment and inflation, such that at lower levels of unemployment there would be a higher inflation rate and vice versa. . . . Thus, the government could choose among many combinations of unemployment and inflation."[2]

Labor denied that any trade-off existed between inflation and unemployment. Following Leon Keyserling (who had been CEA chairman under Harry Truman and later ran a labor-supported think tank), it defined inflation as too much money chasing too few goods. As long as some industrial capacity was unutilized (and there almost always seemed to be some, by labor's account), the solution to inflation would be to produce more goods by hiring more workers. Conventional economic thinking to the contrary, this procedure would not increase inflationary pressures but would actually do the opposite because maximizing utilization of manufacturing capacity would reduce the relative cost of overhead. Similarly, whereas conventional economists held that interest-rate hikes would reduce inflationary pressures by reducing demand, labor argued that the opposite was true because increasing interest rates raised the cost of borrowed money and therefore the total cost of production.

Labor also deviated from conventional economic thinking with its longstanding view that most blame for price increases rested with oligopolies, to which labor attributed price-fixing powers far greater than those detected by any mainstream economist: One reason is that American industry has never been as concentrated as labor made out. Nobel Prize-winning economist George Stigler calculated that as of 1939, 75 percent of American industry was competitive.[3] That percentage has since increased, because to the decline of concentration of virtually all industries that were organized by the industrial unions in the 1930s and 1940s.[4] A second reason, as Peter Drucker has pointed out, is that even the leaders of uncompetitive industries lowered prices to discourage potential competitors form entering their market.[5] Finally, there was Joseph Schumpeter's process of "creative destruction" whereby entire industries were replaced over time (for example, carriages by automobiles), accounting in Schumpeter's view for the fact that there have been no "major instances of long-run rigidities of prices."[6] Thus Barry Bosworth, President Jimmy Carter's chief inflation expert, pointed out in 1978 that "we have reached the point where the fear of unemployment is not an adequate restraint on wage increases . . . [union members] have insulated themselves against the cost of inflation, and they have insulated themselves against the cost of unemployment." Unions, he observed, were strong in concentrated industries, "which cooperate with inflationary union wage demands in order to avoid disruptions to business." He added that only imports restrained prices and wages.[7] Another senior economic adviser to Carter, Alfred Kahn, defined the economy's problem as self-interest, with total disregard for the national well-being. Kahn decried "the fundamental piston thrust of wages upward, ever upward, and the resistance of the unions to any halt or downward flexibility."[8]

The New Egalitarianism

Another basic difference separated the labor movement's approach to macroeconomic policy and that of every presidential administration after Truman's. That difference became fully manifest during the Kennedy administration, which advocated policies to restrain consumption and increase investment so as to speed up the rate of economic growth. Organized labor scorned the approach as trickle-down economics. An AFL-CIO Executive Council statement in 1957 had warned of an existing "imbalance between investment and consumption,"[9] due to increases in investment coming before increases in consumer demand. The council feared that, if productivity increases outran increases in consumer demand, unemployment would result. From labor's perspective, then, the Kennedy administration's attempt to increase the rates of savings and investment was a recipe for recession.

Thus, labor fought attempts to stimulate the economy with tax cuts or incentives for business. The AFL-CIO recommended tax cuts for low- and moderate-income workers and tax hikes for corporations and the wealthy, thus redistributing income while providing what labor claimed would be a more solid basis for economic growth. As resistance grew to the higher taxes required to pay for the government programs supported by labor, such reform was proposed to stave off cuts in spending. In the 1970s, public-employee unions took up this call with a vengeance (see appendix 3–A).

Few noticed labor's emphasis on tax reform. Thus, in commenting on the tax reforms proposed by George McGovern as the Democratic presidential candidate in 1972, Irving Kristol traced them to the struggle for status and power that the "new class" of symbol-manipulating professionals was waging against the business community. He noted that the "American working class" was "far less consumed with egalitarian bitterness or envy than are college professors or affluent journalists": most Americans preferred "regressive" sales taxes to income taxes and the "tax rebellion" of 1972 was "provoked mainly by the rapid growth of . . . [the] . . . welfare state."[10] But Kristol failed to appreciate that the leaders of organized labor were far more committed to egalitarianism than were the professional classes.

Anachronistic Economics

The rift between labor and mainstream economics continued after the Kennedy administration. In the mid-1970s, labor initiated new full-employment legislation, the Humphrey-Hawkins Act, that would have required the federal government to implement policies to ensure that the unemployment rate rose no higher than 4 percent. At this time, the "natural" rate of unemployment (meaning that a lower level would be inflationary) was thought to be 5 or 6 percent. The higher figure took into account the entry into the job market of large numbers of youths and women, whose commitment to full-time employment was generally less intense than that of adult male heads of households. According to the *Congressional Quarterly,* "with a few exceptions, liberal economists began to attack it [Humphrey-Hawkins] as vague, inflationary and generally unworkable."[11] Herbert Stein wrote that "every informed person knew that the whole idea—including the 4 percent unemployment—was nonsense and that the bill could be stomached only on the assumption, which proved to be correct, that it would be forgotten as soon as it was enacted."[12]

Acting on labor theoretician Gus Tyler's theory that the worker's paycheck contained the elixir of the economy, labor tried time and again to raise the minimum wage. Spending by any worker, union or not, would give a boost to the economy. Raising the wages of the lowest-paid workers would have a doubly positive effect: it would increase their own income and would push up the wages of workers above them on the income ladder.

But as labor enthused about new minimum-wage legislation, the doubts of economists and policy makers increased. Liberal economist Alan Blinder—before he was appointed to President Clinton's Council of Economic Advisers—explained that "raising the minimum wage . . . . simply raises the price of unskilled and inexperienced workers. Employers naturally react by hiring fewer of them. And so society succeeds in raising the wages of some by forcing others to pay the ultimate economic penalty: loss of their jobs."[13] The argument was identical to the one against unions raising wage rates in excess of increases in productivity. As such thinking gained currency, general support for increasing the minimum wage diminished. Throughout the 1960s and 1970s, even when liberal Democrats controlled the White House or one or both houses of Congress, minimum-wage legislation was postponed and passed in a diluted form, if at all.

There was as great a divide between labor and even former allies on monetary policy. The AFL-CIO unrelentingly argued for expansionary monetary as well as fiscal policies. Not only did labor advocate low interest rates and increasing the money supply, it urged structural reforms to politicize monetary policy. This stand was consistent with its past policy. Labor had always argued that monetary and fiscal policy should be linked and consistent with each other. Thus, in the 1950s, the movement had been on the losing side of the fight that resulted in the Federal Reserve Bank's independence. When labor returned to the fight in the 1970s, it had fewer allies because of the growing recognition that the Fed would be far less likely to keep the lid on inflation if elected officials were pulling the strings. But that consideration hardly dissuaded labor from making its case, with no moderation of its views.

The problem with the economy, labor said in 1971, was largely caused by "the amount of credit going to the blue-chip corporations and the wealthy for mergers, conglomerate takeovers, land speculation, gambling casinos and investments in foreign subsidiaries." Instead, this credit should have been used for "housing and community facilities." Accordingly, labor called on Congress to

> direct the Federal Reserve system to establish selective credit controls, to establish maximum interest rates on specific types of loans, and the allocation of credit to where it will do the most good for America—to direct the flow of available credit, at reasonable interest rates, into housing, public facilities and the regular operations of business.[14]

At first, the AFL-CIO urged legislation that gave the president the authority to restrict loans for nonproductive uses while lowering interest rates to redirect credit to home building and the like. Then, labor urged Congress to pass legislation that would require the president to act so. If adopted, this proposal would have put the Federal Reserve directly under the control of Congress, the institution where the AFL-CIO wielded the most political clout.

In 1975, the labor movement proposed legislation that would give it more direct control over the Federal Reserve Board. The labor-backed bill called for a total restructuring of the Fed. Under its provisions, the Federal Reserve system would have fewer governors serving shorter terms, and organized labor would participate on the governing bodies and advisory committees of the system. Such a change would force the Fed "to promote maximum employment, production and purchasing power."[15] This was pure and simple populism. It was seen as such and never gained significant support.

An Ever-Growing Role for Government

Throughout the 1950s, labor continued to speak in Keynesian fashion of government as the economic balance wheel whose fiscal and monetary policies were supposed to stimulate private-sector growth. In its 1957 statement on the national economy, the AFL-CIO suggested that the executive branch needed to improve its balancing of investment, consumption, and government spending precisely to avoid "growing dependence on government intercession."[16] The AFL-CIO looked with suspicion on the Left liberalism of those like John Kenneth Galbraith, with its contempt for the consumer tastes of most Americans. "Some have argued," George Meany wrote, "that we are so 'affluent,' so well off, so occupied in creating a multitude of frills and furbelows that the solution is not growth and greater production, but a mere shift in attention to those who have not shared in the fruits of prosperity."[17] Labor disagreed. For it, the problem was still too little, rather than too much, consumption.

Soon, however, labor began to entertain doubts about the capacity of the private sector to provide enough new, well-paying jobs. In a pamphlet distributed by the AFL-CIO's Industrial Union Department, socialist Tom Kahn maintained that the only answer to automation was government-funded job-creation programs. Similarly, in a 1962 pamphlet, Leon Keyserling argued that automation, which precluded much additional employment in some heavy industries, mandated "an immense housing program plus urban renewal involving private and public efforts . . . [offering] by far the greatest single opportunity to translate our burgeoning productive powers into more jobs, rising consumption and living standards and enlarged business opportunities."[18] Organized labor's thinking now considered private investment as part of the problem, not the solution.

Meany took up the new line. "Due to existing overcapacity, the country can't rely on private investment to take up the economic slack," he opined. "Rather the situation calls for public investment in America."[19] By public investment, he meant government spending on the construction of schools and hospitals, sanitation systems, community centers, and new publicly financed housing in slum neighborhoods—all spending that, whatever its other merits, would clearly benefit workers in the highly unionized construction and mass-production industries.

A 1973 executive council report reviewed eras of economic growth, each characterized by investment in new industries, for example, railroad and steel industries in the late nineteenth century and auto and radio industries in the 1920s. "In the 1970s," the report continued, "America's new economic frontiers are in a major emphasis on public investment to rebuild areas, to strengthen the foundation of American society and provide the investment and employment base for a new period of national economic expansion."[20] That is, in the future the driving force would be not private but the public sector and, more specifically, the federal government. An executive council report of 1975 maintained that "especially in times of economic crisis it is the federal government—which represents all of the people and can marshal the nation's resources—that holds the key." Labor was now characterizing virtually every problem as a national challenge that deserved a national effort and national coordination: "America's most pressing problems—employment, housing, energy, conservation and development, poverty, pollution, health care, education, public transportation and the like—are nationwide in scope and impact. They require national leadership, federal programs, and federal financial support."[21]

As part of its larger plan for tax reform, labor advocated a large increase in the tax rate on corporations. Irving Kristol noted that "the consequence—and, one can only suppose, the purpose of—any sharp increase in the tax burden of corporations would be to shift . . . control [over investment] massively towards the political authorities," driving the country thereby away from a "system of liberal capitalism" and toward "the system of state capitalism which some call 'socialism.' "[22] But, Kristol failed to point out that the American labor movement was the most important proponent of this kind of tax reform.

Redefining Investment

Labor's use of the words *investment* and *growth* in connection with increased federal spending has long meant the opposite of the standard definition. Increasing productivity was eroding the labor movement's base in the mass manufacturing and construction industries. Real government investment, that is, investment made with an eye to maximizing returns, would simply have increased job losses in these labor strongholds. Government investment of the AFL-CIO sort was designed to use monies taken from the private sector in the form of tax revenues to fund expensive, yet not necessarily productive, projects requiring workers from the most highly unionized sectors of the economy.

A case in point is the AFL-CIO's constant bemoaning of the state of the country's physical infrastructure. Lane Kirkland, Meany's successor as president, charged in 1983 that Ronald Reagan had promised to lead the way to a shining city, but, in reality, "the streets of that shining city are riddled with potholes and its bridges are falling down. Its rotting water system threatens an epidemic and its waste pollutes its streams."[23] If AFL literature was to be believed, things only worsened during the subsequent nine years of the Reagan and Bush administrations. In defending the AFL-CIO's proposal for a $60 billion stimulus program in 1992 (more than three times as large as the stimulus package that the Democrat-controlled Congress rejected in early 1993 on the grounds that it would be economically irresponsible), Kirkland returned to the theme of a crumbling infrastructure. He cited a study by the economist David Aschauer that purported to show that "the nation's infrastructure needs have been neglected so badly that every additional dollar spent on infrastructure at this time would stimulate between two and five times as much economic growth as would an additional dollar of private investment."[24]

In fact, America's infrastructure was not crumbling in 1992, partly due to increased spending during the Reagan-Bush years. As Heywood Sanders noted, "total investment in streets, highways, mass transit, airports, and water and sewer systems came to $43.66 billion in 1991, . . . 41 percent above the 1982 low point in capital spending."[25] Further, he charged, 40 percent of the endangered bridges eligible for federal aid were in six states, with highway problems similarly concentrated. Sanders concluded that "a major federal spending program would obviously help a few poorly managed states, but only at the expense of others that have done a good job of maintaining their own bridges and railroads."[26] The same would be true of federal programs to alleviate other infrastructure problems.

As for the supposed economic payoff from a massive federal investment in infrastructure, the *New York Times* reported that "few economists find [Aschauer's] claim credible."[27] On the contrary, the preponderance of evidence indicated that billions spent on new highways would be money wasted. There was a growing consensus, never acknowledged by the AFL-CIO, that the optimal plan was to fix existing roads, which would require nowhere near the amount of money the AFL-CIO wanted spent. Economists—again ignored by the AFL-CIO—increasingly agreed further that the problems of traffic congestion could best be alleviated, not by a massive new road-building program, but through user fees on existing highways (new technology could eliminate the need for toll booths). Fees would be highest during rush hours, thus giving motorists an incentive to drive at other times.

Regarding the economic effects of spending on mass transit, another of the infrastructure investments that the AFL-CIO has advocated for many years, the *New York Times* commented, "The worst examples of excesses with federal money involve urban mass transit."[28] The *Economist* pointed out: "There is no more wasteful investment . . . than in urban public-transport systems. Again up to three-quarters of the cost is paid by the federal government; this has tempted many cities to push for glitzy systems that are used on average, to only a fifth of their capacity."[29] To deal with this particular problem, the AFL-CIO in 1980 suggested "no fare" experiments, which would surely have increased ridership—at an enormous cost in public funds.

The sheer wastefulness of such spending is compounded when one considers the opportunity cost of the funds that it diverts from real capital investment. By the mid-1970s, Kristol argued, the problem of waste in the name of job creation had gotten so bad that the United States was suffering an actual net reduction in capital investment. Virtually all economists agreed that the level of investment from the early 1970s on through the next decade and a half was far too low. The AFL-CIO thought otherwise. By 1975, it was sounding its old alarum about a capital goods boom. In contrast not just to conservative thinking but to liberal economic thinking, labor now saw capital—on which the wealth of the nation ultimately depended—as a threat to the survival of the union movement.

Regulation and Jobs

Labor's present approach to government regulation reveals even more clearly its new, negative attitude toward economic growth. The rising environmental movement of the 1960s and 1970s often accused labor of favoring economic growth whatever the cost to the environment. Labor aimed counterblasts at "no-growth advocates who want to clean up every form of pollution except the human pollution of unemployment."[30] For the AFL-CIO, growth was still the highest priority.

An about-face began in the 1970s. A growing number of econo-

mists—by no means all of them free market conservatives—
questioned the wisdom of many environmental regulations of the
sort that labor had long opposed. But in executing its turnabout, the
AFL-CIO made itself an advocate of measures that others now found
ill conceived. Labor leaders had discovered that the environmental
regulations they once feared could be a source of union jobs.

The AFL's 1971 statement on the environment addressed the
concerns of many trade unionists who were worried that costly environmental regulations would take away jobs in at least some industries. The AFL proposed transferring administration of federal anti-
pollution efforts to the Environmental Protection Agency and then
imposing strict national emission standards on all existing station-
ary sources of both air and water pollution. Furthermore, labor
called for legislation providing "that any employer, alleging that an
abatement order will cause layoffs, dismissals, or cessation of operations, must prove its case before an administrative hearing called
by the federal agency involved."[31] Any federal agency was unlikely
to accept the blame for layoffs. Clearly, the idea was to force companies to swallow increased costs, which would lower profit margins
and therefore decrease funds available for productivity-enhancing
investment. Labor, having long argued for lower profit margins, was
now less keen than ever on labor-saving investment.

The AFL urged that Congress spend "3 billion annually for five
years for federal grants to assist municipalities in the construction
or modification of sewage treatment plants," a program that "could
create more than 250,000 jobs." In 1977, the AFL reported that "the
pollution control industry, with over 600 manufacturing firms, has
been operating at high levels of employment during the recession,
with 1.1 million on their payrolls in 1976. The Council of Environmental Quality estimated that in 1976 the pollution control effort of
this nation provided 400,000 jobs." That employment, apparently,
was reason enough for the AFL-CIO to support environmental con-
trols.

Labor's preoccupation with increasing union jobs explains why
the AFL lined up with the no-growth wing of the environmental
movement in scoffing at green taxes—effluent charges designed to
give companies an incentive to reduce pollution with maximum efficiency—as "licenses to pollute," even though virtually all economists, liberal as well as conservative, thought otherwise. The alternative favored by the AFL and its environmentalist allies was a

government requirement that companies use the best available technology.

The AFL, for instance, supported acid-rain legislation requiring the installation of gas-scrubbing equipment to cut sulfuric-acid emissions even though it was unclear whether reducing such emissions would reduce the acidity of rain and despite the existence of cheaper methods, such as washing coals before combustion. It is easy to understand why no-growth advocates would favor this legislation: raising the costs of doing business puts a damper on economic growth. But why did labor?

EPA standards on new plants are stricter than for old plants. The EPA correctly reckons that it is cheaper to include new technologies (like smoke scrubbers) in new plants than to retrofit old plants. But the EPA does require the use of the best available technology, in this instance, the scrubbers in new plants, precluding them from using cheaper means of complying with emission standards, for example, by using low-sulphur content western coal. The effect, as Alan Binder points out, is to raise "electricity costs in the West and South, which retards the shift of industry to the Sun Belt. It also protects the market for high-sulphur Eastern and Midwestern Coals, which might otherwise be displaced by Western Coal."[32]

This process serves the interest of the AFL in a variety of ways. First, the United Mine Workers represents many eastern but few western miners. Second, the trade union movement is generally stronger in the Rust Belt; there is cultural resistance to unions in the Sun Belt. Third, this concept favors old businesses and industries that are more likely to be unionized than startups. Fourth, lots of union labor can go into the building of scrubbers, whereas washing coal, or using low-sulphur coal, requires less or no such labor at all. Without any specific reference to unions, Blinder concluded that "in effect environmental regulations act as a perversely discriminatory tax that deters innovation and favors outmoded plants with low productivity."[33]

The same dynamic can be seen in occupational safety and health, where labor also supports regulations requiring the best available technology. Six years after passage of the Occupational Health and Safety Act in 1970, political economists Albert Nichols and Richard Zeckhauser found no evidence that OSHA had resulted in "significant gains in worker safety and health" despite such costly measures as "OSHA-mandated work practices, the purchase of expensive new equipment, and the extensive modification of existing facilities."[34] Coke-oven emission standards, for example, would "increase employment by 5,000 or more because of a productivity decline in coke-oven operations of between 18 and 29 percent," according to Nichols and Zeckhauser.

Labor also supported legislation to require the clean-up of allegedly hazardous waste-disposal sites, such as the Love Canal in Niagara Falls, New York. According to the *New York Times,* "almost everyone involved, including community and local environmental groups, agrees that the toxic waste program stands as the most wasteful effort of all."[35]

European Attractions

The more American labor became attracted to government regulation and control of the economy, the more attractive European social democracy appeared. Labor leaders in the United States envied the benefits that European unions had won through collective bargaining and envied their legislative accomplishments. In contrast to the United States, unemployment benefits in most of western Europe were extremely generous over long periods. Thus, the AFL-CIO noted that, "in Germany, unemployment benefits amount to 66 percent of normal wages for up to 18 months. After that the level is reduced to 58 percent for an unlimited time." The Integrated Fund of Italy "guarantees jobs at affected companies (ones that need to restructure or go bust) for at least half pay for three years." Vacation pay seemed much better: "As a general rule, EC countries grant between 4 weeks and 5 weeks of mandated vacation pay as contrasted to a *U.S. average of only 12 days.*"[36]

The contrasts were so great that the AFL-CIO could compare the United States only with apartheid-era South Africa. Only these two industrialized nations failed to "provide a wide range of social benefits from universal health care to maternity leave (with pay)."[37] The labor movement concluded that, if the European nations could do it, the United States could and should follow suit.

By the early 1990s, however, serious problems surfaced in the economies of western Europe. Over the prior two decades, they had created far fewer jobs than the American economy. Shortly after the AFL-CIO touted the ample benefits extended to European workers, the economies of those countries plunged into a deep and prolonged recession, which nearly all commentators blamed on the kinds of programs that the AFL-CIO praised. Employee benefits increased labor costs, reduced competitiveness, and decreased new jobs.

Much of the trouble seemed attributable to the strength of European unions, especially as compared with their American counterparts. C. Fred Bergsten, of the Institute for International Economics, commented that "the United States has kept labor costs down and created 40 million jobs over the past twenty years. In Europe, wages have risen about 60 percent during that span but only 2 or 3 million jobs have been created."[38] The recession in Germany, long considered the strongest economy in Europe, was beginning to be seen as not just another temporary dip but much more, because of deep structural problems, including high labor costs, low productivity, lengthy vacations, and the shortest working hours of any industrialized nation.[39] German companies started to build their plants abroad, many in the United States, in particular in the less unionized southern states: "A survey of 10,000 businessmen last November [1993] indicated that 30 percent of those now polled are considering shifting part of their production outside Germany."[40] Virtually all European countries have started cutting back on the benefits that the AFL-CIO had so recently praised.

Economic Planning

To its other turnabouts, organized labor added a flip-flop on economic planning. Once again, considerations of self-interest were paramount. In the mid-1960s, George Meany vowed that "labor would join with business in fighting a planned economy." Official AFL-CIO policy was not as hostile to planning as Meany made out. "Experience has shown," declared a 1963 convention resolution,

> that we cannot rely upon the blind forces of the market place for full employment, full production and effective use of our resources to meet our most urgent needs. Other advanced free and democratic . . . nations have found that they can achieve their economic and social objectives through a rational national economic planning process involving the democratic participation of all segments of their populations.[41]

By the mid-1970s, labor had become the nation's foremost advocate of economic planning. A 1977 Executive Council report claimed that there should be

government planning to forestall future shortages and bottlenecks which contribute to inflation would foresee potential shortages and allow for the buildup of stockpiles to diminish shortage-induced price increases. Potential sources
of inflation pressures could be identified through detailed
investigations of the various industrial sectors. With such
advance information, programs would be undertaken to
eliminate potential bottlenecks before they can become
forces for inflationary pressures.[42]

Peter Schuck, among others, has pointed out the inadequacies of
every one of the numerous economic indexes that one would have to
use to predict bottlenecks, including such basic ones as the "whole-
sale price index, the consumer price index, the unemployment rate
and business inventory levels." Worse yet, "often the deficiencies of
these indices will become apparent only long after they have seriously misled policy makers."[43]

This is exactly what would have happened had policy makers
followed AFL-CIO advice. In the late 1970s, the AFL-CIO, for example, called for "effective export control on agricultural commodities
and other raw materials in short supply" to reduce prices. But, soon
after, the prices of raw materials declined because of the discovery
of new technology that allowed old sources to be used more effi-
ciently and created new substitutes for old resources.

Nonetheless, labor's new-found faith in planning only strength-
ened. In 1981, the AFL-CIO called for rebuilding the U.S. economy,
urging the creation of a government–business–organized labor
board to oversee the investment of "public and private funds in necessary reindustrialization projects."[44] By 1989, labor was arguing
not just for a reconstruction bank but for a more grandiose "demo-
cratically controlled, publicly accountable renewal strategy" that
would necessitate the establishment of a "National Strategic Planning Board which assesses the importance of various industries for
the economic future of the country and formulates long-range plans
for these industries."[45] AFL-CIO President Kirkland subsequently
proposed that "the industrial policy board and the bank . . . have the
authority to limit the wasteful bidding war between the states."[46]

The Return to Class Struggle

In conjunction with the call for ever more government regulation
and control of the economy, the AFL-CIO has increasingly employed

the rhetoric of class struggle. Unlike his predecessors, Kirkland had little good to say about American democratic capitalism. In 1978, he complained that "since 1969, when Richard Nixon and his game planners deliberately established a set of policies designed to reduce the buying power of workers and to inflate profits and interest rates, wage earners have been under economic siege."[47] Three years after this remark, with a Republican once again in the White House, the executive council charged that the Reagan administration's policies "add up to class warfare against the disadvantaged, the poor and the working people of America."[48] In 1982, Kirkland described the economic policies of the Reagan administration as "an attack on American working people." Such policies were "a conscious attempt to respond to a particular constituency whose solitary commitment is to enhance the position of class, privilege, and wealth in America."[49] Kirkland argued "that were it not for the labor movement American politics would be completely taken over by the most narrow and greedy special interests. . . . both parties would be controlled by the bankers, the oil barons and the admen, lawyers, consultants, and lobbyists for corporate greed,"[50] whom he identified at another time as those who "profit from monopoly, economic chaos and human suffering."[51]

The Impact of the Public-Employee Unions

The first purpose of all public-employee unions, as labor economist Leo Troy has argued, is to "socialize income" and thereby "to shift decision making from the individual to the state. That position puts them at odds with private-sector unions, which "historically . . . stressed the acceptance of capitalism."[52] But that view confuses the past with the present and the membership with the leadership. The members of private-sector unions may not want to pay the high taxes needed to finance the salaries that public-employee unions demand for their members—many working-class Americans have been active in the tax revolts of the past two decades. Still, the leaders of today's private-sector unions have no such objections to higher taxes and spending. Besides, many private-sector unions, from the Teamsters to the Steelworkers, have recently taken up organizing and representing public employees: at least thirty-two AFL-CIO unions now represent some public employees.

No public disagreements over government spending between public-sector and private-sector trade union leaders are worth noting. The growing influence of public-employee unions has done nothing fundamentally new but has accelerated, reinforced, and perhaps make irreversible the strong trend toward statism that has long been present within the American labor movement.

The Intellectual Case

America's public-employee unions do more than flex political muscle for self-interested reasons; they present an objective intellectual case for increasing government spending. The Public Employee Department (PED) of the AFL-CIO, to which all unions that represent public employees belong, argues, for instance, that "private investment cannot take place without public investment leading the way"[53]: public spending directly and indirectly creates demand for goods and services provided by the private sector and also creates the infrastructure that companies need to survive and grow (public school systems would be an example). In line with this thinking, the PED holds that there can hardly be too much government spending. Thus, it supports more and higher taxes: raising property taxes on commercial and industrial property owners, extending the property tax to intangible property like stocks and bonds, and transforming "regressive local wage taxes through such means as piggy-backing on existing state income taxes."[54] This is the public-employee unions' prescription for fiscal health in every state, including those, like New York, that are widely thought to be overtaxed.

In New York State in 1992 (before Republican George Pataki defeated Democratic gubernatorial incumbent Mario Cuomo, largely by calling for lower taxes), local representatives of the American Federation of State, County, and Municipal Employees (AFSCME) and the Fiscal Policy Institute (AFSCME's think tank) argued that the notion of exorbitant corporate taxes in New York was a myth and that New York's taxes on corporations were actually lower than those levied by many other states: "Rhetoric aside, many New York corporations are getting a bargain."[55] The Fiscal Policy Institute then proposed to eliminate the investment tax credit; pass a sunset law for all corporate tax breaks; stiffen financial-reporting requirements to catch alleged abuses such as shifting profits out of New York (to lower-tax states); and extending sales taxes to services. The PED adamantly rejected arguments for cutting or, in some cases, eliminating taxes to attract business investment. Claiming that cutting taxes on business would merely result in higher taxes for individuals, the PED warned that businesses would actually leave when "lessened public spending reduces the desirability of a region or state, [and] undermines education, training, research and other elements critical to a healthy economy."[56]

Fighting Privatization

The flip side of the public-employee unions' struggle for increased funding of state and local governments is their newer battle against the privatization of government services. Privatization has become the *bête noire* of public-sector unionism. In recent years, each issue of the PED's newsletter has included a "Privatization Update" insert. No convention or conference of public-employee unions goes by without denunciations of and resolutions against privatization.

Why has this issue come to supersede all others? Clearly, it is not because of any imminent danger of privatizing all or most public services. The real threat is that the public-employee unions might see their monopoly broken. What they fear, then, is the same competition from which the private-sector unions are now suffering.

At bottom, the public-sector unions' arguments against privatization are inescapably anticapitalist. An AFSCME broadside called *Passing the Bucks* argues that "private companies exist to make a profit; the necessity of a profit drives up the costs." The same publication claims that "contracting out results in poorer service, because in order to make a profit the private contractors are also looking for ways to reduce their costs and frequently this has meant they 'cut corners' by hiring inexperienced transient personnel at low wages, by ignoring contract requirements, or by providing inadequate supervision."[57] Another AFSCME publication argues that "contracting out is all too often associated with bribery, kickbacks, and collusive bidding."[58] In other words, there is no good reason for contracting out.

In fact, an overwhelming case has been made for the privatization of a host of government services. An international review of fifty-two cases showed that private provision of a service was more efficient in forty cases; in only three cases was public provision clearly more efficient.[59] Other studies have shown that the costs of water, street cleaning, ship maintenance, housing construction, school bus operation, and railroad track repair were all lower when done by private firms rather than by government agencies because of lower labor costs and more effective management. Both factors are, in turn, products of greater competition in the private sector that the PED warns against.

The Exception That Proves the Rule

For decades, even conservatives have pointed to the American Federation of Teachers as an exception proving that public-employee unions need not be cast in the mold just described. What distinguishes the AFT from other public-employee unions, however, is mostly due to one man, its president, Albert Shanker. Almost all educational reformers have great respect for Shanker. Chester E. Finn, Jr., former assistant secretary of education, calls him "one of the authentically insightful and imaginative figures in American education, casting a much larger shadow than anybody else in what is commonly dubbed the 'education establishment.' "[60]

Finn's praise is appropriate; Shanker's commitment to high-quality public education is undisputed. But, on issues of government spending and privatization, there is no fundamental difference between the AFT and the other public-sector unions: all are enthusiastic friends of the former and staunch foes of the latter. The AFT is perhaps more cautious in making claims about the educational benefits of increased spending than the rival National Education Association. But it is no less committed than the NEA to educational spending as a means of improving the quality of schooling. In 1993, for example, Sandra Feldman (who succeeded Shanker as president of the AFT's huge New York City local and is considered more in the Shanker mold than any other possible successor) chaired an AFT Task Force of Children in Crisis, whose purpose was to "study and suggest solutions to the problems of young people who need so much more from our schools at the very time our schools are being forced to make do with less." The solution was "more," $10.5 billion more. According to Feldman, "most of this money would be used to expand existing, proven successful—but never fully funded—programs such as Chapter 1 [funds schools attended by underprivileged students] and Head Start [funds preschool education for the same group]."[61]

Both Chapter 1 and Head Start are popular programs, but neither has been nearly as successful as Feldman claimed. Shanker himself acknowledged as much regarding Head Start, after Bill Clinton was elected president. At that time, the AFT president admitted that, before the 1992 election, "many of us saw its shortcomings, but we were reluctant to open up the issue, to raise doubts. We were afraid that if we offered suggestions for improving Head Start, the end result would be no improvements and the program might suffer cuts instead of being expanded."[62]

Even then, Shanker would not admit the extent to which Head Start had failed. The evidence that Head Start worked was based on the success of a small program in Ypsilanti, Michigan, that was not even part of the Head Start programs. All research on actual Head Start programs shows that whatever effect they have on children disappears altogether within three years. The program was performing so poorly that its founder, Yale professor Edward Ziegler, "recommended against putting more money into it unless it improves."[63] Still, Shanker and the committee had called for full funding.

Chapter 1, which Shanker once described as the federal government's "most successful program for disadvantaged children,"[64] had been no more successful than Head Start, maybe less. A report for Congress determined that the program's method of pulling students out of regular classes for intensive instruction was ineffective for several reasons—among them, students received on the average only ten minutes of additional instructional time each day; the schools they attended were not performing well in general; in many instances they received instruction from teacher's aides who were not fully literate or numerate themselves; and sometimes they were pulled out of classes in basic subjects so that there was no increase in instructional time in reading.[65] In sum, more than $6 billion per year was being spent to little effect.

Feldman asserted that, despite underfunding (nearly $8,000 per student per year, thousands more than are now spent in affluent school districts in California), "we're saving enough [students] to know that if only we could make an adequate investment in programs that work, it would be possible to save almost all of our young people. . . . Money does make a difference." She continued:

> For instance, in New York City, state and local education funding increased throughout the late 1980s and per-pupil expenditure grew by more than $1500 in the last half of the decade. The money was targeted to a few well-defined objectives, and it worked. Attendance is at its highest level in twenty-four years, and the dropout rate has been edging steadily downward. A special math initiative raised math scores five percentage points, the largest one-year gain in twenty years. And perhaps most gratifying, reading

achievement for those with the least skills soared ten percentage points.[66]

But things were not quite as Feldman described them. The year following the AFT report, New York City's school superintendent, Joseph Fernandez, reported yet another reduction in the dropout rate. Yet, "the significance of the decline was immediately disputed by other educators, who viewed the figures as a statistical irrelevancy. Even as dropout rates were declining, they said, a smaller percentage of students were earning high school diplomas than only a few years ago." According to one authority, "more students were spending more years in school, but with little to show for it."[67] (Another *New York Times* report related that students may have been spending more years in school, but the number graduating from high school in four years had actually declined during Fernandez's tenure.)

Math scores did rise as Feldman said but then fell in a year. The next year, they dropped precipitously "when a new math test with more up-to-date national norms was administered."[68] The "improvement" cited by Fernandez and Feldman was due to teachers becoming more familiar with the old test and thus better at showing students how to score well on it; it was not due to students actually learning more. As for reading scores, "since the reading test . . . was last calibrated against a national sample of students in the late 1980s, performance on the test has moved within a narrow range, just at or below the national average."[69]

Reviewing all the numbers, Raymond Damonico, a former data analyst for the New York City Board of Education and then director of the Manhattan Institute's Center for Educational Innovation, concluded that "on all three of these important indicators, the system has been stuck at the same level for the last six or seven years. This despite a budgetary increase of $2.4 billion, or 40 percent in per-pupil terms, over those same years."[70] So much for Feldman's altogether typical claims for the educational benefits to be derived from increasing spending on education.

No evidence shows that increased spending will improve the quality of education. In an exhaustive review of 180 studies conducted over the past decades, Eric Hanushek found a "consistency to the results: *There appears to be no strong or systematic relationship between school expenditures and student performance.*"[71] Neither reducing class size nor increasing teacher pay had any positive effect on student achievement.

Like other public-sector unions, the AFT teams support for more funding with opposition to privatization. For years, its top political priority (a life-or-death issue, according to Shanker) has been fighting privatization in the form of school choice. The AFT was probably the first union in the antiprivatization fight. As early as the first half of the 1980s, the union was making a candidate's position on tuition tax credits or vouchers a litmus test.

A resolution passed at the AFT's 1992 convention pledged the organization to be at the "forefront of the public policy debate . . . in shaping policy designed to combat privatization and contracting out."[72] The AFT includes the Public Employees' Federation that represents workers who do not provide educational services. Moreover, the union realizes the inescapable, logical connection between privatization and school choice.

Like other proposals to reinvent government—including the National Performance Review prepared under the direction of Vice President Albert Gore, Jr.—school choice is based on the idea of treating clients (in this case, the parents of school-age children) as customers who are assumed to know better than a government bureaucracy what best serves their needs and interests. The AFT is as irreconcilably opposed to this approach as any public-employee union.

For customers to have choices, more than one provider of a service or product must compete for business. For public-employees' unions, whose members are monopoly providers of public services, competition is a threat, as it is to any monopolist. "There is little doubt," Shanker concedes, "that competition would force schools to be sensitive to what customers (parents and students) want," but he argues that "there's precious little evidence that what they want is a rigorous education." Under a school-choice regime, then, all schools both public and private would wind up selling themselves on the basis of the wrong criteria: "Creative marketers with schools to sell would find plenty of ways that had nothing to do with producing real learning to attract kids to their schools—'Get a free trip to Disneyland.' 'Come to the school that produced last year's state champs.' 'Swim in our new Olympic pool.' "[73]

The mind-set that this critique reveals is troubling. That some parents may be taken in by hucksters is no more an argument against allowing parents choice among schools than the propensity of some Americans to buy too much junk food for their children is an argument against supermarkets and for government-run food-distribution centers that stock only nutritious foods.

Many parents may not know how to distinguish between good and bad schools for their children, and others may not care. But some will know and care, and these demanding "customers" may well push up the general quality of education in the same way that in the more competitive automobile market of the 1970s and 1980s, the more demanding buyers forced American carmakers to improve the quality of not just some but all cars that they manufactured. That competition will bring similar improvements in educational quality is not certain. As James Q. Wilson writes:

> We do not know the effect on values, educational attainment, or operating efficiencies, of a true market in publicly-supported education in which there are strong incentives for parents to make choices and strong incentives for schools to adapt to these choices. We do know that many organizations speaking for public-school teachers. . . . are determined that we not find out.[74]

Prominent among such organizations is the American Federation of Teachers, which in this very important respect is at one with other public-employee unions in opposing any challenge to public sector monopoly.

4
The Foreign Policy of American Labor

F or Gompers, as for the radicals of his era, the crucial problem of foreign policy was imperialism and its wars, which they all vehemently opposed. But the significance of one crucial difference would become apparent only decades later. For Lenin, imperialism was "the last stage of capitalism," during which the capitalists essentially bought off the labor aristocracy of the advanced countries through profits derived from exploiting colonial workers. Gompers, too, saw imperialism as a form of class warfare, but, unlike Lenin, he understood imperialism as a capitalist frontal assault on the working class in America and other developed countries. He complained that the

> systematic policy of the capitalistic class as exhibited in its persistent efforts in breaking down the ancient civilizations of India and China, the introduction of labor-saving machinery, of modern methods of production in the less-advanced countries of the world, is a form of deviltry far more menacing to the well being of the working class of America, than negro slavery was in Dixie.[1]

Gompers opposed all instances of imperialism, making no exception for the United States. He opposed the annexation of Hawaii (most important then as a stopover for ships on their way to China) and the acquisition of the Philippines, Puerto Rico, and Cuba following the U.S. victory in the Spanish-American War. He blamed such expansionism on the greed of capitalists for whom "when there is a question between liberty and profit, liberty is thrown to the dogs as a worn out and threadbare thing of the past."[2]

Like most Americans, including President Woodrow Wilson, Gompers adamantly opposed U.S. entry into World War I—at first. In 1914, he condemned the war as nothing more than a capitalist plot "to divert the attention of the people from their domestic problems and to demoralize organized labor so that it would no longer be a threat to the entrenched dynasties."[3]

Within a few years, however, his thinking about America's involvement in the war, and indeed about American foreign policy altogether, had changed greatly. Gompers became a proponent of an all-out U.S. effort to defeat Germany and an ardent nationalist generally. His left-wing critics have charged that calculation played a role in this reversal. Of course, Gompers realized that continued opposition to the war would have disastrous consequences. He had long been at pains to portray the AFL as a distinctly American institution, indeed as no less than the bulwark of the existing order. To persevere in opposition to U.S. involvement would have shattered that image. Withholding support from the American war effort would have meant associating the AFL in the public mind with the Socialist Party, which in March 1917 had decried the U.S. declaration of war as "a crime against the people of the United States and against the nations of the world."[4] For three decades, Gompers had been putting as much distance as possible between the AFL and the Socialists; he could not stand by and see that work ruined. He sought to prove his movement's patriotism by arguing effectively against pacifism and the pacifists in labor's own ranks. He even called a special trade union conference for the express purpose of putting the labor movement "before the public in a patriotic light."[5]

Gompers told a receptive Wilson administration that the American workingman's whole-hearted support of the war effort depended on union representatives being appointed to all commissions and committees that dealt with labor matters. In recognition of labor's contribution to the war effort, Wilson made such appointments. Under the protection of the boards on which the unionists served, union membership rose rapidly, as did wages.

Institutional self-interest coincided with but does not explain Gompers's obviously heartfelt conversion to the idea that the U.S.

role during and after the war should be to promote democracy. "I was convinced," he wrote in his autobiography,

> that the real issues of the war concerned those who believed in democratic institutions and that the time had come when the world could no longer exist part democratic and part autocratic. It was an issue upon which there could be no real neutrality, and therefore propaganda for neutrality was propaganda to maintain autocracy. Those not actively for democracy were in effect against it.[6]

Henceforth, the promotion of democracy would be the touchstone of his own foreign policy and therefore of the AFL for as long as he lived.

Gompers's conversion to an activist, prodemocracy foreign policy grew out of his conviction that free trade unions were essential to the establishment and survival of democracies. The spring of 1917, for instance, found him supporting the first phase of the revolution in Russia. His letter to the labor representatives in the Russian Duma on the overthrow of the czar read in part: "The splendid proclamation of your provisional government declaring for free speech and press and the right of workers to organize and if necessary strike for their rights guarantees to Russian workers opportunity for freedom and progress and assures the new Russia her future greater glory."[7]

Yet when the Bolshevik coup of that autumn overthrew Aleksandr Kerensky's provisional government, Gompers minced no words: "These pirates ran up the black flag over helpless Russia and declared war upon the established order about which the fabric of civilized life had been woven and Russia had been transformed from an Ally into a menace."[8]

Previously, Gompers had argued that "in the last analysis the masses of the people of every country have it in their hands to exert their own will and power against international war, and . . . if otherwise thwarted they will not hesitate to exert it."[9] But now he took a very different tack, arguing that strong trade unions were the best defense against revolution:

> Were there an American Federation of Labor in Russia there could have been no bolshevism. Were there no organized labor movement in America devoted to the ideals of liberty and right and justice and unshaken in its faith in progress through the orderly processes of democracy, there would be bolshevism in America.[10]

Had Russia possessed a trade union federation analogous to the AFL, there might have been no October Revolution.

If free trade unions were as important as Gompers believed, then, as he argued, the AFL had an extremely important role to play in promoting the foreign policy interests of the United States as defined by President Wilson. Thus, after the war, he actively participated in the establishment of the International Labor Organization of the League of Nations and in the reorganization of the International Federation of Trade Unions (IFTU) that the AFL had joined before the war.

After Gompers died in 1924, the AFL stepped back from active involvement in international affairs. The Soviets had organized the Third (socialist or Communist) International in 1919 and then their own Red International of Labor Unions (RILU) in 1921 to compete with the Second International (democratic-socialist) and the IFTU, respectively. Moreover, both the Second International and the IFTU moved left in response to the Communist challenge. The IFTU issued a manifesto for a general strike to socialize industry (a radical step beyond the parliamentarism of the German Social-Democrat Eduard Bernstein) and also for an embargo on arms shipments to Poland but not to its enemy in war, the Soviet Union.

In his classic *Labor and Internationalism*, the usually sympathetic Lewis Lorwin criticized the leadership of the post-Gompers AFL for not differentiating among trade unionists, Socialists, and Communists, and he probably was correct to do so. But labor's leaders, living in the shadow of the great red scare of the years after World War I, were acutely sensitive to public attitudes and, therefore, put as much distance as possible between their movement and the events in Europe. Moreover, Gompers's foreign policy views were based on the assumption that Wilsonian internationalism would be the future U.S. posture in the world. When that proved wrong, the AFL, in tune with the temper of new times, slipped into what some leaders happily called splendid isolation.

The Totalitarian Threat

Labor's interest in international affairs revived with the approach of World War II. David Dubinsky, the social-democratic president of the International Ladies Garment Workers Union, was active early.

The ILGWU raised $20,000 from its membership for unions under siege in Italy and Germany in 1933 and $64,000 the following year.

But the rest of the AFL was not so involved in opposing fascism. The AFL as an organization was in no way sympathetic to facism. As early as 1933, it expressed its concern about the new Hitler government's repression of German trade unionists and supported a call for a boycott of German goods. And, because of the efforts of Dubinsky and his allies, labor committed itself in the mid-1930s to funding a Labor Chest for the Oppressed Peoples of Europe. Although the AFL resolutely continued to favor U.S. neutrality (even after the start of the war in Europe), Dubinsky believed that the labor chest represented the start of a new federation effort to support trade unions.[11]

The CIO shared the AFL's antifascist sentiments but felt even more intensely that the United States should stay out of war. John L. Lewis even belonged to the America First Committee. The Communists who had penetrated the CIO also opposed U.S. involvement, at least between August 1939, when Germany and the USSR signed their nonaggression pact, and June 1941, when Hitler invaded Russia. Because of their influence, the CIO resolution in favor of neutrality did not even "mention the antagonists in the European war by name. . . . Sympathy for the victims of Hitler's terror, growing by millions weekly as Nazi troops cut across the Polish plains, is studiously avoided."[12] Communists also saw to it that, unlike the AFL, which by 1940 had come out in favor of aid to the Allies, the CIO in that year "unanimously adopted a position which discouraged even non-military aid."[13]

The support of some in the CIO of the Allied cause equaled that of the AFL, preeminently Walter Reuther of the Automobile Workers and Sidney Hillman of the Amalgamated Clothing Workers. But neither matched Dubinsky's activism. Reuther was preoccupied with fighting Communists in the UAW. Hillman, according to his sympathetic biographer Stephen Fraser, was consumed with thinking about how to get the CIO "invited permanently inside the highest policy-making and strategy-making circles of the Democratic Party and the national regime."[14]

During the war years, Dubinsky supplemented his antifascist activism by taking a lead role in mobilizing labor to fight the spread of communism. In 1943, he organized a protest meeting against Stalin's execution of two labor leaders, the Polish Jews Henryk Ehrlich and Victor Alter. Matthew Woll and William Green, Gompers's successor, both attended, as did former CIO president John L. Lewis. Reuther lent his support. Yet CIO President Philip Murray and Sidney Hillman stayed away for fear of alienating the Communists in CIO ranks. In Hillman's case, his refusal to speak out publicly for two leaders of a movement to which he had belonged before emigrating to America was considered despicable even by many of his closest associates, some of whom broke with him over this incident.

Dubinsky was also responsible for the establishment of the AFL's Free Trade Union Committee in 1943 and for encouraging the appointment of Jay Lovestone, the one-time Communist turned anti-Communist, to direct it. The committee's first purpose was to help prepare Europe's democratic, Socialist-led trade unions to work on rebuilding their societies after the war. Its second purpose was to make clear the difference between free trade unions and Soviet-style trade unions, which Dubinsky understood to be "instrument[s] of a dictatorial government . . . whose . . . only goal on the labor front would be to subvert the unions of all other countries into instruments of Soviet dictatorship."[15]

International Workers' Organizations

The CIO, following Hillman's lead, did everything possible to blur the distinction between democratic and Communist trade unions. Late in 1944, when victory over the Nazis was certain, Hillman led in organizing the World Federation of Trade Unions, a new working-class coalition including Communist and non-Communist trade unions. The Soviets and Hillman working together managed to elect a Communist, Louis Saillant, general secretary of the WFTU, which included all the significant trade union movements of the world except the AFL, which stayed away because of anti-Communist conviction.

At war's end, Hillman warned a popular-front rally at Madison Square Garden of "powerful and unscrupulous forces" that were "jockeying for positions from which to launch a new imperialist scramble for power . . . seeking domination of world markets and dream[ing] of an American Century" and spreading "anti-Soviet and anti-British poison." But Hillman was confident that the WFTU would stop them. In a conversation with Secretary of Labor Frances Perkins, he was full of praise for the Soviet labor commissar and the Soviets in general and expressed his conviction that the WFTU "would penetrate and dominate the UN, would end all future wars and plan the world economy."[16]

Perkins took this as grandiose nonsense, but the appalled AFL leadership took it seriously. Believing as strongly as Hillman did that control of international labor would be decisive in the conflicts ahead, the AFL was concerned about the WFTU and harbored high hopes for the International Confederation of Free Trade Unions (ICFTU), which it helped establish after the WFTU broke up over the Marshall Plan. For the AFL, victory in the East-West conflict would go to whichever side controlled labor. The leadership thought that "in mid-century . . . the chief totalitarian threat was that of Communism, which, in some respects, was far more dangerous than fascism because its chief appeal and its false claims were directed mainly at workers and their organizations throughout the world."[17] Equating control of the internationals with control of their member unions, the AFL believed the former to be decisive.

The breakup of the WFTU proved both Hillman and the AFL's leaders equally wrong about the importance of controlling international labor organizations. Communists controlled the WFTU, but all the non-Communist unions in it supported the Marshall Plan despite Soviet opposition. In the U.S. Congress, meanwhile, the bill passed easily; even Republican isolationists voted for it. Opposition to such a popular plan would have been futile and probably even self-destructive, as the CIO's leaders recognized. Other trade union movements found themselves in a similar bind: because of such strong support of the Marshall Plan, even some Communist unions wanted to back it. Communists in France and Italy were expecting to support the plan until the Soviets gave them contrary orders. And had not Stalin told them no, Poland and Czechoslovakia would have taken part in the European Recovery Program.

Thus, the ICFTU's Communist counterpart, the WFTU, had a limited capacity to further the aims of the Soviet Union. The AFL's high hopes for the ICFTU were dashed almost immediately. The AFL remained far more resolutely anti-Communist than any of its European counterparts. Unions almost everywhere outside the United States identified with the Left, and, after the first few years of the cold war, the Left was less anti-Communist than the Center or Right. Differences between the AFL-CIO and the British Trades

Union Congress (TUC), according to U.S. diplomat George Lodge, were "one of the most debilitating divisions" in the ICFTU structure:

> Many leaders of British labor do not feel that because a man is a Communist he is necessarily an agent of a foreign power. . . . An official British source estimated that one out of every ten British trade unions officials is a card-carrying member of the party. . . . The TUC feels that if a trade union leader in Africa, for example, is doing a good job, ably assisting a democratic worker organization, he should not be deprived of ICFTU assistance just because he happens to be associated with the Communist Party. The Communist Party, they argue, is just another political party.[18]

Such differences increased over time. Indeed, the AFL-CIO quit the ICFTU in 1969—returning in 1980 after the ICFTU reversed course—because other movements were increasingly relating to and working with Communist trade unions, even with the state-controlled unions of the Soviet bloc.

Victor Feather, the first president of the European Trade Union Committee, the European division of the ICFTU, said in 1973 that "ETUC's doors are open to all the trade unions of Europe."[19] Lodge pointed out that there were "other differences too. The Americans feel many British and European trade unionists have an insufficient realization of the need for an improved and expanded NATO defense system. The 'better Red than dead' philosophy of Bertrand Russell, shared by some trade unionists, is completely unacceptable to Americans."[20]

The AFL also grossly overestimated the political importance of any given country's trade union movement. Labor leaders strove to convince America's opinion leaders and policy makers that control of a nation's trade unions was decisive in a nation's future. "As the war in Europe came to an end," wrote David Dubinsky, "it became increasingly obvious that the question of whether democracy was to revive in the countries overrun by Hitler and Mussolini lay in the trade unions."[21] But what seemed obvious then, does not seem so in retrospect.

In postwar Eastern Europe, the most important factor turned out to be the balance of international forces, which determined whether the USSR could send in the Red Army to support a Communist takeover or to put down an anti-Communist insurrection. The balance of forces within a country was also crucial. Marxist-Leninist theory aside, the Soviets "knew that ultimately the outcome of the struggle depended on seizing control of the secret police, the army, their radio, the press and the Ministry of the Interior."[22] After that, the most important task was to crush all opposition parties. This is not to say that Communists did not try to take over trade unions and then use them to gain or consolidate power. By definition, totalitarian movements aspire to eliminate any and all independent sources of economic, social, and political power, including unions. But absorbing or destroying independent trade unions was just one of many important objectives.

The West European Battleground

American labor's parallel claim that in Western Europe, too, the future depended on control of the trade unions proved untrue. The AFL warned in 1947 that "if the German trade unions [are] captured by the Communists and their stooges, they will be coordinated as part of a giant war machine run by the Russian dictatorship in its drive for world conquest and war."[23] The warning was repeated in 1948 by AFL Vice-President Matthew Woll in a letter to Secretary of the Army Kenneth Royal.[24] In 1949, David Dubinsky wrote that "had it not been for the extensive educational activities of the AFL . . . the Communists . . . might by now have seized control of the reviving German trade unions."[25] The left-wing critic Sidney Lens gave credence to Dubinsky's claim: "This might have been true, but it is odd that Dubinsky never asked himself whether the German workers had a right to make their own choice without 'educational activities' from the outside."[26]

But the odds of a Communist takeover of the German trade unions had never amounted to much; by 1947, they were hovering just above zero. West Germans had a front-row seat from which to witness the spectacle of Soviet rule over their eastern cousins. In the Soviet occupation zone, Communist authorities had confiscated any property of value early on, alienating all classes in the process. After doing poorly in local elections in the winter of 1945–1946, they crushed all opposition, arresting political activists and forcibly folding the Socialists into the Communist Party structure. As a result of these actions, Germans from the Soviet zone started streaming into free Germany as early as late 1945.

"The influence of the Communist Party in West Germany," historian Walter Laqueur noted, "dwindled into insignificance. . . . Social Democrats, Christian Democrats, and Liberals were alarmed about the fate of their comrades in the East, and a militant anticommunism spread in their parties."[27] The AFL, to its credit, did help to thwart an effort by Communist infiltrators within the Western occupation authorities to set up the revived German trade unions in ways that would disadvantage Social-Democratic unionists, but that process was only a sideshow. The growing unpopularity of the Communists themselves primarily made a Communist takeover of the West German trade unions impossible.

France—Second in Importance. France was considered second in importance only to Germany. "France," Jay Lovestone, now head of the AFL's International Affairs Department, wrote, "is the key to Russia's control of Western Europe. If Joe [Stalin] gets France he outflanks Germany and then he might allow us to go home or lend-lease us the railroad fare."[28] One legitimate concern was that the French Communist Party (PCF) had strong popular support. Another concern was that the Communists controlled the Confederation Générale de Travail (CGT), the French trade union movement. But that proved to mean far less than feared.

The armed forces, the gendarmerie, and the state apparatus in general all remained in non-Communist hands. The United States stood, moreover, behind the French state and would surely have intervened militarily had the Communists dared to try a full-scale insurrection. And Soviet armed forces were no match for ours at the time.

Subsequently, the Soviets decided to offer up the French Communist Party as a sacrifice in their desperate effort to sabotage the Marshall Plan. The French Communists were ordered to use the only means at their disposal, the trade unions, to create economic instability. A general strike was duly called. The French government remained uncowed and soon moved to stop the disruptions. Jules Mach, the Socialist interior minister, called for legislation mobilizing 80,000 reservists, increasing penalties for sabotage and for violating a worker's right to go to work, and so on. After a five-day filibuster by Communist deputies, the legislation passed. This was too much for the strikers themselves, most of whom were not dedicated Communists. The strike crumbled when the government made it clear that the now-hungry workers would receive no back pay for the time they had missed.[29]

The CGT tried—and failed—again a year later in a strike against the mines. The Communist-controlled unions used tactics, such as calling out the safety and maintenance men (not done even in strikes against the Nazis), that repelled even militant trade unionists. Mach acted decisively once more, sending troops to protect nonstriking miners from assault and the mines from sabotage.[30] The Communists paid heavily for calling these strikes and for the tactics they employed. After the 1948 strike, membership in the CGT plummeted. Of 6 million, 2–4 million members quit. That made the movement and the organized working class an even weaker force to contend with.

American Labor's Role. Up until this point, the AFL itself was hardly in the picture. It had played only a minor role in supporting the anti-Communist French trade unionists, to no great effect. After the defeat of the 1948 CGT strike, the AFL aided in the creation of the Force Ouvrière (FO), a new federation of free trade unions that the AFL hoped would surpass the CGT.

The AFL hoped that the FO would become the dominant trade union federation in France. Irving Brown, the AFL's European representative, argued to no avail that the West should recognize the FO as the official and only legitimate representative of French workers and that, in France, "the CGT should be denied representation rights as an organization which is not independent, but is an agency of a foreign power."[31] Although the FO never approached the size of even the shrunken CGT, FO members and affiliates did help contain and defeat Communist efforts to disrupt or prevent the delivery of arms from the United States in 1949 and 1950.

For this success, too, at least one commentator has given Brown and the AFL more credit than they strictly deserve. Writing in *Policy Review*, former AFL staffer Arnold Beichman noted that "through force and intimidation, and abetted by the high popular esteem of the Soviet role in World War II . . . the Communists had seized the longshoremen's unions. . . . Neither the French nor the Italian government seemed ready to overcome this threat to their sovereignty. . . . Into this breach stepped the American Federation of Labor."[32] Brown helped to organize the Mediterranean Committee that hired laborers (from Italy according to Ronald Radosh; with CIA money according to former CIA agent Tom Braden) to "stand guard while French dockworkers unloaded U.S. arms for NATO in the face of Communist threats to life."[33]

Beichman overstated both the seriousness of the threat and the character of the indigenous response to it. The disastrous strikes of 1947 and 1948 had left the CGT largely a spent force, and the French government (contrary to Beichman's assertion) was more than willing to take on the Communists, in this case with tough new antisabotage legislation. In addition, the British and American governments would have stepped in if necessary. The United States would not conceivably have allowed a relatively small number of Communist dockworkers to prevent delivery of arms considered vital to Western security. As for the Mediterranean Committee, its contribution merits only praise. The AFL played an honorable part here, but in a supporting role.

Frustration in Italy. The story in Italy was similar. The Italian Communist Party (PCI) had a popular following and, after the war, controlled the trade union movement, the General Confederation of Italian Workers (CGIL). But, as in France, the Communists faced constraints. A revolutionary insurrection was not a viable option since they knew that the British and Americans were prepared to intervene against any attempt to seize power by force.

Later that year, the CGIL's Communist leaders received orders from Moscow to go on the offensive against the Marshall Plan. But Communist efforts to disrupt the economy did little damage, and the government for the most part maintained law and order. In response to a general strike the Communists called in Milan, for instance, the government met force with force and arrested violent strikers.

In the runup to the scheduled elections of 1948, the Communists built extraparliamentary, mass organizations of workers and peasants—still to no avail. The February coup in Czechoslovakia made the election a virtual referendum on communism, which de Gasperi's Christian Democrats won big, garnering 48 percent of the vote against 32 percent for the Communist-Socialist electoral alliance. Clearly, the Italian Communists would not obtain power by any means, whether legal or illegal. There were protests that had the look of an insurrection after the Communist leader Palmiro Togliotti was shot in late 1948, but, according to Hugh Seton-Watson, the great historian of international communism, "the machinery of government was never in danger and after two days [and facing Italian police and troops] the Communists called off the strike. Further strikes in the winter of 1948–9 and since had even less effect."[34]

The AFL tried to build a strong anti-Communist trade union movement in Italy, but it was frustrated time and again. The fall of 1947 found Dubinsky, whose ILGWU had taken the lead in Italian affairs, writing scathingly to his representative in Italy, Luigi Antinioni, "telling him that . . . despite all . . . Antinioni's activities in Italy, nothing had been done in the trade union movement and the money had been wasted."[35] Subsequent efforts were as unsuccessful.

Indeed, labor's efforts were so inconsequential that a new initiative was undertaken in Italy after the Christian Democratic leaders in the CGIL split and formed their own trade union federation, the Italian Confederation of Workers' Unions (CSIL). Other anti-Communist, Socialist, and republican trade union leaders later split from the CGIL. The AFL successfully pursued a merger between this group and the CSIL but soon found itself contending with yet another split resulting in the formation of the socialist Italian Labor Union (UIL). Daniel Horowitz notes that "a joint appeal by the AFL and CIO in May, 1952 for [these] two Italian organizations to work together and eventually unify had no effect."[36] The Communist-dominated CGIL, like the CGT in France, remains the predominant trade union federation to this day. Indeed, Horowitz has expressed the view that the course of the Italian labor movement was unaffected by the efforts of American labor.[37]

Backfiring in Japan

In Japan, the other major former Axis power, American labor leaders were assigned to the Labor Division, Economic and Scientific Section (ESS) of the office of the Supreme Commander, Allied Powers (SCAP), General Douglas C. MacArthur's occupation authority. Labor's men saw the growth of a strong Japanese labor movement during the occupation as an essential counterweight to the economic and political power of Japanese industrialists, who had supported Japanese militarism and aggression. Many occupation authorities agreed, but for the wrong reasons.

In his book *Exporting Democracy*, Joshua Muravchik called the creation of a trade union movement in Japan after the war a "big success," according to the head of SCAP's Labor Division: "By the end of 1946, a total of 4.5 million Japanese—ten times the prewar peak—were union members."[38] But they belonged to unions that were themselves threats to democracy. As Richard Deverall, the AFL's representative in Asia, acknowledged, "Communist influence was all-pervasive during the first year of the occupation, . . . generally, Marxist thought patterns set the tone for the development of the postwar labor movement in Japan."[39]

American labor continued working to establish a pro-Western labor movement in Japan, but with little success. Asian scholar Robert Scalapino wrote that "SCAP, American labor (both the CIO and AFL), and ICFTU officials worked hard to bring about the formation of Sohyo [a new trade union federation]." But the hopes for the new federation "dissipated when Sohyo and the Socialist Party with which it was linked, attacked the American proposals for peace and security. . . . In the international arena Sohyo has expressed heavy criticism of the United States while treating the Soviet Union leniently. The by-words are 'neutralism' and 'Afro-Asian solidarity.' "[40]

The turning point in SCAP's attitude toward the trade unions came in 1947, when the Japanese labor movement, led by the Communist-allied Sanbetsu, called a general strike against government and management. The United States throughout the period had taken the position "that the success of the recovery program will in large part depend on Japanese efforts to raise production and to maintain high exports through hard work, a minimum of work stoppages, and internal austerity measures."[41] Not surprisingly, General MacArthur banned the strike.

To deal with the general problem of labor unrest, SCAP proposed new labor legislation that would deny government workers collective-bargaining rights and would deny workers in government enterprises the right to strike. Richard Killen, who had been chosen chief of SCAP's Labor Division with the blessing of both the AFL and the CIO, responded by resigning in protest. Later in the year, both U.S. labor groups passed resolutions condemning what they considered an antilabor policy that would drive Japanese workers and their country into the waiting arms of the Communists. Fortunately, this prediction proved wrong. Under the leadership of the conservative Liberal Democratic Party, Japan remained solidly within the Western camp.

The Third World

Lenin, as noted, viewed imperialism as the last stage of capitalism, an endgame during which advanced capitalist countries would strive to escape the fatal contradictions that Marx had foreseen by going to the underdeveloped world for cheap raw materials and captive markets for goods that could not be absorbed at home. "The surplus value extracted from the colonies is the principal . . . resource of contemporary capitalism," the Second Congress of the Communist International said in 1920. "By exploiting the colonial population, European imperialism is able to offer a quantity of compensatory gratuities to the labor aristocracy in Europe." Knocking out the colonial props that supported the domestic capitalist order, then, seemed a fair bet to further revolution in the developed countries, hence the Comintern's "great stress on the need to incite colonial rebellions."[42]

After being burned by the Soviet-trained Chiang Kai-Shek, Stalin shied away from supporting non-Communists in the underdeveloped world. The late 1950s, however, found his successors returning to the strategy of supporting nationalist revolts against the West, directed against colonialism and then neocolonialism, with the goal of breaking the West's hold on resources located in what was becoming known as the third world.

American labor leaders believed that trade unions were destined to play as important a role in the underdeveloped world as they thought incorrectly they had played in the developed world. Labor's reasoning was that, first, the Soviets, the third world Communists, and their allies presented themselves as the opposition to Western colonialism and exploitation. Second, any defense of colonialism was bound to be futile; its days were numbered. To stop the Soviets, the West needed to declare itself in favor of the right of self-determination for non-European peoples. More than that, it should give whatever assistance it could to non-Communists who were fighting for full national freedom. Finally, the West should above all aid unions, which were the most effective of the forces fighting for independence. With national liberation achieved, the unions would presumably become the most effective and reliable of the forces fighting for economic and social policies to benefit the broad mass of people rather than a narrow elite. Unions would cut the ground out from underneath Communists, who thrived on the misery of the masses.

The AFL was certainly right that movements for liberation from colonialism were both just in their basic demand for independence and unstoppable. It was also correct that Communists aimed to exploit these movements to further Soviet foreign policy goals. As events would show, however, labor was tragically wrong about everything else.

Algeria. The AFL was a consistent and vocal advocate of independence for the Arab countries, for instance, and never more prominently so than in the case of Algeria, where nationalists warred against French rule starting in the early 1950s. This advocacy continued long after it had become clear that in Algeria, at least, terrorists had had the upper hand from the start. Neither free trade unions nor democracy stood much of a chance after French president Charles de Gaulle let Algeria go in 1962. Paul Johnson summed up the postliberation situation as follows: "The regime, composed mainly of successful gangsters, quickly ousted those of its members who had been brought up in the Western tradition; all were dead or in exile by the mid-1960s."[43]

As for the trade union movement, the Union Générale des Travailleurs Algériens, it was quickly and easily taken over by the ruling party, the Front de Libération Nationale. The FLN simply stacked the first postindependence UGTA conference with its supporters. At the first meeting, FLN leader Ahmed Ben Bella warned the delegates that "trade unions . . . had to defer to the decisions of the party in power."[44]

So much for the independent trade unions that the AFL had cast as the bulwark of democracy in Algeria. The UGTA, henceforth, took its orders from the FLN government, soon disaffiliating from the ICFTU and later joining regional trade union organizations that had close ties with the WFTU, which, by then, was totally under Soviet control.

Sub-Saharan Africa. Consistent with its position on North Africa, U.S. organized labor argued strongly for the fastest possible decolonization in sub-Saharan Africa, both to deprive the Communists of an issue and to give the people of Africa a foundation for democracy and prosperity. From the point of view of both democracy and free trade unionism, however, the story in Algeria was surpassed in sadness by the tale of sub-Saharan Africa. Many of the postcolonial depredations there were the work of men who got their start in the trade unions.

One of these was Sekou Touré of Guinea, who first developed his political skills within the trade union movement. "It was . . . as a labor leader," Lodge noted, "that he first demonstrated his ability to command an almost religious devotion from his followers"; he remained head of the official union movement even after he became prime minister.[45] On the international stage, Touré was a nemesis of the West in general and the AFL-CIO in particular. He became president of the officially neutralist, but in fact anti-Western, African labor federation (UGTAN) and then a leader of its successor, the All-African Trade Union Federation (AATUF), which tilted even more toward the East bloc.

In his international work, Touré was a close ally of the Ghanaian dictator Kwame Nkrumah, who did not come out of the trade union movement but had received strong support from organized labor in both America and his own country (the former British colony of Gold Coast) as it struggled for independence. Nkrumah's successful rise to power in Ghana was "due in no small measure to the support which he received from the Ghana labor movement."[46]

To express its great expectations, the AFL-CIO dispatched its top-ranking black leader, A. Philip Randolph, to represent it at Nkrumah's 1957 inauguration as president. (One indication of the significance of Randolph's presence: there was not to be another official AFL-CIO delegation to Africa for another eleven years.) But Nkrumah quickly showed that any faith in his democratic bona fides was misplaced. He soon brought the Ghanaian labor movement to heel as part of his larger dictatorial strategy. On the rare occasions when workers got out of line, Nkrumah cracked down hard. When dockside and railway workers went on strike in 1961, he arrested the strike leaders and held them without trial. A member of his cabinet publicly denounced the strikers as "despicable rats."[47]

Worse yet, Nkrumah used the trade unions as a vehicle to promote his anti-Western foreign policy. Perhaps more than any other African leader, he was responsible for the ICFTU's humiliating retreat from Africa. In 1959, the Ghanaian trade union movement disaffiliated from the ICFTU and announced the organizing conference of what would become the AATUF. This meeting was deliberately scheduled at the same time as the African Regional Conference of the ICFTU.

Guinea and Ghana both demanded from the start that disaffiliation from the ICFTU be a condition of membership in the AATUF. They did not get their way immediately, but, by 1961, the charter of the AATUF included a disaffiliation provision. Within a few years, virtually all African trade unions had disaffiliated—even the Kenyan federation, which had the closest ties to the AFL-CIO.

Postcolonial Latin America

In Latin America, too, the AFL saw conflicts in the context of the cold war and argued once again that the best way to defeat communism was to support trade unionism. Once again, events refused to cooperate, though not because of any shortcomings on the part of Serafino Romualdi, the AFL-CIO's gifted representative in Latin America after the war and the first head of the American Institute for Free Labor Development (AIFLD). Romualdi devoted his great talents and energy to the defense and promotion of democracy in Latin America and deserves far more credit and public recognition than he has received.

The notion that U.S. organized labor played a significant role in South American politics comes from an ironic source: the AFL-CIO's critics on the left. In the 1960s, leftist scholars wrote numerous books and essays making the case that U.S. labor, in league with the Central Intelligence Agency, had defeated "progressive forces" (meaning Communist or pro-Communist movements) throughout Latin America. The AFL-CIO certainly opposed communism everywhere, but a review of the charges reveals that neither the AFL-CIO itself, nor the unions it supported, made any but the most minor difference in the conflicts under discussion.

Most left-wing accounts focus on the cases of Guatemala, Cuba, British Guiana, and the Dominican Republic. Let us briefly review them in chronological order.

Guatemala. In Guatemala, the AFL-CIO and the Guatemalan labor movement played a bit role in the June 1954 overthrow of the pro-Communist Arbenz regime by a CIA-funded and equipped "liberation army" led by Colonel Carlos Castillo Armas. After Armas's victory, George Meany issued a statement which read in part that "the A.F. of L. rejoices over the downfall of the Communist-controlled regime in Guatemala" and expressed "the hope that [the new regime] would soon restore all civil liberties, including the right to organize unions."[48] Instead, Armas turned almost immediately on the trade union movement and other democratic forces. Eight years later, Lodge wrote that Guatemala had "a number of small, uneconomic trade unions . . . [with] little structure, no national cohesion, and little effort at dues collection. These unions can be destroyed as quickly as they are established, and are easy prey for any rabble-rouser."[49]

British Guiana. "Communism had both targets of priority and targets of convenience in Latin America. . . . The main target of convenience in 1961 . . . was a small country, still an English colony, British Guiana," according to Schlesinger.[50] In the runup to independence, the Communist, Chedi Jagan, won three straight elections. The AFL-CIO became involved in a serious way following the last election. Immediately thereafter, Jagan renewed his assault on the trade union movement, the Guiana Industrial Workers' Union (GIWU), proposing legislation that would have allowed the government to decide which union was "representative" of any group of workers. In defense, the GIWU called a strike that lasted for eighty days before Jagan backed down. CIA money funneled through AFL-CIO representatives enabled the strikers to stay out as long as they did.

The next election in Guiana was won by Forbes Burnham and the People's National Congress (PNC), a breakaway group from Jagan's People's Progressive Party (PPI). In Arthur Schlesinger's account, the Kennedy administration had assumed that Burnham was "as the British described him, an opportunist, racist and demagogue intent only on personal power." The administration began to question this characterization of Burnham, however, partly because "the AFL-CIO people in British Guiana thought well of him."[51] It probably would have been better if policy makers had not rethought the matter. According to a 1982 State Department publication, the PNC had "declared itself a socialist party, operating on Marxist-Leninist principles."[52] Eight years later, Burnham declared the "paramountcy" of the PNC over all other institutions, requiring civil servants, for example, to take political indoctrination courses in Marxism-Leninism.[53]

Cuba. In Cuba, the labor federation, the Confederación de Trabaja-dores de Cuba (CTC), had a tacit deal with the dictator Fulgencio Batista. The CTC refrained from criticizing Batista's rule, and, in return, Batista allowed it to function in a nonpolitical way. The AFL-CIO did not like this arrangement but could do little about it.

After Fidel Castro took power in 1959, Meany "hailed the over-throw of the Batista dictatorship."[54] But then, on orders from Cas-tro, the CTC disaffiliated from the ICFTU, and Castro established a new labor federation under his own control. From then on, the only function of Cuba's unions was to meet production quotas and agree to pay cuts. Both before and after Castro's takeover, then, independent democratic trade unionism was irrelevant in Cuba.

Dominican Republic. In the Dominican Republic, dictator Rafael Trujillo had successfully intimidated the trade union movement. Even during the last year of the regime, all Serafino Romualdi could say for the leaders of Dominican labor was that they had "begun to shake off the fear that has paralyzed them for so many years."[55] Only after Trujillo's assassination in 1961 did a free labor movement begin. But the movement never played much more than a cameo role.

In 1962 elections, the centrist politician Juan Bosch was elected president. Communists took his election as a signal to start working toward a takeover. They instigated disruptions; the AFL-supported union, Confederación Nacional de Trabajadores Libres (CONA-TRAL), responded with force. But then CONATRAL stood on the sidelines when Bosch was overthrown by a military coup in 1963.

Nonetheless, organized labor's left-wing critics took out after it. Sidney Lens alleged in *The Nation* that CONATRAL's criticism of Bosch had helped to undermine him. Lens also claimed that "labor movements are so pivotal in revolts and counterrevolts that AFL-CIO strategy can sometimes be enough to tip the scales."[56] Yet he provided no evidence that it tipped the scales here or anywhere else. By the time of the military coup, Bosch had squandered all the sup-port that he started out with. The scales hardly needed any tipping by the AFL-CIO or CONATRAL.

Brazil. In Brazil, President Joao Goulart, described by Romualdi as a demagogic Peronist, won the 1961 election with strong working-class backing. Although courted by American labor, he rejected it for an alliance with Communist trade unionists. The economy then soured, costing Goulart the support of the vast majority of Brazilians, including Brazilian workers. The army then took over.

Trade unionists trained by the AFL-CIO participated in what William Doherty, U.S. labor's man on the scene, described as a "revolution," but their role was minor. Labor tried courting the new regime, but with little effect. Soon, the regime "curtailed civil and political rights and liberties," forcing the labor movement "back to its original status—an integral part of the state."[57]

Failure in Vietnam

Events in South and Southeast Asia cast yet greater doubt on the proposition that trade unions were destined to play a crucial role in the worldwide struggle against communism. At the height of the cold war, the *AFL-CIO News* regularly carried gloomy reports by Harry Goldberg, the federation's representative in Asia. In Indonesia, the Communist Party (PKI) had a lock on the trade unions that the AFL-CIO could not break. The AFL also had to acknowledge that it had little, if any, influence over the Indian trade unions. In 1955, N. G. Ranga lamented in the *American Federationist* that his hopes of seeing the Indian Trade Union Congress (INTUC) become the "common nonpolitical platform for all democrats in the labor field" had not been realized.[58] He described INTUC (whose only serious competitor was the union wing of the Indian Communist Party) as a weak handmaiden of the ruling Congress Party with few dues-paying members.

Perhaps the greatest test of labor's theory was in Vietnam. There labor once again argued that building trade unions was key to the success of the U.S. effort, which it supported. But this turned out to be yet another tragically incorrect understanding of the conflict.

The real war was a military struggle. Pro-Communist propaganda claims notwithstanding, neither the North Vietnamese nor the Viet Cong (VC) ever stood any chance of winning the support of most Vietnamese. A million or more people fled (mostly to the South) after Ho Chi Minh's Communists defeated the French at Dien Bien Phu and took over the North in 1954. Twenty-one years later, as armored formations of the North Vietnamese Army (NVA) bore down on Saigon, hundreds of thousands tried desperately to escape the country altogether.

As North Vietnamese officials admitted after the war, the Viet Cong, far from being an indigenous national liberation movement run solely by South Vietnamese patriots, was created, supplied, and commanded from the North. The test of whether the VC had won the "hearts and minds" of the South Vietnamese people at large came in early 1968, when the VC urged them to support the Tet Offensive. This operation, timed to coincide with the festivities surrounding the Vietnamese New Year, featured numerous assaults (including a guerrilla attack on the U.S. embassy in Saigon) designed to spark a massive urban insurrection by the South Vietnamese against their government and its American allies. "Far from rising up to join the Vietcong . . . the people of South Vietnam fought; and by the time the offensive was over, the Vietcong cadres had been decimated. From that point on, North Vietnamese troops did 80 percent of the fighting in the South . . . the Communists had lost the 'people's war.' "[59]

After Tet, writes one-time *Foreign Affairs* editor William Hyland, the war became "a conventional battle between two large armies." The U.S. forces were clearly superior to the NVA, but President Lyndon Johnson did not press the advantage. Hyland offers an explanation for this failure: "As a New Deal Democrat [Johnson] wanted to believe that the social revolution and nation building he was encouraging in South Vietnam would create a new sense of purpose and would thus win the war."[60]

But not only Johnson wanted to believe this. The AFL-CIO had argued strongly for social reform as a means of winning the war and had thereby unwittingly undermined support for a military solution to what had been a military problem all along. In December 1968, the *American Federationist* proclaimed that the Confederation of Vietnamese Labor (CVT), as the democratic trade union federation was called, "stands now as the largest mass membership civilian organization and represents the major force for national unity and for social, political and economic reform in the developing nation."[61] In reality, the CVT amounted to far less than that. South Vietnam was, after all, a primarily agrarian society. Accordingly, CVT's major affiliates were associations of tenant farmers, plantation workers, and fishermen; the first and third of these were not even organizations of "workers" as the word is normally defined.

The CVT engaged in some well-meaning social welfare programs. It also lobbied the South Vietnamese government for land reform, the most important being the Land-to-the-Tiller Law of 1970. Moreover, the AFL-CIO lobbied the U.S. government to press the South Vietnamese to enact land reform. Yet these efforts to win hearts and minds ran the risk of becoming counterproductive. "The beneficial effect of American aid and of many social and economic reforms (e.g., land reform) undertaken at the instigation of the Americans was bound to be countered psychologically and politically through resentment, felt at several levels of Vietnamese government and society, of interference by foreigners," Adam Ulam observed. "It was imperialism without even the redeeming feature of the straightforward source of authority and responsibility which a colonial relationship implies."[62]

Moreover, even if such efforts did not backfire, they were destined to remain a sideshow, diverting attention from the harsh but essential task of meeting the military challenge from the North. If American social aid and nation-building efforts were a sideshow, the South Vietnamese labor movement on which the AFL-CIO pinned its hopes was a sideshow within a sideshow: in most histories of the conflict, the CVT is relegated at best to a footnote or two.

5
The Defeat of Communism

After the U.S. defeat in Vietnam, the will of labor's liberal allies to resist communism diminished, in some cases to the vanishing point. But the AFL-CIO remained committed to a foreign policy of active anticommunism. Indeed, labor took a position to the right of the Nixon, Ford, and Carter administrations, all of which supported a policy of détente with the Soviet Union. Labor persistently and relentlessly criticized détente and pointed out at every opportunity that communism remained the main threat to freedom in the world. It did that most effectively by championing the cause of Soviet dissidents, such as the novelist Aleksandr Solzhenitsyn and the physicist Andrei Sakharov, and by sponsoring speaking tours of well-known Russian emigrés, such as Vladimir Bukovsky.

The first discernible change in the AFL-CIO's own foreign-policy outlook came only after the election of Ronald Reagan. In principle, labor remained as opposed to communism as ever. Nonetheless, its support of actual anti-Communist policies began to flag as the federation's leadership responded to the growing strength of trade union leaders whose views on defense and foreign policy issues reflected those left-wing political alliances they had established. This shift in policy eluded many. Former Reagan aide Peter Rodman, for instance, has written that the AFL-CIO backed the administration's efforts to defeat Marxist-Leninist forces in Central America. In reality, the AFL-CIO did not support the U.S. military efforts in the region.

El Salvador

The AFL-CIO's enthusiasm for land reform as a spoiler of Communist ambitions, however, survived the U.S. defeat in Vietnam. In El Salvador, for example, land reform was the centerpiece of the policy that labor advocated. The Salvadoran Communal Union (UCS), which AFL-CIO representative William Doherty helped organize to represent landless peasants, was by all accounts an effective lobbyist for land reform legislation in El Salvador. In the United States, meanwhile, the AFL-CIO provided strong and crucial political backing for the land reform program that El Salvador adopted under President Napoleon Duarte. *Time* magazine (May 4, 1981) was not far off when it titled an article on the land reform program "What the AFL Has Wrought in El Salvador." As in Vietnam, the intent in El Salvador was to win the hearts and minds of the peasants by depriving the Communists of a key issue. The consequence, though, was to reduce agricultural production.

In addition to pushing land reform, the AFL-CIO supported the non-Communist trade union movement of El Salvador, which was closely associated with Duarte's Christian Democratic Party. Before the 1984 elections, this movement agreed to support Duarte's presidential bid in exchange for his promise to accede to a social pact that included a series of populist measures, such as nationalization of the banks (which the unions called the "democratization of credit") and the nationalization of the coffee export industry. The AFL-CIO supported the social pact, saying that its measures would "strip the guerillas of their social base."[1]

Once again the consequences were negative. The nationalized banks bailed out the failing land reform cooperatives, but they were still badly run and kept losing money. "Since recipients of these loans were either cronies of newly politicized bank officers or merely inefficient managers . . . millions of dollars were lost in bad loans."[2] Throughout the 1970s, under a corrupt military regime, El Salvador's per capita income had consistently risen but then dropped to 1950 levels in the 1980s.[3] The ill-fated reforms were not fully to blame—there was a destructive guerilla war going on at the same time—but they did contribute to the economic decline.

Criticizing the Carter administration's Latin American policy, Jeane Kirkpatrick wrote that "in theory, the reforms will vaccinate the masses against Communism by giving them a stake in the society" but that, in practice, it is impossible to "fight howitzers with land reform and urban guerrillas with improved fertilizers."[4] Kirkpatrick's criticism of the Carter policy applied to the AFL-CIO's similar approach (she noted the role of AIFLD in directing the implementation of reform). In the actual war between the Salvadoran government and the leftist Farabundo Martí National Liberation Front (FMLN), the AFL-CIO opposed a Communist victory, as it had in Vietnam and every other conflict during the cold war. But now union support of U.S. military efforts was conditional. In 1982, labor called for the suspension of military aid pending more progress on land reform and human rights. In 1985, it reiterated that its support of military aid was conditional. In 1987, labor called for a reduction in military aid "if there are not further improvements in human and trade union rights."[5] A year later, it called for the suspension of military aid until there was judicial reform and the killers of two AIFLD workers were brought to justice. By 1989, the labor leadership had moved to the left of the U.S. Senate on the issue, calling for a suspension of aid while the Senate was voting to increase it from $85–90 million per year. The Senate also voted down an amendment that would have put conditions on military aid, an amendment that labor declared was "largely in accord with AFL-CIO policy."[6]

What accounts for labor's less than wholehearted support of U.S. policy in El Salvador? The AFL-CIO leadership was fighting a rearguard battle against an internal Left that was desperately trying to be part of a "progressive" political coalition in the United States. Operating under the name of the National Labor Committee in Support of Democracy and Human Rights in El Salvador, this labor Left included unions representing approximately half of the membership of AFL-CIO–affiliated unions. Although the national labor committee sometimes talked in the same language of conditionality as the AFL-CIO, it was understood by all that what it really supported was an absolute cutoff.

Nicaragua

Like their Cuban counterparts under Batista, the Nicaraguan unions had made their peace with the local dictatorship—in this case that of the Somoza family. Pliant organized labor gained "many benefits in welfare and legislation" under the Somozas, reported Serafino Romualdi, and also welcomed the dictatorship's respect for the "freedom of trade unions."[7] Therefore, unions did not actively oppose strongman Anastasio Somoza in the 1970s. But since there were so few real workers in factories and such, the absence of working-class support made little difference.

After ousting Somoza and seizing the reins of power in 1979, the Marxist-Leninist Sandinistas easily took over the existing trade union movement. Nicaragua in 1981 had only about 70,000 union members, and about half belonged to the Sandinista federation. Democratic trade unionists resisted, but their role in the anti-Sandinista struggle was insignificant.

The two most important opposition forces were the Roman Catholic Church, led by the highly respected Cardinal Miguel Obando y Bravo, and the peasantry. Latin American specialist Mark Falcoff observed that "as in Poland, the church has become an opposition party *manqué;* though unable to overthrow the regime it is the most important instrument of serious resistance within the country."[8] The armed resistance came from the contras, who drew most of their support from peasants who sought ownership of land and from small landowners who feared that their farms would be expropriated or that they would be forced to join state-run cooperatives.[9]

The AFL-CIO was highly critical of the Sandinistas. Moreover, criticism was the extent of the AFL-CIO's opposition; it never supported aid to the armed resistance. As they had in El Salvador, unions that were part of the "National Labor Committee" prevented the AFL-CIO from supporting the military dimension of U.S. policy in Nicaragua.

Defense Spending

The leftward-shifting internal balance of power that influenced labor's position on Central America in the 1980s was also reflected in its new attitude toward U.S. defense spending. In the past, the AFL-CIO had supported defense programs almost as a matter of course. In the 1970s, for example, it supported funding for the B-1 bomber, neutron warheads, the cruise missile, and the MX mobile strategic missile—all controversial defense initiatives. Moreover, labor rejected the notion that there was or should be a trade-off between defense and social spending. In 1979, the AFL-CIO's Executive Council held that "the level of our defense spending should depend on our assessment of the military threat to our interests, not on a comparison with social spending."[10]

In the early 1980s, however, labor began to hedge. In 1982, the executive council declared that *if* Congress saw a need for more defense spending, then

> this increase should be fully financed by a progressive surtax on income. At least one-third of this tax should be provided by an inescapable levy on gross corporate earning. In this way defense needs can be met without adding to the federal deficit or cutting food stamps, unemployment benefits, job and training programs, mass transit, or other already battered social programs.[11]

Not long after, the AFL-CIO's Defense Committee issued an interim report that called outright for caps on defense spending. The committee opposed the 9–10 percent defense-budget increase that the Reagan administration was asking Congress to approve, calling instead for a 5–7 percent real-term increase. "A number of members of the Executive Council," noted the committee's report, "have expressed the strong opinion that the increase should be held to the lower end of this range or below."[12] Almost identical wording found its way into resolutions passed by the AFL-CIO convention that same year.

In early 1985, the executive council took the more radical position that "if vital [domestic] programs are to be cut or frozen, defense spending must also be frozen."[13] Then, in May, the council went further, arguing that "the Pentagon should not be exempt from spending reductions equal in severity to those forced on domestic programs."[14] Spending was no longer to be based solely on actual defense needs.

Declining support for defense spending was evidenced also in Labor's changing attitude toward the arms race between the United States and the USSR. As late as 1979, the executive council noted that "whatever restraint we have seen [in arms building] has been in the form of unilateral U.S. decisions to cancel or delay new weapons systems, while the Soviet Union has engaged in the most massive military buildup in peacetime history."[15] The defense committee in 1982 rejected proposals for a nuclear freeze, which would have simply locked in Soviet superiority in certain categories, particularly mobile strategic missiles and mobile intermediate-range missiles in the European theater. But attitudes were changing. By

1982, labor journalist David Moburg reported that "two public-employee unions (AFSCME and AFGE), two rival electrical unions (IUE and UE) and the NEA are part of a budget coalition that calls for military spending to be transferred to people's needs. The UAW, the Steelworkers and the United Food and Commercial Workers are supporting Ground Zero, an effort to educate people on the dangers of nuclear war."[16]

The 1983 convention was forced to acknowledge that "among our membership, as in our society, a majority favor a verifiable nuclear freeze." Maybe so, but the real reason for the statement was that the leaders of six of the ten largest unions in the AFL-CIO had declared themselves in favor of the proposal. The pro–defense spending consensus in the AFL-CIO had evaporated. From this point on, the AFL-CIO would merely pretend to be the defense stalwart it had once been.

This pretense was revealed most clearly by organized labor's reaction to the Strategic Defense Initiative, a plan for space-based missile defense that Reagan first proposed on March 23, 1983. Don Oberdorfer of the *Washington Post* has written that the Soviet Union in the 1980s was frightened at "the prospect of being forced into an expensive high-technology race with the United States that it could not afford and probably could not win."[17] This conclusion was confirmed in February 1993, when Soviet officials admitted publicly that "Soviet President Mikhail Gorbachev was convinced that any attempt to match Reagan's Strategic Defense Initiative that was launched in 1983 to build a space-based defense against missiles would do irreparable harm to the Soviet economy."[18]

This is the background to the report and recommendations of the AFL-CIO Defense Committee (later accepted by the AFL-CIO Executive Council), a committee often said to be stacked with hardliners. The committee began eccentrically, accusing SDI proponents of deliberate obfuscation: "It is impossible to debate the question of SDI intelligently if there is no agreement on what is being debated. This is not the fault of critics of SDI. The blame rests clearly on the back of the Reagan Administration." According to the committee, what President Reagan had proposed and what his SDI Organization (SDIO) was working on were "so completely different as to have completely opposite purposes and strategies."[19] In fact, neither SDIO nor the White House was aware of any difference, nor were the overwhelming majority of proponents and opponents of SDI.

"The President's proposal would do away with deterrence," the committee alleged, without providing any evidence. Moreover, the president's ideas "played into the hands of those who argue for unilateral disarmament and nuclear freezes," meaning, presumably, that those who were really prodefense would fight SDI.[20] On each specific question at issue, the committee sided with the opponents of SDI. Thus, it rejected arguments of SDI proponents for a liberal interpretation of the Anti-Ballistic Missile Treaty, which would allow proper testing. Instead, the committee suggested, the United States should meet with the Soviets afresh to "negotiate a clarification of the testing to be permitted," which would give the Soviets an effective veto on the full development of SDI. Then, the committee called for delaying the decision whether to deploy SDI until "there is something to deploy,"[21] which there never would be so long as the Soviet Union was allowed to prevent testing.

In the years since the publication of this curious report, labor's support for defense spending has continued to decline. Once the foremost advocate of guns and butter, it now shared the view of its liberal Left allies that social spending be financed by deep cuts in the defense budget.

The Defeat of State Communism

Even as the United States approached victory in the cold war, U.S. foreign policy was getting less and less support from the AFL-CIO. Yet, labor claims major credit for communism's defeat. "No one," Lane Kirkland declared, "can deny the primacy of free trade unionism in the defeat of state communism."[22] The truth, however, is that trade unionism had remarkably little to do with the fall of the Soviet empire.

Let us start our review with Poland, where, by all accounts, trade unionism was a more important factor than anywhere else. There is no denying the role of Solidarity, which was a trade union, or of the AFL-CIO, for that matter, which championed Solidarity's cause from start to finish. But Solidarity was more than a union of workers. If it had been only a union, it would have failed, as had previous worker rebellions in Poland and elsewhere in Eastern Europe.

There were sporadic worker rebellions in Poland from 1956 on. The cycle of protest and quiescence might have continued indefinitely had it not been for the introduction of a new and, as it turned out, revolutionary element, namely, a transformed Catholic Church. Starting in the 1970s, Samuel Huntington observed, "the church almost invariably opposed authoritarian regimes," and in some countries, including Chile and Poland, "it played a central role in the efforts to change such regimes."[23] In Poland, this made possible a rapprochement between the church and the intellectuals on nationalist and anti-Communist grounds. This new alliance, in turn, formed the basis for the birth of Solidarity as a liberation movement, as distinguished from an ordinary trade union. The ability of the church to act as a bulwark of opposition was huge, owing in no small part to the 1978 election of Cardinal Karol Wojtyla, the archbishop of Cracow, as Pope John Paul II. His pastoral visit to Poland in June 1979 was epoch making. In Walesa's words, "millions of unorganized and unaffiliated Poles had suddenly seen themselves as a community under the leadership of the church—an experience that a year afterward had led to the creation of Solidarity."[24]

When the workers at the vast Lenin Shipyard in Gdansk went out on strike in the summer of 1980, the difference from previous protests was palpable. As Polish philosopher Leslek Kolakowski puts it, "It was obvious from the outset that the workers' revolt was not only against poverty and wretched working conditions; it was essentially a revolt against the rule of lies."[25] A workers' movement had been impregnated, as it were, with the ideas and spirit of the church-intellectual alliance. That is what allowed Solidarity to play the leading role in the struggle against state communism.

The AFL-CIO's role in the Polish struggle, while certainly important, has been much exaggerated. It was Solidarity's most vocal supporter in the United States, but Solidarity was not an unpopular cause. On the contrary, it had the support of the Right and most of the Left. In Poland, the federation by all accounts widely used government money it received for its support of the democratic struggle. But it was far from alone. By some accounts, for example, the Communist-dominated CGT gave similarly effective assistance to Solidarity.

The Rest of Eastern Europe

In other East European satellites of the Soviet Union, American labor's contribution to the freedom struggle was minimal, at best. This is no reflection on the AFL-CIO: it would have helped if it could have, but opportunities for significant involvement were virtually nonexistent. Behind the iron curtain and outside of Poland, independent workers' groups, to the extent that they existed at all, followed the lead of intellectuals, students, and churches, most often from a great distance.

Czechoslovakia's Velvet Revolution, for instance, began with a student demonstration in Prague in the fall of 1989 and spread to other universities throughout the country. Vaclav Havel, then a distinguished playwright, essayist, and leading dissident, called intellectuals together to discuss the situation. They quickly formed the Civic Forum, which was to lead the struggle for democracy. As historian Theodore Draper explains: "If it was revolution, it was largely set off by students and intellectuals. Workers were gradually drawn in by flying squads of students who went from factory to factory explaining, exhorting, entreating. When the workers came out, they were following, not leading."[26]

In East Germany, resistance to the Communist regime was initiated in the early 1980s by Socialist intellectuals who wanted to reform the Communist system. Others then joined them—peace activists, greens, the Evangelical Lutheran Church—but not the workers, who became active only after it had become clear that the Soviet Union would not use any of the thousands of its troops stationed on East German soil to suppress dissent. Then, virtually the entire East German people joined in public protests against the ruling Socialist Unity Party and its extensive police state. At the most memorable of these, hundreds of thousands demonstrated in Leipzig, demanding the full panoply of institutions, free trade unions among them, that mark a free and democratic society.

In Hungary, too, intellectuals took the lead. Tension marred relations between them and the workers, for the regime's longstanding policy of so-called goulash socialism had met with some success in buying off industrial workers with high wages and high status to give them the impression that they were indeed the ruling class. According to the Romanian émigré scholar Vladimir Tismaneuanu, the workers saw intellectuals "as trouble makers, while the intellectuals considered the workers the main social base for a most suffocating regime."[27] Some of the bad feelings on both sides dissipated after the 1956 revolt, in which workers had played an important role before it was crushed by a Soviet invasion. In the end, though, in

1988 and 1989, the main opposition groups were the Magyar Democratic Forum, a conservative populist organization, and the Free Democrats, which was organized by free market liberals and social democrats. There was no equivalent of Solidarity.

In Romania, "the revolution against Communist rule began in Timisoara, sparked by the courage of one man, the Reverend Lazslo Tokes, a pastor of the Reformed (Calvinist) Church."[28] A December 1989 attempt by the Securitate—dictator Nicolae Ceausescu's dreaded secret police—to evict the ethnic-Hungarian pastor from his rectory in that western city sparked massive demonstrations. Unrest spread quickly to the capital, Bucharest, where, with the help of the army and disaffected Communist Party members, Ceaucescu was captured, hastily tried by a military court, and executed (along with his wife Elena) on Christmas Day 1989.

Much about this chain of events remains unclear—what at first appeared to be a spontaneous mass uprising later began to look like an inside job carried out by various elements of the power structure that had come to fear and despise the erratic, megalomaniacal Ceausescus. Clearly, however, neither Romania's unions nor its workers played any distinctive part in Ceausescu's overthrow.

The Fall of Soviet Communism

What happened in Eastern Europe had an impetus of its own, but it is hard to think that any of the freedom movements could have succeeded had the Soviet Union clung to the Brezhnev Doctrine, under which it claimed the right to invade any country that attempted to exit its empire. The Red Army had always been the ultimate guarantor of Communist rule in Eastern Europe. The crucial question, then, is what destroyed the Soviets' will to maintain their imperial sway? And another question that needs to be asked is, what role did trade unionism (or, more accurately, independent labor activism) play in the ferment within the USSR?

The answer to the second question is that labor activism played almost no role whatsoever—in any account. There were a few strikes, mainly by miners, but no one claims that they shook the regime. To the extent that masses of people were involved, their participation usually took the form of expressions of ethnic and national feeling. Such demonstrations occurred in the Baltic states, Georgia, and elsewhere. But even those events came late in the day, after the

Soviet elite had determined that communism represented not the future but the past; that it was not progressive but reactionary.

Nikita Khrushchev really did believe that the Soviet Union would bury the advanced capitalist countries; he also believed that the Hungarian Revolution of 1956 was fascist-inspired. But this kind of confidence eroded in the years following Khrushchev's removal. The new elite saw the Soviet Union fall further and further behind in numerous significant areas. Its unwieldy command economy in particular simply could not keep up with the pace of technological change. The authorities were thus forced to allow Soviet intellectuals access to information from and about the West. What they learned delegitimized Soviet communism in their eyes. They were confronted with the inescapable "contradiction between ideas and reality" that led directly to *perestroika*. "The *perestroika* revolution," according to Charles H. Fairbanks, Jr., "was a revolution begun not by the deprived but by the owners and operators of the Soviet system and their children."[29] The game was over when it became clear, as it soon did, that *perestroika* was a nonstarter.

Speaking before the Socialist International, as in other forums, Lane Kirkland maintained that "the mouthpieces and organs of business enterprise would have you believe that freedom and democracy are borne on the wings and in the pockets of capital. Yet, they were nowhere on the battleground where freedom was born again, except as distant co-conspirators with the forces of oppression."[30] All too many corporations were happy to do business with the Soviet Union, no matter what the foreign policy consequences. But the importance of that trade policy in comparison to the decisive role played by the free enterprise systems of the West, and, most important, of the United States, was demoralizing the Soviet elite.

6
Labor and Economic Development Abroad

T he Right has praised, the Left damned, American labor for defending and promoting the private enterprise system throughout the world. Both the praise and the blame, however, flow from a serious misreading of labor's position, based on the misconception (particularly common on the Left) that anticommunism and procapitalism are opposite sides of the same coin. In fact, those who formulated labor's foreign policy after World War II went to great pains to distinguish the two and to argue that procapitalist policies were, objectively speaking, pro-Communist.

Irving Brown, the AFL's European representative after World War II, contended that the region's unionists (supposedly the key to the cold war in Western Europe) "reject what they term 'capitalism' and accept some form of Socialist ideology." With the Soviets broadcasting the message that they were for socialism while the United States opposed it, "any attempt on the part of America to impose or glorify its [economic] system would play into Russian hands."[1]

A recent account of labor's position on economic policy in occupied Germany mistakenly asserts that "in the debate over the future of Germany that took place continuously after 1945, the AFL argued for a functioning democratic capitalist Germany."[2] In 1947, the AFL's man on the scene, Henry Rutz, was highly critical of the conservative economic policies adopted by Konrad Adenauer's Christian Democrats. In 1949, Rutz dismissed the new government that Chancellor Adenauer headed as a "reactionary coalition" that "does not represent the will of the majority of the German people."[3] Adenauer was committed to a federal state, "conceived with the view to an eventual creation of a United States of Europe."[4] His coalition partner, Ludwig Erhard, believed in a "free market economic philosophy, based on low tariffs, free trade, cheap imports and high exports."[5] The next year, Rutz criticized the government's currency reform, which he described as one of many antilabor policies. With this reform,

> At first prices rose and unemployment increased, but both were brought under control and gave way to stability and full employment . . . production rose by 50 percent within six months, and it . . . in the following year. It was a most spectacular turning point in postwar German history, the beginning of the 'economic miracle' of the fifties.[6]

Far from adopting a right-wing posture, American labor began to criticize the new industrial relations structure in Germany and the German trade union movement itself from the left. In 1954, for instance, Brown applauded an outbreak of strikes in Germany. They represented, he said, a new militancy that stood in contrast to the "philosophy of a number of German union leaders who believe that through codetermination and a moderate wage policy, the general economy will so improve that the workers will naturally benefit."[7] Brown argued, time and again, the contrary proposition, that prosperity in Europe, just as in the United States, depended on the creation of expanding markets based on increasing mass consumption funded by higher wages for workers.

Germany, instead, chose the opposite route. "Thanks to the restraint of the unions, wages remained at a relatively low level . . . and salaries did the same, amounting (1950–60) to only 47 percent of the GNP as compared with 58 percent in Great Britain . . . and . . . the propensity to consume was the lowest in Europe. The rate of saving was high while the profits of firms were ploughed back in fresh investment."[8] Had AFL economic theory been correct, this path would have have caused a recession or worse. Instead, it produced spectacular economic growth.

In Italy, too, American labor supported social-democratic, redistributionist economic policies, warning that if they were not adopted, the workers would be thrown into the laps of the Communists. Brown complained about the "incomprehension and evil practices of both employers and the government in the field of labor relations,"[9] and then about the unemployment situation, which he attributed to the austerity policies of the De Gasperi government. But the policies he so disliked soon produced the Miracolo Italiano.

Third World Socialism

Conventional wisdom also holds that American labor supported capitalism in the third world. The following is an altogether typical characterization of U.S. labor's supposed policy: "The AFL-CIO's economic perspective on Latin America [which was no different from its perspective on any other economically underdeveloped area] was based on unequivocable support for capitalism in general, and for U.S. business investment abroad in particular. Regional development was to be exclusively pursued within capitalistic frameworks."[10]

This is what the Left believed, and may even be what some U.S. policy makers believed. Yet, it was never true. On the contrary, in the underdeveloped world, much as in postwar Europe and Japan, labor took strong exception to the view that the United States should encourage the adoption of free market economic policies.

In organized labor's view, the key to economic growth in the underdeveloped no less than the developed world is rising wages. "We have steadfastly urged for Latin America, as well as for the underdeveloped countries of the world," read a resolution passed by the AFL-CIO's 1959 convention, "a policy of economic expansion based primarily on the increasing purchasing power of the people. The economic difficulties stem precisely from the failure to extend to the great mass of agricultural, mining, and industrial workers a fair share of the profits of the land owners, local industrial concerns and foreign investors." The solution to this problem was the organization of strong trade unions that would negotiate higher wages and lobby for minimum-wage legislation and the like.

But labor unions in underdeveloped countries were in no position to practice trade unionism pure and simple. Organized workers had little bargaining power, for there was a huge reserve army of the unemployed ready and willing to take their jobs at lower pay if they struck. With collective bargaining a nonstarter, these workers and their unions turned to the state for help. Therefore, labor historian Walter Galenson concluded in 1959,

> it should be apparent that the outlook for nonpolitical unionism in the newly developing countries is not bright. We may expect, rather, a highly political form of unionism, with a radical ideology. Indeed, so strong is the presumption that this will be the prevailing pattern that, where it is absent, we may draw the conclusion that unionism is, in fact, subordinated, to the employer or the state . . . that we are dealing either with a company union or a labor front.[11]

As it did following World War II, American labor followed the lead of the foreign unions. Testifying before Congress in 1963, George Meany maintained that while labor had always strongly supported the American economic system, this system could be maintained "only within the larger framework of a democratic society which has developed strong countervailing forces to private capitalism," for instance, strong trade unions and regulatory agencies, both rarities in the third world. There was, Meany sensed, "an acute danger that we will witness a repetition of the exploitation and anti-labor practices which threatened America in the early years of the Industrial Revolution."[12]

He then attacked a report on foreign aid issued by a committee headed by General Lucius Clay (a similar debate had also taken place when Clay administered Germany after the war). What especially troubled Meany was the report's cardinal thesis, which, as Meany put it, held that the United States "should insist on free enterprise in the recipient countries, with primary emphasis on private capital." Professing American labor's agnosticism as to the relative merits of competitive capitalism and its statist alternatives, Meany questioned whether a public enterprise need be any less efficient than a private corporation. And he challenged the Clay report's assertion that there were "countless instances" of "politically operated, heavily subsidized and carefully protected inefficient state enterprises in less developed countries." This was a matter, he argued, that should be left up to the people of the third world to decide for themselves: "The people may choose to concentrate on government ownership, control and planning; that is up to them."

In reality, underdeveloped countries that adopted organized labor's favorite economic views invariably met with disaster. The belief that private or public ownership of enterprises was irrelevant led directly to the proliferation of state-owned enterprises (SOEs). But "public-sector enterprises were a negative factor for economic efficiency both because of their own inefficient use of resources (they acted according to political imperatives) and because they placed pressure on government budgets."[13] The magnitude of the difference in efficiency between public- and private-sector companies was staggering. A study of the Turkish economy, for example, by Anne Krueger and her associate

> found that SOEs were invariably—regardless of sector— employing more than three times as much capital and about four times as much labor per unit of output as private firms, and we feared that no one would believe us. . . . Turkish economists reacted to our numbers by asserting that we had vastly overstated the efficiency of Turkish State Enterprises.[14]

In retrospect, it is clear that labor's basic views on economic development were fundamentally flawed. But labor's thinking about development was not too different from mainstream development economics in the 1960s. Relatively few development economists or policy makers then believed that free enterprise had much to offer underdeveloped countries.

In his chronicle of the Kennedy presidency, Schlesinger writes that the administration wanted to move away from the dominant policy of the Eisenhower era, when "Washington had been deeply convinced of the superiority, not to say sanctity, of the system of free private enterprise." The task force charged with making plans for the Alliance for Progress between the United States and Latin America held that

> while private enterprise "has a major part to play," the United States should give greater relative emphasis to indigenous as against foreign capital and end its "doctrinaire opposition" to loans to state enterprises. The hemisphere is large enough to have diverse social systems in different countries. . . . Our economic policy and aid need not be limited to countries in which private enterprise is the sole or predominant instrument of development.[15]

Trade Unionism and the Asian Miracle

Subsequently, the astounding economic success of the Four Little Dragons of Asia—Hong Kong, Singapore, South Korea, and Taiwan—forced development economists and policy makers to reevaluate their thinking. The powerhouse East Asian economies, in contrast, depended for much of their success precisely on the adoption of policies that labor opposed and which, in turn, required the regulation of independent trade unions.

The Four Little Dragons practiced what the AFL-CIO has disparagingly referred to as trickle-down economics. In complete contradiction to AFL-CIO economic theory, "it was possible simultaneously to pay scarce workers rapidly rising real wages even while exploiting them—in the sense of paying them less than their marginal productivity . . . leav[ing] the surplus in the hands of business for investment."[16] The Little Dragons started in low-wage, labor-intensive industries and worked their way up. "South Korea's electronic and machinery industries often began as assembly plants for parts produced in Japan. . . . But as quickly as possible Koreans learned to make more of the parts for the products they assembled, and then went on to assemble more complex products."[17] This was higher value-added work, and wages rose as a result. In Taiwan, wages rose at the phenomenal average rate of 18.1 percent a year throughout the 1970s.[18] Since 1988, South Korea has boasted the world's fastest-rising wage rates.[19] Per capita income in Hong Kong climbed from $999 in 1970 to $12,000 in 1990.[20]

Even in the course of denouncing the Little Dragons' labor policies, the AFL-CIO has implicitly acknowledged their centrality. Thus, Kenneth Hutchinson complained that "workers' rights in developing countries are often sacrificed to 'neocolonialism'—the process by which multinational corporations dictate labor policies to third World governments."[21] Whether multinationals dictate labor policy is open to question, but labor unions have indeed been put on a short leash. In Hong Kong, trade unions are weak and divided and have little influence over economic policy, which caters to business interests.

In South Korea, the Federation of Korean Trade Unions (FKTU) and its affiliates were tightly controlled by the government until 1987, when the country had achieved industrialization.[22]

In Taiwan, the Chinese Federation of Labor was not active until 1975. Even then their collective bargaining rights were limited, and they were denied the right to strike. Strikes were legalized only in 1988, long after Taiwan had become an industrial power.

Subsequently, Malaysia, Thailand, and Indonesia emulated the Four Dragons by, among other things, strictly regulating trade unions. In Malaysia, according to Walter Galenson in 1992, "the labor movement has been weakened in recent years by the growth of company unions, particularly in the public sector, with the encouragement of the Prime Minister who is an advocate of the Japanese model of enterprise-level unions."[23]

In Thailand, half or more of trade unionists belong to the public-sector unions, "whose main concern is to prevent privatization of such state enterprises as the airlines and the telephone system." These unions have been denied the right to strike. Organization of private-sector unions has been limited by a "number of legal and cultural factors conspiring against further organization . . . such as ineffective legal bars to unfair dismissal and traditionally paternalistic relations between employer and employee."[24] The result: Thai labor costs are one-sixth of those in Taiwan, but Thai workers are more than one-fourth as productive.[25]

The labor policies that U.S. organized labor has complained about have made it possible for Indonesia to use its comparative advantage of cheap labor (wage rates in textiles, one of its strongest export industries, average one-tenth of wages for similar work in South Korea) to attract investment by multinationals. The payoff, according to the *Economist*: poverty rates dropped from almost 60 percent in 1970 to 15 percent in 1990.[26] Other Dragons similarly benefited from keeping their trade unions under control. Incomes in Malaysia, for instance, rose 40 percent from 1987 to 1991.[27]

The Chilean Path

In Latin America, Chile was the first country to follow the East Asian way. In Chile, before the implementation of neoliberal economic reform, the state acted as a redistributor of wealth to those sectors of society with the greatest political clout. Prominent among these was the Chilean labor movement, which represented the "aristocracy" of the working class. Workers employed by the state (where featherbedding was rampant) or by corporations were protected by the state from stiff economic competition. The privileged, unionized workers received "annual salary adjustments, social security, [and] housing subsidies," as one of the groups that had "carved out for themselves a perimeter of safety within which, through a variety of means, they could survive inflation, devaluation, and periods of low or negative economic growth."[28]

The trade unions, therefore, had no interest in fundamental change. On the contrary, all they wanted was more, which is what Salvador Allende promised them in his successful 1972 presidential campaign and what he tried to deliver after his election. In office, the Allende government was the "ultimate populist government. It froze prices; it increased wages by decree. As a result it completely distorted the productive process and created enormous shortages."[29]

The spectacular failure of these policies, as evidenced by 600 percent inflation and a deficit amounting to more than 23 percent of GNP, made virtually inevitable the military coup that brought General Augusto Pinochet to power, with initial support from all sectors. Privatization then proceeded, over strenuous objections from the Chilean labor movement, which called a general strike in 1989 to protest the final stage of the process.

As in Asia, labor law reform that was opposed by trade unions there facilitated economic change. One of the architects of Chile's policy makes the point that "there was a labour law which abolished the 'closed shop' to the detriment and horror of a cushioned union elite but to the ultimate benefit of real workers. For anti-trust reasons the new labour law prohibited collective bargaining by industrial sector."[30] As Elliott Abrams, former assistant secretary of state for inter-American affairs, has written, "by ending the stranglehold of several unions on whole sectors of the economy, flexibility for both workers and employers was increased."[31]

Labor's Response

Predictably, labor's response to the Asian miracle and Chile's economic reforms has been purely negative. "The record shows," Kenneth Hutchinson, former executive director of the AFL-CIO's Asian-American Free Labor Institute, stated, "that the multinational corporations in developed countries and their partners in Hong Kong, Taiwan, Singapore, and Korea have profits as their goal and sweatshops as their result."[32]

The AFL-CIO has taken a similarly critical stance toward economic reform in Latin America, for instance toward the highly successful economic reforms in Chile. These policies worked so well that, as Mark Falcoff points out, "economic reform in Latin America these days means following the Chilean path."[33] But the AFL-CIO has yet to acknowledge Chile's extraordinary achievement. To the contrary, AFL-CIO leaders, such as AIFLD Director William Doherty, steadily criticized the reforms and denied their positive effect. Typically, Doherty, labor's chief spokesman on Latin America throughout the Kirkland era, commented that

> Paul Sigmund, the noted Princeton University political scientist, has said that the much-extolled Chilean privatization was carried out because of the extended Pinochet dictatorship and because of the weakening and partial destruction of the unions e.g., the banning of industry-wide strikes. And what did they privatize? The education system. The welfare system. And at what cost? Real wages fell by 26 percent during the decade of the 80s.[34]

Like his colleague Hutchinson, Doherty was attempting to deny the undeniable. Take the issue of wages. Socialist President Allende had recklessly increased wages (out of ideological conviction and to buy the political support of workers), which was a major reason why Chile was plagued by astronomical inflation. The only way to tame the inflation rate was to cut government spending and tighten the money supply. Predictably, this action caused a recession, and real wages fell. Yet, once the reforms took hold, economic growth resumed, and real wages increased. Average annual growth in the late 1980s was an impressive 6 percent; in 1992, the Chilean economy grew 10.5 percent. Chile's average per capita income nearly doubled between 1985 and 1990, rising to U.S. $2,111 in the latter year.[35]

Opposing Privatization Abroad

In 1990, American labor joined in a statement issued by a conference of the ICFTU and Organización Regional Interamericana de Trajadores (ORIT) that called for a reassessment of privatization, which it described as a "buzz-word currently popular among Latin American neo-liberal conservatives, who seem to think it could cure everything from government budget deficits to acne."[36] Doherty compared it to contracting out of public services, which the AFL-CIO opposes in all instances. Elsewhere he described it as the counterpart to deregulation, which the federation has also opposed.

"If inefficient bureaucracies and padded payrolls are an obstacle to development," Doherty asked, "who knows that better than the nationals of the suffering country?"[37] The people themselves must decide.

According to a monograph prepared by Doherty and AFL-CIO research director Rudolph Oswald, a key consideration is "whether for reasons of history, custom, and social policy the public believes that a given economic activity requires public accountability and therefore should remain in the public sector."[38] As the bulletin of the International Affairs Department has put it:

> Many of the privatization schemes currently being presented in Latin America also violate social norms prevailing there on the proper division between the public and private sectors. In the United States, for example, it is considered customary and proper that police forces, fire departments, and schools are in the public sector. In Latin America many workers view it as improper for railroads, airlines, telephone systems, and power networks to be in private hands.[39]

To ensure that decisions to privatize "broadly reflect a national political consensus," Doherty and Oswald argued that "unions must obviously be involved in this process."[40] But if they are, and if a consensus is a precondition for action, then there will be little privatization as most Latin American unions strongly oppose it.

The AFL-CIO itself is concerned that U.S. corporations will invest overseas rather than in the United States: "As many developing countries have recently turned to what the World Bank calls 'market-friendly' policies, privatization and a more welcoming attitude toward [foreign direct investment] have often gone hand in hand."[41] Now, as opposed to twenty years earlier, virtually all developing countries welcome such investment. Yet, the AFL-CIO officials continue to castigate American corporations that invest abroad. Former Secretary-Treasurer Thomas R. Donahue cautioned that "we can not accept blindly the structure that is presented by international capital and its apologists."[42] In speeches such as "Privatization—for the People or for the Capitalists?" Doherty refers darkly to "unscrupulous businessmen who would seek to take investment advantage of the poverty that exists in the world, maintain that poverty through a commitment to abysmally low wages, and in the process to enrich themselves through the exploitation of other human beings" and "Captains of Industry who send their capital overseas."[43] There is a conspiracy of sorts, Doherty argued, between these businessmen and some governments that would "turn the Western Hemisphere into a huge bazaar where each nation is trying to sell a cheaper work force than its neighbors. The businesses in this vast bazaar would be the multinational corporations. They can prosper while the workers suffer as their wages and living conditions are kept low."[44]

From the AFL-CIO's perspective, U.S. workers also suffer from neoliberal polices in Latin America because economic restructuring inherently relies on the promotion of economic growth through development of export industries. Labor has criticized the outward orientation of the Pacific Rim dynamos and Chile, as it has their neoliberal economic policies. Yet, a World Bank study of the Four Little Dragons plus Japan, Malaysia, Thailand, and Indonesia attributed their success in large measure to their pursuing "policies to enhance the competitiveness of their industries in the world economy with only secondary attention to domestic affect."[45]

From the AFL-CIO's perspective, the problem with an outward orientation is that such a large chunk of developing-country exports is imported by the world's largest economy, the United States, where they often replace domestically produced, union-made products. A growing trade union movement might not mind this, for, after all, employment in the United States has continued to grow. But for a union movement in serious decline, it is a virtual call to arms.

Thus, when Doherty says that "export-promotion policies depend on . . . low wages which are considered by their advocates to be a 'comparative advantage' and . . . on access to the developed-country markets," he does not mean merely to state facts but to offer a critique.[46] "If Third World economies are not to be dependent on production for export," Lane Kirkland argued, "they must develop domestic markets for their goods and services. This requires consumer purchasing power—that is, higher wages."[47] In other words, the experience of the past twenty years has simply not made a dent in labor's thinking about development.

7
The Struggle against Free Trade

I n the early days of the AFL, the issue of international trade was left up to the affiliated unions, which supported protectionist measures or opposed them, depending on how they would be affected. After World War II, however, labor moved decisively into the free trade camp. It seemed, at the time, as if America's unionized industries could only benefit from the lowering of trade barriers. As George Meany argued in the pages of an official AFL publication in 1954, "America can not prosper alone, our prospects increasingly depend on export of farm commodities and industrial products abroad." Moreover, he continued, "Our ability to produce is increasingly dependent on the supply of raw material from across the seas . . . foreign trade has become the balance wheel which keeps . . . the forward motion of our country's economic machine."[1]

Since the productivity of American industry after the war was so much higher than anywhere else, it was assumed that we would dominate world trade in manufactured goods. Thus, neither Meany nor any other trade union leader of the time expressed any concern that our own markets would be penetrated by foreign producers. As late as 1959, David McDonald, the president of the United Steelworkers, still had no idea of what the future held. Upholding the principle of free trade, he wrote that "imports didn't add up to a hill of beans."[2] Within a matter of years, though, imports that competed against American-made products started to add up to far more than that.

Still, the AFL-CIO continued supporting free trade well into the 1960s. But it then based its support primarily on foreign policy considerations. It made the following argument, for instance, for increasing imports of manufactured goods from developing countries: "We must also assist the newly developing countries, to whom we are giving economic and technical assistance, to obtain markets for the products of their new industries. . . . Exports can actually mean as much or more to the less developed countries than all the foreign aid they receive."[3] Labor supported trade with more developed countries for similar reasons. It argued, for example, that "as an island nation, Japan must literally trade to live. Japan is a bastion of strength to the free world in the Far East. For both political and economic reasons, therefore, it is important that we keep open our trade lines with Japan."[4]

The first sign of the change to come was a new, more critical attitude toward the export of capital. Because foreign aid after the war was minuscule (with the exception of the Marshall Plan), labor expected that needed capital would be obtained from the private sector. Indeed, Meany argued at the time that the government should encourage private investment abroad by underwriting it.[5] But, by 1962, labor was calling for "more investment in under-industrialized countries and less in industrialized" to stop the "export of jobs."[6] And, in 1963, it asked that consideration be given to restricting investment of U.S. firms abroad and the raising of capital in the United States for investment overseas.[7] Inroads into U.S. markets by firms of other advanced countries were clearly putting labor's commitment to free trade to the test. It did support the Trade Expansion Act of 1962 but only after the Kennedy administration agreed to a provision that promised to make assistance available to workers who lost their jobs because of imports.

By the late 1960s, the AFL-CIO started to express alarm about imports from developing nations. The AFL-CIO's 1968 platform proposals (submitted to the Democratic and Republican Parties) favorably mentioned the sixth successful round of tariff reduction negotiations under the General Agreement of Tariffs and Trade. But it also called for the enforcement of fair labor standards in trade policy and for the protection of endangered industries. Labor was concerned with the production for export of labor-intensive goods (clothing, shoes, etc.) in underdeveloped countries where wages were far lower than in the United States. In 1968, the federation's Industrial

Union Department complained that "such operations (investments abroad) obviously displace U.S. produced goods in both American and world markets."[8] It was now evident that labor's support of free trade would not survive the development of a competitive world market in manufactures. But, after supporting free trade for two plus decades, it could hardly attack the underlying principle.

Attack on the Multinationals

Instead, labor launched an attack on corporations, specifically, on the multinationals. In 1972, Gus Tyler, ILGWU leader and intellectual, wrote in his seminal article, "Multinationals: A Global Menace," that "giant conglomerates" were "moving their investments massively overseas," thereby, stripping America bare of good manufacturing jobs (1 million according to George Meany) in a "compulsive search for profits" that enriched "the top 1 percent of the shareholders who own about 75% of personally held corporate stocks and about 85% of the corporate bonds. This process becomes a way to redistribute the income of America from the bottom to the top." Only the rich benefited. Any benefit to the consumer was short-lived; it lasted only during that "time span when a foreign-made import enters the American market to knock out a competitor. But once that is done, the price goes right back to where it was and higher as the import takes full advantage of its monopoly position in the United States."[9] (Tyler cited no evidence to substantiate this claim.)

These "stateless, soulless, anonymous multinational corporations," Tyler further warned, could and did "order governments," the U.S. government not excepted, "to comply with corporate needs—or else." If a multinational did not like our labor laws, for instance, it could just pack up and leave. (Or if it did not like "America's Fair Employment Practices Laws, it can set up shop in South Africa.") As Tyler described the situation, unless something were done to prevent it, our entire manufacturing industry would be leaving, sooner or later, for underdeveloped countries where it could exploit workers without governmental interference.

This has remained the labor line on the multinationals ever since. When he became president of the AFL-CIO, Lane Kirkland would over and over again accuse the multinationals of lacking the patriotism that came naturally to the labor movement. He decried those who "stalk the planet in search of the cheapest and most re-

pressed labor, trampling on human and national values while seeking to pit the world's workers against each other in the interest of
pure profit."[10] Their investing overseas, he charged, amounted to
nothing more than "heed[ing] the beckoning pimps and pursue[ing]
the prostitution of other lands and peoples."[11] He also echoed Tyler's
claim that international competition did not lower the price of products to American consumers.

Labor made out as if it opposed only investment that "exploited"
desperately poor people in the most underdeveloped countries. But
it first raised concerns about investment in the most advanced countries. And its opposition has extended to investment in virtually all
foreign countries. In a 1973 publication, for example, labor attacked
the "greed trip of multinational corporations that have gone to low
wage areas." But it then included such high-wage countries as
France, Italy, and Japan.[12]

Labor was, clearly, wrong in its prediction that multinationals
would strip America bare of its manufacturing industries. To the
contrary. As economist Michael Porter has written, "the international strength of multinationals was self-enforcing. One U.S. industry pulled through demand for the products and services of other
U.S. industries."[13] And, as Peter Drucker has argued in a similar
vein, "Every dollar invested in a subsidary abroad leads to many
dollars of American exports within a very short time, in addition to
a flow of dividends. In fact, investment abroad during the last
twenty years has fueled full employment in the United States."[14]

Why Labor Fears Free Trade

But free trade did threaten union jobs. Resolutions adopted at the
1993 convention, for example, explicitly demanded protection for the
auto, steel, machine tool, telecommunications, electronics, shipping,
defense, textile, apparel, and shoe industries and, in addition, of
"office and other service sector jobs." Exports had been a different
matter. Meany certainly thought they were good for the economy,
and for unions, back in the 1950s. But today exports do not look as
good to labor.

The problem for labor is that protected industries cannot compete in the world market. To be competitive, industries must be in a
competitive environment themselves. The McKinsey Global Institute's detailed study of nine different manufacturing industries

showed in each instance that "global competition breeds high productivity; protection breeds stagnation."[15] Thus, to be competitive in exports, the United States must

- encourage direct foreign investment that is of no benefit whatsoever to labor since it has succeeded in organizing so few workers in the factories of foreign subsidiaries. The United Automobile Workers, for example, has organized a total of 3 percent of workers in the plants of foreign automobile manufacturers, and the percentage is on the decline.[16]
- facilitate, not penalize, U.S. corporate investment overseas because, as Drucker argues, in today's world "to maintain a leadership position in any one developed country, a business—whether large or small—increasingly has to attain and hold leadership positions in all developed markets."[17] This cannot be done unless "one has a physical presence as a producer. Otherwise, one will soon lose the 'feel' of the market."[18]
- and, worst of all as far as labor is concerned, open up our markets to imports because world-class exporters must import from world-class suppliers.[19] Compounding this problem is the fact that some U.S. exports increase imports as a matter of course. The export of U.S. goods, for instance, airplanes, machinery, and medical equipment (the United States is the number one exporter of capital goods in the world),[20] clearly enhances the ability of other countries to produce more goods for export.

In other words we are very far beyond the halcyon post–World War II days, when we could export the products of our industries in exchange for raw products. And thus, economically speaking, American labor supports what amounts to a fortress America.

"Fair Trade"

But labor will not acknowledge that it opposes the principle of free trade, especially with poor, developing countries. So the position, as expressed by Kirkland, is that labor still believes in the principle of free trade but that free trade is nonexistent. He challenged "anyone to name for me a single product, commodity or service, including money, that moves in commerce under conditions that Adam Smith or David Ricardo would have recognized as free trade, unlevered by state policy or intervention."[21]

But, if that is the case, why did the AFL-CIO support free trade in the postwar period, when it was much less free than it has since become? Immediately following the war, Anne Krueger wrote, "the U.S. economy was already highly open, with tariffs as the only significant barrier to trade. By contrast, both the European countries and Japan employed quotas, in part because of U.S. pressure under the Marshall Plan. Quota reductions spurred their economic growth, which in turn permitted further liberalization. . . . [by] the early 1970s . . . the major nontariff barriers—European and Japanese quantitative restrictions—have been eliminated."[22] Tariffs were also reduced: "In the United States, the average tariff declined by nearly 92 percent over the 33 years spanned by the Geneva Round of 1947 and the Tokyo Round (of the 1970s). By the early 1980s, the tariff level had gone down to 4.9 percent in the United States, 6.0 percent in the European Community, and 5.4 % in Japan."[23]

The lowering of trade barriers, quantitative restrictions and tariffs alike, was negotiated under the auspices of the General Agreement on Tariffs and Trade. GATT has been described by Jagdish Bhagwati as a "*contractarian* institution. Its underlying essence is a concept of symmetric rights and obligations for member states, rather than unilateralism in free trade"; under this system, "oneness of markets and fair access are measured by reference to rules, not judged on the basis of results."[24]

Historically, the U.S. government provided crucial support for this system of opening markets and increasing world trade. In the 1970s and 1980s, however, the United States reversed course. Sometimes under the prodding of, and always with the full support of, the AFL-CIO, the United States began backtracking from its commitment to the principle of free trade. Thus, labor was the primary backer of the Hartke-Burke Bill of 1971. This legislation, labor argued, would "restrict the pell-mell rush by corporations to go abroad for profits" by denying them tax credit for taxes paid overseas. Double taxation would make them less competitive at home and abroad. The bill would further discourage firms from moving production abroad by restricting multinationals' access to the huge U.S. market by regulating the "torrent of imports that have smothered U.S. production and cost hundreds of thousands of U.S. jobs." It would do that by setting "an annual import quota based on the level of imports during 1965–1969."[25] The relationship of imports to internal production of any given product would be frozen as of that time.

From this point forward, labor supported every piece of protectionist legislation that was put before Congress.

All the broad labor-backed protectionist legislation, like Hartke-Burke, has failed. But, with the full backing of labor, Congress has passed narrower protectionist bills, for example, the Super 301 legislation that represented a retreat from contractarianism and reversion to unilaterism. It also adopted and used its economic might to enforce trade laws that permit the government to take unilateral action against dumping (antidumping, or AD, provisions) and foreign subsidies (countervailing duties, or CVDs).

These provisions have been captured by protectionists. Dumping, for example, has been defined as occurring whenever the price of goods in a foreign market is higher than the price of any sale in the United States. Fred Smith, Competitive Enterprise Institute, was quoted as saying of U.S. practice that "if the same anti-dumping laws applied to U.S. companies, every after-Christmas sale in the country would be banned."[26] And so would many, if not most, U.S. exports. More than 90 percent of U.S. exports of nonspecialty steel would be banned if they were subject to such laws.[27] Or as a *Washington Post* editorial argued, "since most of the major producers (steel) lost money last year, they were clearly selling below cost— one of the definitions of dumping."[28]

Once these protectionist measures were adopted with its strong backing, labor used them as the basis of the more general argument that restrictions on the Right to take unilateral action posed "profound problems for the ideal of self-government." Thus, the movement took exception to a provision in the Uruguay Round agreement of 1993 that would, in its view, restrict the United States from "imposing sanctions on nations which do not adhere to international worker rights conventions" and "to protect American workers and their employers from unfair trading practices."[29]

Ironically, partly because the AFL in Gompers's time opposed legislating such matters, the United States did not have any government requirements covering these employment conditions until passage of the Fair Labor Standards Act in 1938. Before that time, the United States was violating worker rights, as the AFL-CIO now defines them. Consider, too, the issue of the freedom of association, which is defined by the AFL-CIO as including the right of workers to organize as well as the "right of workers to withhold labor without government sanction, and without fear of being replaced."[30] Before passage of the Norris-LaGuardia Act in 1932, U.S. courts could enforce "yellow dog" contracts that prohibited a worker from joining a union. It is not even clear that the United States could meet AFL standards today. Lane Kirkland has charged that our present labor laws do not afford protection of workers' right to organize and that labor would be better off going head-to-head with business. If so, the United States would be subject to unilateral retaliation on these grounds as well.

As far as the right to strike is concerned, not a worker in the United States can go on strike without fear of being replaced. In *NLRB v. Mackey Radio and Telegraph Co.* (which labor is seeking to overrule through legislation), the Supreme Court ruled that employers in the private sector have the right to replace strikers. Moreover, few public employees in the United States have any right whatsoever to strike. (With AFL-CIO encouragement, the ILO is investigating this matter to determine whether the country is thereby denying workers rights.)

Bhagwatti has observed that "the notion of unreasonable, unfair trade practices *has been extended* to areas as diverse as domestic antimonopoly policies, retail distribution systems, infrastructure spending, savings rates, worker's rights, and so on." But, "if *everything* becomes a question of fair trade, the likely outcome will be to diminish greatly the possibility of agreeing to a rules-oriented trading system. 'Managed trade' will then be the outcome, with bureaucrats allocating trade according to what domestic lobbying pressures and foreign political muscle dictate."[31] Labor seeks precisely that: a foreign trade regime that is the analogue of the domestic economic order it now advocates. The economic rule of government bureaucrats (with the participation of Big Labor and Big Business) would replace both the free market and free trade. Labor admits as much. According to Lane Kirkland, "American workers cannot and should not be asked to compete with foreign workers making a buck and a half a day."[32]

The Battle over NAFTA

At first glance, the labor movement's total opposition to the North American Free Trade Agreement made little sense. By any rational calculation, the net number of jobs at stake was inconsequential. Those jobs that would be lost were in highly labor-intensive industries, such as apparel manufacturing and light electronics, in which employment had plummeted over the past several decades. The decline of those industries in the United States would continue, NAFTA or no NAFTA.

In the days of the AFL, unions such as the International Ladies Garment Workers would have lost by such a treaty and would have opposed it. Conversely, unions that would not have been affected would not have taken sides; those that would have gained would have supported it. But all unions opposed the NAFTA agreement. The heads of the major public-employee unions, which would not have been directly affected, took strong anti-NAFTA stands. And the president of the UAW, the union that had the most to gain, was reportedly one of the fiercest opponents of the agreement.

In attempting to account for the union reaction, the *New Republic* argued that "Lane Kirkland is not stupid, and he is not a hysteric. There is a larger question here."[33] That larger issue was free trade in general. If NAFTA went through, the United States would sign free trade agreements with other Latin American countries and, then, with countries on other continents as well.

The *New Republic* was right. But there was a still larger question than free trade per se. The union leadership understood that the NAFTA debate was only a small part of a larger, ongoing debate over the structure of the American and international economies. Labor itself drew the connection between the philosophy underlying the deregulation of the initiatives first undertaken during the Carter administration and NAFTA. As labor saw it, "the withdrawal of effective government regulation in the domestic market over the past 10 years can be seen as the driving force behind this nation's current approach in the international arena."[34]

The Link between Liberal Reform and Free Trade

Labor also drew the connection between NAFTA and liberal economic reform throughout the world. Thus, in February 1991, it denounced NAFTA as the "most recent, albeit extreme, manifestation of an ideological world view that believes overall progress can only be achieved if the organization and structure of economic and social affairs is left entirely to private capital."[35]

NAFTA, thus, took on a broader significance. From labor's perspective, it was a crucial, if not decisive, battle against neoliberalism, or competitive capitalism, which unions correctly saw as a grave threat to their effectiveness and their survival. Public-employee unions had just as much to fear from the ideas that motivated NAFTA as the private-sector unions. After all, they were threatened by efforts to deregulate, and, in many instances, to privatize government services—and so was the UAW. It might gain a slight advantage from the NAFTA agreement but would lose much more if the principle underlying NAFTA were extended to trade with Japan, Korea, and other countries where the advantage might well go to foreign producers.

This reasoning explains why Lane Kirkland frequently used extreme rhetoric in opposing NAFTA. In a *Wall Street Journal* op-ed, Kirkland even compared the maquiladoras (factories that produced for export) to the worst excesses under Joseph Stalin.[36] This was at odds, to say the least, with all objective reports out of Mexico. A typical *Washington Post* story reported that "workers interviewed around Tijuana said they are thankful for the employment, which pays more than they could get in other parts of Mexico." Further, "Mexican government statistics show that the states (in Mexico) with the lower levels of unemployment, highest living standards and smallest gap between rich and poor are those with a heavy maquiladora presence."[37]

Kirkland also accused NAFTA's proponents of waging class warfare. He charged that NAFTA was "conceived and drafted by and for privileged elites." The American businessmen and companies that would invest in or trade with Mexico if NAFTA were confirmed he referred to as "gringo bankers and flagless, empire building corporations." Their intended victims were workers on both sides of the border. Mexican workers would become, if they were not already, their indentured servants, and American workers would be reduced to "peonage."[38] U.S. workers would suffer this fate because they either would lose their jobs or their wages would be pulled down in order to compete with lower-paid Mexican workers.

There was no evidence for this conclusion. The "productivity ratio between U.S. and Mexican workers (7.9 times as high in the U.S.) is higher than the ratio of hourly compensation (compensation in the U.S. was 6.9 times the Mexican average). These ratios indicate that the balance between productivity and wages modestly favored the U.S. workers, not Mexicans."[39] But international competition would work to the disadvantage of any company that paid a union premium—without which there would be little reason for workers to pay dues to unions.

In a more ideological vein, Kirkland warned that NAFTA put at risk nothing less than American democracy itself. The question, he said, was "whether the American people are going to retain their ability to shape change and to have a say in creating the world of tomorrow." The clue to understanding the import of Kirkland's remarks lay in his description of the emerging era, when "people will decide for themselves, in a democratic manner, how to fashion their societies and their economies in their own interests."[40] He, clearly, was implying that if government did not own, control, direct, or regulate an economic activity, it was abdicating its democratic responsibility. If so, both free market economics and free trade were antidemocratic. Labor's opposition to NAFTA and free trade, then, should be understood as yet another indication of its conversion to the critique of capitalism.

8
Labor and American Values

R esponding to conservative critics of the American labor movement, Samuel Gompers argued that it did not undermine but
rather was a mainstay of cherished American values—
especially the emphasis on individual initiative and self-reliance:
"New World individualism and initiative have shaped our thinking
and activity."[1] According to Gompers, a major purpose of law was
"to free people from the shackles of the government" and give them
the opportunity "to work out their own salvation."[2] He feared not
only that government would "exercise tyranny over the people" but
also that the people would come to rely on government rather than
on themselves. "Permanent change and progress," he argued, "must
come from within man. You can't save people; they must save themselves."[3]

Yet, there was tension from the start between these principles
and Gompers's advocacy of the closed shop (outlawed by the Taft-
Hartley Act for this reason), in which prior union membership becomes a requirement for employment. Neither he nor his successors
expressed any concern for the rights of workers who did not want to
join unions or participate in union actions: "The man who is selfish
enough and is ignorant enough to fail or refuse to join the union of
his grade wherever he may live, is not the man about which it is
necessary to so much concern ourselves."[4]

Compromising with Racism

There were other contradictions between Gompers's expressed principles and the practice of the trade union movement he led. For reasons both principled and pragmatic, Gompers believed in equal treatment of minorities: "If we do not make friends of the colored men," he warned, "they will . . . be . . . our enemies, and they will be utilized . . . to frustrate our every effort for economic, social, and political improvement."[5] Accordingly, he refused, at first, to allow unions that excluded blacks to affiliate with the AFL. But when, by the turn of the century, it became clear that many unions would refuse to affiliate if they had to admit blacks, he relented. From then on, the AFL admitted unions that discriminated, either by running separate black and white locals or by excluding blacks altogether.

After accommodating himself to the prejudice of white trade unionists, Gompers took to blaming blacks for the prejudice of white workers. He remarked in 1901 that "colored workers have allowed themselves to be used . . . by their employers . . . as 'cheap men,' "[6] undercutting the wages of white union workers, thus giving the latter an objective cause for their racism. On occasion, Gompers even played on the racial attitudes of white workers, as when he referred to blacks as darkies[7] and warned about the threat that blacks allegedly posed to "Caucasian civilization."[8]

Gompers's explanation of the AFL's hostile attitude toward Asians tracked closely with his statements about blacks. "[T]here is no antipathy on the part of American workingmen to Chinese because of their nationality," he averred.[9] Stating "emphatically" that he harbored "no prejudice against the Chinese people,"[10] Gompers defended the AFL's demand for the exclusion of Chinese coolies who worked for wages way below those of unionized white workers by noting that labor had no desire to see Chinese students, businessmen, and professionals barred from the United States.[11]

Gompers claimed that the problem with Chinese workers was not racial but cultural. If all the workers of the world were organized, he maintained, he would not object to any of them emigrating to America.[12] But the Chinese were not merely unorganized, they were a people who "allow themselves to be barbarously tyrannized over in their own country, and who menace the progress, the economic and social standing of the workers of other countries."[13] Here again, Gompers and the movement he led were not above using the language of racism to further his purposes. The AFL's 1914 convention declared that "the racial incompatibility as between the peoples of the Orient and the United States presents a problem of race preservation which . . . can only be solved by a policy of exclusion ."[14]

The presence in the United States of immigrant workers from Eastern Europe elicited a similar lack of enthusiasm from the father of the AFL. East Europeans, he contended, were used to being cowed by the authorities in their native countries and, therefore, were likely to allow themselves to be taken advantage of in the United States as well. The steel industry was not organized, in his view, because it "filled its mills with workers from Eastern and Southeastern Europe, creating difficulties of Americanization and unionization."[15] Gompers supported legislation to restrict immigration from Eastern Europe. Anticipating the argument that this would violate the concept of America as a refuge for the oppressed from all over the world, he asserted that denying entry to immigrants would actually do more to further the cause of freedom since those who would have emigrated to an already free America would now be forced to join the struggle for freedom in their native lands.

In stark contrast, the CIO never discriminated against blacks. Racism went against the grain of the CIO union organizers, many coming out of left-wing movements that were philosophically opposed to discrimination. Still, if goaded strongly by self interest, leftist movements in the United States and elsewhere had shown themselves ready, willing, and able to exploit white racism.[16] The far more important reason for the lack of discrimination in industrial unions was that industrialists themselves did not discriminate. The "Negro is now recognized as a permanent factor in industry and large employers use him as one of the racial and national elements which help to break the homogeneity of their labor force,"[17] one of their purposes being to increase the difficulty of organizing trade unions. A case in point was the AFL-affiliated UMW, which was organized at the turn of the century under the leadership of the Gompersite moderate John Mitchell. Because the union had to contend with an already integrated work force, to succeed it had to sign up black and white miners alike.

Representing as they did mostly unskilled workers, the industrial unions knew of the danger that blacks could be used as strikebreakers. They had been involved in the massive—and, for the unions, ultimately disastrous—steel strike of 1921; as the leaders of the auto workers and other industrial unions greatly feared, they would again be involved in the organizing strikes of the 1930s.

Many craft unions continued to discriminate against minorities well into the 1960s. Thus, George Meany, in violation of the strong tradition of demanding that government keep its nose out of union business, demanded that unions be brought under the fair employment provisions of the 1964 Civil Rights Act.

But as far as public policy was concerned, differences between the AFL and the CIO had narrowed long before, as the number of industrial unions in the former began to increase in the late 1930s. While perhaps less vigorous in doing so, in the 1940s the AFL supported the same types of civil rights legislation as the CIO: both opposed poll taxes in federal elections and favored antilynching bills and similar legislation. By the time of the merger in 1955, therefore, the sole remaining difference between the two organizations was one of practice rather than principle.

The Labor–Civil Rights Alliance. A few years later, the former AFL leader and now president of the merged organization, George Meany, had begun referring to the AFL-CIO as nothing less than a civil rights force. This was more than rhetoric, for labor was indeed instrumental in organizing and funding the Leadership Conference on Civil Rights, which coordinated lobbying for civil rights legislation, and labor provided lobbying muscle for all of the landmark civil rights legislation of the 1960s.

Only a few years before, in 1959, Meany had admonished A. Philip Randolph—the president of the all-black Brotherhood of Sleeping Car Porters and a leading civil rights activist—to "stay a little closer to the trade-union movement, to pay a little less attention to outside organizations that render lip service rather than real service."[18] What happened between 1959 and 1964 to change Meany's attitude?

Although Meany was reluctant to admit it, labor was outgrowing its Gompersite origins. Influencing public policy had taken on an importance at least equal to collective bargaining, and winning at politics required building coalitions with groups, like the civil rights organizations, that had much in common with labor. Moreover, civil rights organizations were now more reliable supporters of labor's political agenda than organized workers themselves. As labor historian Alan Draper writes, "Unable to depend on the support of secondary labor leaders, labor's Committee on Political Education (COPE) implemented its partisan strategy (registering voters it was certain would vote its way) by working regularly outside the labor movement, particularly with civil rights organizations to broaden support for the Democratic Party."[19] Labor worked in Harlem and Detroit with black ministers and started the same sort of work in the South. There blacks were even more vital, since many white Southern unionists opposed the AFL-CIO's integrationist stands. In 1960, COPE focused its efforts on 12 states, which were selected because they were home to two-thirds of all AFL-CIO members and because each "contained large minority populations that COPE predicted could be registered and brought to the polls to vote."[20]

The Appeal to Civil Rights Leaders. Like the civil rights establishment, the AFL argued that the legal equality achieved through Supreme Court decisions such as *Brown v. Board of Education* (1954) and the civil rights legislation of the 1960s was insufficient to guarantee or even permit black economic and social progress. Abandoning Gompersite philosophy altogether, the AFL held that the progress of blacks depended not on their taking full advantage of new opportunities but rather on the adoption by government of organized labor's favorite policies.

As the AFL put it in the 1968 platform proposals that it submitted to the two major parties, "the right to equal service in a restaurant, hotel or any other public accommodation is of great importance to the dignity of an individual but the enjoyment of that right is limited by the ability to pay one's way." A little more than a decade later, mere legal rights had become altogether worthless. From the 1980 platform proposals: "The right to eat in a restaurant is valueless if the person cannot afford to pay the check." Generalizing on this theme to that year's convention of the National Association for the Advancement of Colored People (NAACP), Lane Kirkland declared that "fair-housing laws hold meaning solely for American families who have not been priced out of the market. Equal employment is an empty promise to nearly ten million workers of both sexes and all races and colors who need and want jobs and cannot find them."[21]

Freedom and equality for blacks were invested with new meanings. Bayard Rustin, who argued labor's case in the civil rights movement, said that "for many young Negroes, who are learning that economic servitude can be as effective an instrument of discrimination as racist laws, the new 'freedom' has already become a bitter thing indeed."[22] The 1980 platform proposals claimed that "economic discrimination [i.e., disparities in economic outcomes between the races]—because it traps greater percentages of black and Hispanic Americans in poverty—has racial overtones resulting from past failures of our society. To ignore that fact is to subscribe to discrimination but under supposedly more enlightened and color-blind premises."

According to this line of reasoning, the promise of civil rights legislation could be realized only through the implementation of labor's economic program. Lane Kirkland went so far as to proclaim at a 1979 Urban League convention: "The members of this organization know what it means to see brown-shirted Neo-Nazis and white-sheeted Klansmen parading in public places. You should be aware that the aims of the Proposition 13 cultists [referring to a California referendum on lowering property taxes] add up to much the same thing."[23] In the same vein, Kirkland later told an NAACP gathering that the minimum wage was no less a civil rights issue than a labor issue.[24]

This basic concept was readily expandable. Labor, for example, convinced organizers of the 1993 "civil rights" demonstration in Washington—held to commemorate the August 1963 March for Jobs and Freedom at which Martin Luther King, Jr., gave his famous "I Have a Dream" address—to include among their demands the defeat of the North American Free Trade Agreement, which labor opposed. In his speech to the demonstration, Norman Hill, Rustin's successor at the A. Philip Randolph Institute (now officially part of the AFL-CIO structure), alleged that "NAFTA is the Jim Crow of the 1990s."[25]

The Political Imperative

Not surprisingly, the support that labor received from civil rights quarters came with a quid pro quo, that labor support the civil rights establishment's own agenda. This payback created an internal political problem, first in the form of white union members who resisted demands for integration. This particular obstacle was overcome as the country as a whole came to accept the principle of equal opportunity. But, almost immediately thereafter, the civil rights movement abandoned the principle of nondiscrimination in favor of preferential treatment for minorities, which neither the American people as a whole nor white workers ever accepted as legitimate.

For a while, labor tried resisting the race-conscious approach, but on strategic rather than principled grounds. It argued, for example, that preferential employment policies would pit blacks against white workers and, therefore, would defeat the goal of building a labor–civil rights alliance to fight for full employment. Some in labor, including Meany, saw such initiatives as the 1971 Philadelphia Plan (a Nixon administration measure that attached race-based quotas to federally funded construction projects in that city) as a ploy to sow dissension among white and black workers and drive a wedge between the labor and civil rights movements. One of labor's best friends in the civil rights movement, NAACP lobbyist Clarence Mitchell, agreed, calling the plan a "calculated attempt coming right from the president's desk to break up the coalition between Negroes and labor unions."[26]

Race-Conscious "Remedies." But most civil rights leaders were far more critical of labor than Mitchell. In the rhetoric of the civil rights establishment at that time, any person or group opposed to the establishment's race-conscious agenda was called reactionary and racist. Labor, in particular, received heaps of scorn as a racist institution. Many construction unions deserved criticism, but even unions like the ILGWU, with its impeccable civil rights credentials, came under attack.

Meany tried to dismiss the problem, blaming only a few unnamed "wild men in the NAACP."[27] This was wishful thinking, for virtually the entire NAACP leadership joined in the harsh rhetoric. The crucial alliance between organized labor and the civil rights movement was in jeopardy. How crucial was indicated in a 1971 debate between Donald Slaiman, then head of the AFL's Civil Rights Department, and Herbert Hill, its nemesis within the NAACP. Everything positive that has happened in this country since the time of FDR, Slaiman argued, was due to the coalition of labor, blacks, and like-minded liberals.[28] That being so, the coalition was worth just about anything to preserve it.

Within a few years, however, and without any public explanation of the change, labor reversed course and became a strong supporter of affirmative action. The most telling example was its support in the seminal *Weber*[29] case (1979) of a race-conscious personnel policy against the challenge raised by a white member of the United Steelworkers. Labor seemed not to remember its reservations about race-conscious policies. It denounced even those who were still committed to the principles of nondiscrimination and equality of opportunity as racists and reactionaries. The new line was that adherence to color-blind policies was nothing more than an excuse for what the civil rights movement called "institutional racism,"[30] the label for practices that had a disparate impact on the races.

In 1990, the AFL endorsed not just the original decision in *Griggs v. Duke Power* (1971) but the whole line of cases that followed as a "forceful yet balanced way of sorting through the merits of discrimination cases."[31] Whether decided rightly or wrongly, *Griggs* and its progeny made it increasingly easy to press discrimination complaints by dispensing with any requirement to prove discriminatory intent. A prima facie case could now be made on the basis of statistical disparities alone. Consequently, validating any kind of eligibility requirements became increasingly difficult. As Nathan Glazer was to write four years after *Griggs* about requirements of the Equal Employment Opportunity Commission (EEOC) for validation: "Analysis . . . by various authorities had led to the conclusion that just about no test that shows differential achievement really can be validated."[32] When the Supreme Court attempted to correct for this unintended effect years later in *Wards Cove Packing Co. v. Atonio* (1992), however, labor quickly joined other civil rights forces in lobbying for a bill to overturn the Court's decision.

The Workers' Revolt

While white workers, in general, were surprisingly quiescent in the face of racial preferences in hiring and promotions, they took strong exception to race-conscious policies outside the workplace, such as forced school busing and certain open-housing programs. This, Glazer theorized, was because they were "in the path of black residential movement (as against earlier ethnic groups who are already further out in the suburbs) and their children are subject to the requirements for racial balancing, since they are still more heavily concentrated in the central cities." Their concern was not with race per se but with "significant differences of life-style, of 'culture,' that is 'different ways of life.' " White ethnics "emphasize strongly a neighborhood-centered, family-centered, job-centered life, respect for authority, close attachment to local institutions," whereas among "black families today there is a higher rate of illegitimacy, and . . . a higher rate of crime among the young."[33]

In a special issue that the socialist journal *Dissent* devoted to the labor movement in 1972, Joseph Epstein described an illustrative case. Epstein wrote that Cicero, Illinois—the close-in, blue-collar suburb of Chicago where Martin Luther King had led marches for integration in the mid-1960s—was on the verge of being inundated by a spillover of problems from Lawndale, a slum just across the city line on Chicago's West Side. For their concern about their neighborhood, the white working-class ethnics of Cicero were called honkies by blacks to the applause of Chicago's liberal elite.[34] Scenarios like this played themselves out all across the country. Jonathan Reider examined the opposition that working-class whites in a modest Brooklyn neighborhood mounted against the busing of children from the slum of Brownsville. Here, as well, the reaction for the most part was not racist. The majority of Canarsie's residents distinguished those blacks who lived by "middle-class values"— meaning merely law-abidingness, civility, and a general attitude of responsibility—from those who did not and opposed only the busing of the latter.[35]

The intensity of antibusing sentiment in working-class neighborhoods may be gauged by noting that even the staunchly liberal Democratic representatives whom these areas tended to elect almost invariably opposed busing. In 1972, for example, all the congressional Democrats representing heavily unionized districts in the Detroit area voted in favor of antibusing amendments.[36]

By contrast, the top officials of American labor—the self-proclaimed spokesmen for the working class—strongly supported all such policies. Indeed, even while Meany was being labeled a racist by the Left (for backing the civil rights establishment against black-nationalist radicals), he condemned President Nixon's call for a moratorium on busing as "political chicanery."[37] Labor said that it supported busing to improve the quality of education, even though no evidence was ever produced to show that busing improved education for any students. The first Coleman Report, produced in 1966, that insofar as educational achievement was concerned, integration (much less busing) was irrelevant.

Busing succeeded only in driving whites, many of them working-class, out of public schools or out of the central cities to the suburbs. The most dramatic example of white flight occurred in heavily blue-collar Boston. In the 1970s, the number of whites living within the city limits dropped from 524,000 to 393,000; the minority population rose over the same period from 116,000 to 215,000. There was a similar change in the school population, from 68.5 percent white in 1968, a few years before Judge Arthur Garrity's busing decision, to 45 percent white in 1976. By 1980, whites were even less in evidence in Boston's public schools.[38]

By the mid-1970s, white flight, clearly, had defeated the efforts of courts and government agencies—cheered on by labor leaders and other bulwarks of establishment liberalism—to force the integration of big-city public schools. At the same time, white withdrawal triggered the decline of precisely the working-class urban neighborhoods that had long nourished trade unionism. In the early 1980s, after the damage was done, COPE Director Al Barkan was to lament that "thirty or forty years ago we had pure working-class precincts . . . [but] not anymore. The old New Deal coalition of ethnics is going. We're losing the Italians, the Irish."[39]

The Conversion to Salvation by Society

Strategic political considerations had driven labor to support school busing and similar race-conscious measures. Labor's long-held views neatly dovetailed with the civil rights establishment's belief that there were governmental solutions to virtually all social and economic problems.

Labor and the Urban Riots. The propensity for structural explanations and government-funded solutions was evident in labor's response to the riots that began to rock American cities in the middle and late 1960s. Rustin, viewed at the time as labor's unofficial civil rights spokesman, took the view that the riot in the Watts section of Los Angeles during the summer of 1965 represented the "first major rebellion of Negroes. . . . with the express purpose of asserting that they would no longer quietly submit to the deprivation of slum life."[40] His recommended antidote to the poison of despair was a massive government spending program outlined in the so-called

Freedom Budget that had been written by Leon Keyserling under AFL-CIO sponsorship and endorsed by a host of AFL leaders.

Yet, Watts then was, in the words of George Will, a "community of adequate single-family homes in Los Angeles, a city which the Urban League then rated first on a list of sixty-eight cities in terms of how blacks fared. . . . A more detached and informed study later concluded that it was a 'collective celebration in the manner of a carnival, during which about forty liquor stores were broken into and much liquor consumed.' " [41] Such studies did nothing to keep labor from singing the same refrain. "No one can condone the riots," Meany said. But then he added, "Nor can anyone condone the conditions in the slums and ghettoes."[42] The rioters surely did wrong, he was saying, but they were not really to blame: the conditions of ghetto life were. Testifying before the Kerner Commission, called by President Johnson to investigate the riots, Meany called for "study [of] the underlying causes of the riots, and remedies to eliminate them."[43]

In its 1972 platform proposals, labor took yet another step away from holding blacks accountable for their own actions and toward assigning responsibility for solving their problems to government: "Foremost we recognize the contribution that poverty makes in creating criminals and we look upon the war on poverty as the *first* line of attack on crime." "Black teenagers," the proposals continued, "whose unemployment rate is upward of 35 percent, face conditions that inevitably affect the entire community. Many individuals turn in despair to crime or drugs."

In the decades since, labor has moved further in the same direction. After the Los Angeles riots of May 1992, the executive council argued that "the explosion of violence, unlike the riots that occurred during the midst of the Great Society era, is symptomatic of more than a decade of policies that favor the rich and privileged while ignoring and injuring the disadvantaged and their communities. . . . It is no accident that violence erupted in Los Angeles, a city that experienced the loss of tens of thousands of high-paying manufacturing jobs over the last two decades."[44] Lane Kirkland went even further: "The Los Angeles case is one in particular. The devastation in the inner cities derives essentially from the loss of job opportunities of that particular kind. We have our own Third World in this country, and our own Third World is the one that is most directly impacted by the writing off of job opportunities of this kind."[45]

One wonders if Kirkland knew when he said this that black labor force participation had decreased over the past generation, at the same time as unemployment. Later Kirkland said:

> The violence in the streets of a major American city is the legacy of the Bush Administration's indifference to the harsh realities of urban life, outside of the country club. . . . While the AFL-CIO deeply regrets the violence and destruction that has erupted in Los Angeles, we see it as the consequence of communities abandoned by an elitist Administration out of touch with the day-to-day reality of workers and the poor.[46]

The facts here, as elsewhere, were inconsistent with labor's analysis. In the first place, communities had not been abandoned. Social welfare spending in 1960 totaled $50 billion and climbed to $593 billion in 1983. During the Reagan years, it continued to climb at a rate that was only 10 percent less than projected and rose again during the Bush presidency. Second, the 1992 riot began "in one of South Central's better neighborhoods," where "covetousness, more than rage, filled the streets," as evidenced by a neighborhood homicide rate near the national average and a robbery rate "nearly four times the national average."[47] Third, the riot started when members of a youth gang decided to steal malt liquor from a Korean-owned liquor store. The rioters made liquor stores special targets, and their stolen contents fueled the riots as much as anything.

Labor and the Breakup of the Black Family. Labor's comments on the breakup of the black family are in keeping with its favored lines of analysis regarding social problems. In 1965, White House aide Daniel Patrick Moynihan wrote his prophetic report on the black family, concluding the "master problem" to be "that the Negro family structure is crumbling."[48] Rustin argued in reply to Moynihan that "if Negroes suffer more than others from the problems of family instability today, it is not because they are Negro but because they are so disproportionately unemployed, underemployed, and ill paid."[49] To have admitted that family breakdown was a cause of social and economic problems, as well as their result, might have undermined support for the government programs that labor supported.

But the issue of the breakdown of the black family could be buried only so long. In 1973, economist Richard Freeman—a liberal and a friend of labor—wrote that "the convergence in economic position [between similarly qualified blacks and whites] in the fifties and sixties suggests a virtual collapse in traditional discriminatory patterns in the labor market."[50] Moreover, Freeman reported, young ghetto blacks admitted, when interviewed, that jobs were available; macroeconomic policies were not the problem. Rather, the problem was the breakdown of the family. By 1971, the median income of Negro husband-wife families was 93 percent of the median income of comparable white families. "If both husband and wife worked," Glazer reported, "an increasingly common development for whites, as it has been for blacks, the figures for the two years (1969 and 1971) were 99 and 101 percent respectively."[51]

No acknowledgment of such realities was forthcoming from the AFL-CIO, which continued to deny the real nature of the problem—even after a nationwide consensus in support of the Moynihan thesis emerged and solidified. "We know what the real family values are," Kirkland said:

> Family values are a home, a job, health care, a decent education for your kids, and protection from the harsher realities of market economics that have thrown millions out of work and have brought millions more to the brink of financial ruin—with only their job and their good health standing between them and joining the ranks of the street people.[52]

Welfare as a Right

In keeping with its penchant for ascribing virtually any and all social problems to gross economic causes, the AFL-CIO opposes efforts to reinforce positive individual behavior, as in the case of welfare reform. Abandoning altogether Gompers's abhorrence of dependence on government, labor declared itself, as early as 1968, in favor of the "principle of welfare as a right."[53] In document after document, labor ignored growing signs that welfare programs were fueling dependency, idleness, and dissolution.

Eight years after Moynihan's controversial but accurate report, the AFL put out a broadside entitled "Welfare: Everybody's Whipping Boy." It argued that the growing opposition to welfare was based in part on a mistaken belief that welfare recipients did not want to work. The truth, it averred, was that only a "handful of potential employables" were on welfare. The far more numerous unemployables included many mothers of young children, most of whom were in dire circumstances and needed welfare through no fault of their own. They were certainly not "churning out" illegitimate children: "Nearly 70 percent of children in welfare families are legitimate." Nor was there any serious worry that they would become addicted to welfare. There was "no evidence to sustain the belief that welfare is necessarily habit-forming, that is that 'once on welfare, always on welfare.' "[54]

This has remained labor's position on welfare. In 1985, the AFL-CIO Executive Council argued that, in the immediately preceding period, the "ineffectiveness of welfare programs in fighting poverty has been largely a result of the [Reagan] Administration's efforts to cut more than $6 billion from the AFDC program since 1981."[55] The remedy was to "establish a national minimum standard which would restore the purchasing power of AFDC benefits and mandate regular benefit increases to keep pace with inflation. This standard should be raised to not less than the poverty level as quickly as possible."

In his 1984 bestseller *Losing Ground*, Charles Murray wrote of an unappeasable "liberal conviction that the recipients [of welfare] were victims incapable of obligation."[56] While most liberals subsequently became persuaded that welfare as designed is part of the problem of poverty in America, organized labor will not brook such an admission.

The historian Gertrude Himmelfarb has written that Keynesian economics emphasizes "immediate and present" rather than future satisfactions, and that this "same ethos is reflected in the Keynesian doctrine that consumption rather than saving is the source of economic growth—indeed, that thrift is economically and socially harmful."[57] The ethos that Himmelfarb describes is uncannily like the one that pervades the American labor movement. It has for decades pressed the notion that there is far too much saving and far too little consumption in the United States. For those who hold such views, casting welfare as a right without qualifications is not much of a leap.

The Stake of the Public-Sector Unions

The public-employee unions, whose weight within the AFL-CIO has continued to grow, have their own particular stake in traditional welfare programs. So far as they are concerned, welfare is far preferable to workfare, condemned by Kirkland as amounting to involuntary servitude and described by the AFL-CIO's Public Employee Department as "cheap punitive workfare which requires welfare recipients to work off their benefits at unpaid jobs."[58] The problem, from the public-employee unions' point of view, is that workfare often takes the form of public-sector jobs that "displace regular public workers."[59]

Labor opposes not just workfare but any program based on the assumption that the taxpayers, who fund welfare, and the government, which administers it, have a right to demand more responsible behavior from recipients. Thus, organized labor was at the forefront of the effort to get "President Clinton to ease off his campaign pledge to 'end welfare as we know it' by making public assistance a transitional entitlement and requiring recipients to work in community service jobs after two years of benefits."[60]

Douglas Besharov has observed that "mandated community service may be the only way to build the job skills and work habits of those who cannot support themselves in the regular job market." Yet, not working at all would be far worse for the poor, if not for unionized welfare workers: "Child abuse, drug abuse, and a host of social problems are associated with long-term welfare dependency. A work requirement will help to reduce their levels."[61] Conversely, it will also cut into the ranks of public employees.

In 1992, New Jersey's governor, liberal Democrat Jim Florio, signed welfare reform legislation that increased the responsibilities of welfare recipients. One provision eliminated additions to welfare payments for children born to parents already on welfare, and another required welfare recipients with children over the age of two "to participate in education and employment activities." Job-placement programs were to be biased toward the private sector. Aside from these provisions, the reform actually liberalized previous legislation. The *New York Times* praised the new measure as "a compassionate, realistic blueprint for dealing with an intractable problem."[62] The AFL-CIO's Public Employee Department, however, denounced it as "deplorable."[63]

As an alternative, the public-employee unions called for more of the usual "voluntary" training programs, noting that "as with all successful assistance programs, those that work best cost money."[64] There was no attempt to explain why expensive programs like the Job Corps raised their graduates' earnings by an average of less than $200 per year. Any money spent, moreover, would have to be spent by and through the poverty bureaucracy. One PED publication pronounced that "the social workers, employment counselors, income-maintenance workers, and other employees know best how to make their programs work better."[65]

And they would also know best that no public employee should ever be displaced. Their putative knowledge of how best to get people off welfare remains a matter of less certainty. The same PED publication highlights Washington State's Family Independence Program, praising it, in part, because public-employee unions were involved in its design. Yet, an Urban Institute study found that the major effect of this program was more frequent recourse and longer resorts to welfare.[66]

Despite the Workers

Workers were also frequently on the opposite side of the welfare issue from the unions that represented them. Although denounced roundly by the AFL as reactionary, the tax revolt of the 1970s ran to a large degree on working-class anger. Journalist Thomas Byrne Edsall noted, "The tax revolt was a major turning point in American politics . . . firmly establishing new grounds for the disaffection of white working- and middle-class voters from their traditional Democratic roots." These previously Democratic voters "including many who considered themselves members of the working class . . . saw their rising tax burdens going to finance programs disproportionately serving the Black and Hispanic constituencies."[67]

With the rise of social issues like busing and welfare, workers became unreliable supporters of labor's program and favorite political candidates. Increasing numbers of workers were more interested in other issues and cold to "the welfare state agenda of the AFL-CIO."[68] Meany was said to be shocked by the results of a poll, taken for labor by Joseph Kraft, that starkly revealed the wide gap separating labor leaders from rank-and-file workers on a number of salient civil rights and social welfare issues.[69]

Labor leaders believed that workers were being duped by politicians like Richard Nixon and George Wallace (whose supporters in his 1968 run for the presidency were more likely than those of Democratic nominee Hubert Humphrey to identify themselves as working class).[70] Labor's 1972 platform proposals held that Nixon's ultimately unsuccessful attempts to name the conservative jurists Clement Haynesworth and G. Harrold Carswell to the Supreme Court were "specifically directed as part of the 'southern strategy' to appeal to anti-civil rights sentiments." Al Barkan put it this way: "Labor's enemies are trying to divert trade unionists from the real issues to trick them into voting against labor's proven friends."[71]

After workers turned against labor-supported candidates in the midterm congressional elections of 1966, Barkan wrote to NAACP head Roy Wilkins that "we in COPE are sharply aware that many of our members deserted liberal candidates for one reason only: In protest against their advocacy of civil rights."[72] But Barkan misunderstood working-class attitudes. "Talk about 'law and order,' 'welfare ethic,' 'immorality,' or 'crime in the streets' may not really be code words for racism at all, but rather they are the cause and essence of the racial attitudes themselves."[73] As time went on, labor leaders would prove less and less willing even to consider the possibility such analyses might be correct.

The increase in the absolute and relative number of blacks in labor's ranks ameliorated its internal problem because they were far more reliable supporters of the leadership's political agenda. This status was revealed most dramatically in the 1984 presidential election, when Walter Mondale, the Democratic challenger, endorsed by the AFL-CIO, received the votes of 55 percent of union members and their families. To reach this figure, he had needed the votes of 95 percent of black union members and their families. A clear majority of white union members and their families had voted for labor's nemesis, Ronald Reagan. Labor was now politically at odds with the working-class constituency that it claimed to represent.

The Entente with Cultural Radicalism

By the 1970s, the only elements in the Democratic Party that supported labor's economic agenda were the civil rights establishment and the cultural radicals, for whom George Meany had contempt. Those who supported the Equal Rights Amendment (ERA), urged the legitimization of homosexuality, supported abortion on demand, and so on agreed with labor's positions.

An alliance with the new liberalism had been inconceivable when Meany was in charge. He proudly avowed his support for traditional American values and had contempt for the cultural radicalism associated with the 1960s and their aftermath. After the 1968 Democratic Party convention in Chicago, Meany said:

> I saw the invaders who came to this city. . . . I want to tell you quite frankly that I think the Chicago police did not overreact, or whatever that means. What would you do if some group advertised that they were coming here to prevent you from . . . holding this convention? . . . I know what you would do with this dirty-necked and dirty-mouthed group of kooks."[74]

After the 1972 convention, Meany was quoted in the *New York Times* as criticizing homosexuals and abortion supporters in no delicate terms.[75] At the convention itself, he had angrily complained that the New York State delegation had "six open fags and only three AFL-CIO people."[76] Barkan shared Meany's sensibilities. In 1982 (the year he stepped down as COPE director), a *Washington Post* piece quoted Barkan's references to "black ingrates," "pansies," and "those women yelling about equal rights in Lafayette Park."[77]

This attitude had clearly become a political liability by the late 1960s, as more liberal trade union leaders like Walter Reuther realized. Meany was scarcely cold in his grave before labor was forging a rapprochement with the left wing of the Democratic Party. Broadsides against cultural radicals were halted. Second, there was a natural narrowing of the gap on some issues as labor became more disenchanted with the market and more enchanted with government. One such issue was comparable worth. From Gompers's time, labor had supported equal pay for equal work because it did not want women undercutting the wages of men.

But equal pay for work of "comparable" value was a horse of a different color, for it meant that unions (and employers) would have to cede much of their authority to determine wages through collective bargaining to outside "experts." Columnist Charles Krauthammer warned about the "judicial and bureaucratic monster (that would be called) into being as through the mechanism of comparable worth (as a first step) we moved away from determination of wages by the market to the fixing of wages by law."[78] But, to the AFL-CIO, that no longer sounded so frightening. The public-employee unions, like AFSCME, found that fighting for comparable worth in the courts helped it to recruit women, who now make up a third of the total membership of AFL-CIO-affiliated unions.

Narrowing the gap on other issues required an even more radical change of policy. Labor had opposed the ERA from the start. The progressive UAW had even quit the National Organization of Women (NOW) over the issue in 1968. In 1970, during the height of the culture wars, Evelyn Dubrow, the longtime lobbyist of the International Ladies Garment Workers Union, wrote a critique of the ERA for the *International Free Trade Union News*, which was distributed throughout the world by the AFL-CIO. Dubrow argued that the ERA would threaten existing legal protections for women workers and that it would also put into jeopardy child-support, divorce, and alimony laws; the law that protected women from the draft; and laws that prohibited homosexual marriages.[79] Just a few years later, however, after protective legislation was found in violation of title 7 of the 1964 Civil Rights Act, labor reversed itself on ERA, even joining the 1979 boycott of those states that had not yet ratified it.

As the old guard died off, labor abandoned nearly all its socially conservative views in favor of more "progressive" ones. The one partial exception so far has been abortion. The AFL never had a position on the issue, probably figuring that it was none of its business. Yet, as the composition of labor changed; as the percentage of women, many professing feminist beliefs, increased; and as the percentage of Catholics decreased, the AFL-CIO started edging toward a prochoice position to improve relations with feminists. With that purpose in mind, it set up a committee to study the issue, with the expectation that it would recommend a pro choice position. But when members heard of this, the sizeable numbers of union members with antiabortion convictions—many, though not all of them, Catholics—lobbied the leadership not to take a position that violated their moral and religious values. The matter was tabled.

Nonetheless, the executive council found other means of signaling that its views had changed. It took issue with the Supreme Court's ruling in *Rust v. Sullivan* (1992) that the government could prohibit health care workers at clinics from discussing abortion with clients. The AFL not only took the position that the decision was wrong in denying access to information about this medical option but, in doing so, used language that indicated exactly where it stood. Speaking to the "broader rights" involved, it declared that its policy was to defer to judgments of the unions (most of the larger ones such as AFSCME, the Service Employees, and Food and Commercial Workers had, by now, come out in favor of choice) and to the membership, which had made it "clear that on reproductive issues they believed firmly in their right to act in accordance with their personal convictions" on what the AFL-CIO called, in the parlance of NOW and Planned Parenthood, "reproductive rights."[80]

All this effort in repositioning itself vis-à-vis the women's movement has paid off. Not so long ago at war with each other, the AFL-CIO and feminists now have a close working relationship. One symbolically important indication of that is a statement published by the Women's Leadership Committee for Workplace Fairness, an organization supported by the AFL-CIO. A ringing endorsement of trade unionism that calls for the "women's movement and labor to work together,"[81] the statement was signed by the likes of the Rev. Joan Brown Campbell, general secretary of the National Council of Churches; Judy Lichtman, president of the Women's Legal Defense Fund; Eleanor Smeal, president of the Fund for the Feminist Majority; and Molly Yard, former president of NOW.

Labor is also trying hard to establish a working relationship with organized homosexuals. Almost as soon as he took over from the socially conservative Al Barkan as COPE director in 1982, John Perkins started mending fences, for example, by attending the banquet of the Gertrude Stein Society of Lesbians. The 1989 convention came out in support of "legislation at the federal, state and local levels that would guarantee the civil rights of all persons without regard to sexual orientation in employment, housing, credit, public accommodations and public services," which the executive council asserted was "consistent with . . . a person's right to privacy."[82] But the purpose of such legislation was not to prevent discrimination against homosexuals, who suffered little of that, but rather to "establish society's official indifference to homosexuality." George Will predicted that "next will come the right of homosexuals to adopt children, to have homosexuality 'fairly represented' as an 'alternative life style' in every child's sex-education classes."[83] Labor's leaders, meanwhile, become more deeply committed to this issue with each passing year. Thus, by 1993, the leadership supported the lifting of all restrictions on military service by homosexuals, even though the entire top leadership of the armed services was opposed. And, as a symbol of how far it had moved in the decade and a half since Meany stepped down, labor sponsored a reception at its Washington headquarters for leaders of the 1993 gay rights march; James Baker, Kirkland's top assistant, represented the AFL-CIO.

Only a few months after Meany's departure, Kirkland had urged his listeners to

> examine what Ronald Reagan opposes: the ERA, busing, abortion, affirmative action, gun control and what he proposes state's rights, prayer in the schools, the death penalty: the sum is prejudice and a lack of respect for human differences. Add that to his economic policies and, once again, the age-old product will be "the rich will get richer and the poor will get children."[84]

Although perhaps a non sequitur, the intention was clear. The only question was how long it would take for labor to revise its views to the satisfaction of cultural radicals. The answer, as it happened, was just a little more than a decade.

9
Unions and the Political Order

T he European trade unionists to whom the Americans have most often been contrasted, the English and the Germans, were hardly Marxist revolutionaries. By the late nineteenth century, revolutionary Marxism had, for the most part, given way in Western Europe to reformism. Samuel Gompers and his mentors saw that classical socialism in the United States had even less working-class support than in Europe. In fact, a working class hardly existed. There was certainly no proletariat, with nothing to lose but its chains. Higher wages here naturally bred a certain contentment. More important, there was far greater social mobility, thus no permanent working class. Even if a worker could not improve his own station in life, his children could.

Given these circumstances, the establishment of a political party based on the working class was not a viable option—hence America's trade unionism pure and simple. American unions would not seek to reorder society through politics; rather, they would use the means of collective bargaining to improve the conditions of workers within the existing order. For this reason, the AFL did not eschew politics altogether. But labor's operating political philosophy would be to reward friends and punish enemies, no matter what the political affiliation. American labor would support either Republican or Democratic candidates, depending on their stand on crucial issues. And, for the most part, these issues directly affected labor's ability to organize workers and to improve their wages and working conditions through collective bargaining.

Before the merger with the CIO, the AFL had stepped up its political involvement. But it justified its increased involvement on strictly Gompersite grounds. Meany said that the passage of the Taft-Hartley Act drove labor into the political arena: "These employers chose the new battleground, the legislative hall, and forced the trade-union movement into the political arena."[1] Indeed, the AFL abandoned its longtime policy of not endorsing presidential candidates only in 1952, when it officially supported Adlai Stevenson— after he pledged to seek outright repeal of Taft-Hartley, while Dwight Eisenhower promised only to support amendments to it.

After the merger of the AFL and the CIO in 1955, the AFL's nonideological philosophy seemed to dominate. The merged organization's first president, George Meany, certainly considered himself in the Gompers tradition. He told his authorized biographer, Archie Robinson:

> I take a very practical view and Gompers took a very practical view that he did not want to run the country. . . . Our job was to be nonpartisan; our job was to try to make progress for the people we represented by economic strikes, by withholding our labor, by boycotts, by using our purchasing power through the use of union labels, and by legislative action.[2]

This did not preclude political action. But it did preclude ideological politics. As Meany put it, "Ideology is baloney. There can be no ideological differences among real trade unionists."[3]

But labor did become increasingly ideological. In general, labor was fighting to realign the Democratic Party, to move with civil rights and liberal forces against the Southerners and machine politicians who had checked the party's liberal impulses. That is, it was attempting to transform the ideologically diverse Democratic Party into a party with a liberal ideology. Labor had opposed putting Lyndon Johnson on the Democratic ticket in 1960 because in its eyes he was for the conservatives.

By 1964, labor was more than happy with Johnson, who had proved even more liberal than Kennedy. For the vice-presidential nomination, "labor leaders—chiefly Reuther, Dubinsky, and Meany—urged the senior Minnesota Senator (Hubert Humphrey) on the President. (Once Johnson asked George Meany, President of the AFL-CIO, who his three choices were for Vice-President, Meany replied that he had only one—Humphrey.)"[4] Four years later, Humphrey had become the *bête noire* of the New Politics movement and New Left radicals for having been President Johnson's vice president and supported the war in Vietnam. But labor leaders knew that he resembled a European social democrat more than any other major political leader in the country and, accordingly, backed him to the hilt.

Journalist and historian Teddy White implicitly criticized the 1964–1966 session of Congress, calling it the "Grandfather Congress of Programs and Entitlement." The AFL-CIO, however, exulted that "on the legislative front . . . we have made greater progress than in any other period of our history." It was "the most productive Congressional Session ever held."[5]

Labor was the strongest supporter of an agenda that "pressed the government's reach into countless corners of American life where federal dollars and federal bureaucrats had never been seen before" and of a process that by 1980 had made the federal government "the center court for every group with a cause to plead, good or bad."[6] Conversely, labor strongly opposed any efforts to reinvigorate federalism. Thus, it adamantly opposed the proposal of Walter Heller, chairman of President Johnson's Council of Economic Advisers, for revenue sharing and has opposed every subsequent effort to devolve more responsibilities to lower levels of government.

Not only that, labor strongly supported efforts to enlarge the powers of the federal judiciary. Robert Bork has argued that "when the Court is perceived as a political rather than a legal institution, nominees will be treated like political candidates."[7] More than any other institution in society, the AFL-CIO has treated nominees as such. It instigated and led the opposition to the distinguished judge, Clement Haynesworth (which, as Bork pointed out, was "very largely political but was presented as a concern about a quite trivial ethical matter"). Later, on strictly political grounds, labor opposed the nominations of the present chief justice, William Rehnquist, and Justice Antonin Scalia, who, because there were no valid objections to his being seated, sailed through confirmation hearings. Most recently, it fought strongly against the nominations of both Bork and Clarence Thomas.

What was the point? White observed that in the early 1970s, "for people who sought new social or political goals, it was far more effective to go to the courts than to go to the voters or move through Congress, where every step forward required the building of a new coalition in House, in Senate, in committee staff, in pressure groups."[8] These decisions mandated or approved integration, state reapportionment, one man–one vote, affirmative action, busing, set-asides for minorities, and abortion and transformed America. In most cases, the AFL-CIO itself did not submit amicus briefs but supported most and did not criticize any. As important, an activist, liberal Supreme Court offered protection and hope to a movement that was so often frustrated in achieving political goals (for example, labor law reform) that were in its own self-interest.

The Faction Fight in the Democratic Party

It is in this context that we should attempt to understand the conflict in the Democratic Party starting in 1968. Class conflict erupted within the party, with the so-called New Class (the new educated middle class) vying for ascendancy, achievable only if it could first defeat the labor movement. Labor seemed capable of meeting the political challenge of the New Politics movement, which was the political expression of the New Class.

There was, indeed, much tough talk from George Meany and a few others in 1968 and in the years following about the New Politics movement. And, in 1972, after the New Politics ideologues captured the Democratic Party in Miami Beach and nominated George McGovern as the party's presidential standard bearer, labor refused to endorse him, just as many New Politics leaders had refused to endorse or work for labor's favorite, Hubert Humphrey, in 1968. The stage seemed set for a battle royal for control of the Democratic Party, with labor leading the resistance to the New Politics takeover. In the wake of McGovern's disastrous presidential campaign, a new organization of traditional liberals (and social-democratic allies) called the Coalition for a Democratic Majority (CDM) was established, on the assumption that labor would be the key element in the fight against New Politics extremists.

But the real problem was not with extremists. Most party activists understood that measures had to be taken to avert a repeat of 1972. Jimmy Carter, then governor of Georgia, for example, came away from the Democratic Party convention of 1972 in a state of disbelief. He thought that most Americans were patriotic and, therefore, while they might be critical of the war effort, they would be repelled by the McGovernite line that the United States played an "evil" role in Vietnam. And he further thought that an issue such as abortion, that the Democrats became associated with in 1972, was a no-win issue that the Democratic Party should avoid identification with.[9] In short, party leaders wanted to take control out of the hands of extremists, if not return it to the center of the political spectrum. To this end, with the support of the AFL-CIO, they elected the quintessential party insider and moderate, Robert Strauss, as party chairman in 1973. The real problem was that, while rejecting the antics of the extremists, the mainstream party leaders and elected officials now subscribed to much of the New Politics ideology. Was the labor movement prepared to take them on?

The Battle That Never Happened

Economic policy was labor's priority; nothing else was nearly so important. It was unrealistic to think that labor would participate in a long ideological battle against the New Politics movement or its representatives over foreign or social policy issues. In this connection, it is worth asking what labor would have done had Hubert Humphrey or Edward Kennedy been nominated instead of McGovern. Undoubtedly the movement would have supported either enthusiastically, even though all indications are that either would have run on dovish foreign policy platforms.

In his campaign for the Senate in 1970, a properly chastened Humphrey had already become dovish. He had endorsed a Brookings Institution proposal to cut $12.5 billion from a defense budget of $76.5 billion, $2.5 billion more than McGovern's final proposal (scaled down from an initial $30 billion) during the 1972 campaign. Such cuts would have "eliminated half the strategic bomber and land-based ICBM forces and most air defense. The Navy would lose four of its sixteen carrier task forces and most of its shipbuilding program, the Air Force its chief new tactical air development, the F-15 fighter, and the Army, six active brigades plus some of its swollen support forces."[10]

Kennedy was, as Gary Hart noted, "uniquely acceptable to both reform and traditional elements of the party." But then the scandal of Chappaquiddick took him out of the running. Had Kennedy won the nomination, labor would have gladly supported him for president, even though his foreign policy views before and since have been indistinguishable from those of what the CDM called the Mc-Governites.

Labor's public explanation of its decision not to endorse McGovern was yet another sign that it did not have the stomach for a broad ideological fight—its tone was pragmatic and conciliatory. According to the Steelworkers president and Meany stalwart, I. W. Abel,

> A lot of the fellows who went all-out for McGovern now appreciate our position and the futility of theirs. . . . they felt so strongly about Nixon that they were ready to support the Devil as an opposition. George and I looked at it more from the standpoint of constructive effort. We felt very strongly that in no way could you defeat Nixon with McGovern. We would have had a hard time in seventy-two defeating Nixon with either Hubert [Humphrey] or Scoop Jackson. With Mc-Govern and the kind of supporters he had, we recognized it as a hopeless situation; we did feel that we could save the Congress and maybe stop some things [that Nixon wanted to do] that way.[11]

The nonideological machine politicians played a similar game in 1968. Assuming that Humphrey would go down to defeat, Chicago Mayor Richard Daley, for instance, committed the resources of his political machine to local campaigns.

Meany himself, who had been rather forthright about his criticism of McGovern before the Democratic Party convention, suddenly became tight-lipped after McGovern was nominated. The executive council passed a one-sentence resolution stating that "given the circumstances" the AFL-CIO would not endorse a presidential candidate. Asked by reporters to explain what circumstances the council was referring to, the usually expansive Meany said in reply, "Under the circumstances in which we find ourselves," nothing more.[12]

Yet another indication that the labor movement was not prepared for ideological warfare was its participation in other political campaigns that year. As Abel indicated, labor did not sit out the election season altogether: it was involved as ever, supporting a myriad of candidates, many with views indistinguishable from Mc-Govern's. In 1972, labor supported Iowa Democrat Dick Clark. The Clark amendment later prevented the Nixon administration from supporting anti-Communist insurgents in Angola; labor opposed the Clark amendment. In Rhode Island, labor was the major boost for the incumbent senator, Claiborne Pell. Pell became a most dovish chairman of the Senate Foreign Relations Committee. Indeed, with the possible exception of McGovern, the AFL-CIO's anti-Communist militancy never stopped it from endorsing any elected officials or candidates for elective office, no matter what their position on either foreign or social policy issues.

After the Democratic Party's midterm charter convention in 1974, the AFL-CIO withdrew from official participation in the internal affairs of the Democratic Party, and labor leaders, such as COPE Director Al Barkan, resigned from their posts on the Democratic National Committee (DNC). This defection was in response to the adoption of rules that labor believed would put it at a great disadvantage vis-à-vis the New Politics. But, according to former CDM leader Joshua Muravchik, it was due as well to labor's divisions; the Left was a minority but strong enough to "lead Meany to call in his troops for fear of splitting the labor movement."[13] Labor used its formal withdrawal from the party to pull the financial plug from CDM. The ostensible reason was that, since labor was no longer participating in party affairs, supporting one party faction over the other no longer made sense. But CDM activists were given to understand that this was a rationalization for labor's withdrawing from a political fight with the New Politics wing of the party, which was its ally on the economic issues that concerned it most.

By the time of the 1974 elections a few months later, it was hard to tell left- and right-wing unions apart. With equal fervor, they supported liberal congressional candidates, once again with no regard as to their views on social and foreign policy. After the elections, the executive council, under Meany's firm control, boasted that "Labor's Political Programs in 1974 were more effective than in any previous election effort. This high level of effectiveness contributed tremendously to a major shift in Congress toward the progressive, proworker position on issues and correspondingly away from the reactionary economic and social policies of the Nixon Years."[14] The report promised a similar effort in 1976.

Labor Moves Left

There would be more frequent debates in the Democratic Party over domestic policy. But labor's move to the left became clear fairly early. The laborites (social-democratic supporters of the labor movement) noticed that on economic issues the New Politics movement was more conservative than labor. Penn Kemble, a leading Social Democrat, noted that in 1968 Robert Kennedy was "experimenting" with a strategy of appealing to lower-income whites or white ethnics through "ethnic appeals, concessions in matters of style, clever handling of the race issue, displays of backbone toward criminals, etc., none of which costs much." And Kemble criticized the middle-class New Politics movement because unlike the labor movement "it has shown little interest in a radical, egalitarian economic program, or in whatever forces in our society might be rallied to promote such a program."[15] He properly suggested that labor was being consistent with the economic policies of the Democratic Party of the past twenty years, which avoided calls for taxing the rich, for planning massive government spending programs, and for more regulation of corporations.

Washington Post columnist David Broder recounted a conversation with Gary Hart (McGovern's campaign manager in 1972) in which Hart was "cold blooded in rejecting the New Deal policies of the past. 'We are not a bunch of little Hubert Humphreys,' he told me . . . in what turned out to be an accurate preview of the economic and social policy revisionism of many of the young Democrats elected to Congress in that Watergate year. They have been far less sympathetic to organized labor, and far more concerned about middle income taxpayers, than many had expected."[16] They were more sympathetic to business, too.

The difference was between those like Humphrey who still thought in terms of the American economy of the 1930s and 1940s and those "new Democrats" who "emphasized American's transition from an industrial economy to an information economy." In terms of specific policy, Hart wrote that "new government programs, requiring large, new administering agencies and bureaucracies, Keynesian tax cuts and government-spending measures, additional volumes regulating economic activities, and looser control of the money supply, all were questioned by the new Democrats of the class of 1974."[17]

Some of this commentary is the reading of present views into the past. The "new" Democrats were mostly willing to go along with big government proposals in almost all instances. But there were seeds of the "probusiness" campaign of Paul Tsongas in 1992 and of

Bill Clinton's "I am a new kind of Democrat" campaign of the same year.

In 1976, Jimmy Carter ran a centrist campaign for the Democratic Party nomination, which only made labor uncomfortable. The platform adopted at the convention, however, was by no means moderate on economic issues. After the convention, the conservative columnist George Will wrote that the platform "expresses the party's consensus. It distills to a four letter word 'More,' more public jobs, more revenue sharing, more subsidies for older cities, more subsidized loans for housing . . . more spending on environmental research, transportation, veterans, arts, the elderly, etc."[18] All this was to be paid for by closing tax loopholes, that is, by soaking the rich. The Democratic left-wing platform belied Carter's claim to be a centrist Democrat.

Political analyst William Schneider explained that "economic problems came into prominence in 1976 when 47 percent named inflation and 31 percent named unemployment as the country's most serious problem. In 1980, according to Gallup, 61 percent named inflation and 31 percent named unemployment as the country's most serious problem."[19] Labor's pump-priming economic policy had become a big part of the Democratic Party's problem in winning back centrist voters. But virtually no one recognized that at the time because labor's champions and detractors were still focused on its anti-Communist foreign policy views.

Labor was true to its new form during the Carter administration. Meany accused Carter of being the "most conservative President since Hoover."[20] While this assessment did not make sense, it did indicate the direction in which labor was headed. Labor not only criticized but organized the left wing of the party against the administration's economic policies. AFL-CIO Secretary-Treasurer Lane Kirkland took the lead in organizing a coalition of 147 organizations, ranging from Americans for Democratic Action through the Citizens against High Blood Pressure, to fight the austerity budgets proposed by the Carter administration and the congressional budget committees." It represented a "liberal-left fusion."[21]

By 1978, there were rumblings from old-guard staffers, preeminently Al Barkan, that labor might not endorse for reelection congressmen who had not supported special-interest legislation during the Carter administration. But that warning was not to be taken seriously. Despite having removed itself from the internal affairs of the Democratic Party, labor was as committed to the party as before, or more. Through the 1960s, a substantial number of union leaders, almost all representing craft unions, considered themselves Republicans. But no more. More than 95 percent of union contributions in 1976 went to Democratic congressional candidates.

Indeed, labor would soon follow the opposite of the course Barkan suggested. The future direction was presaged by the effort of the more liberal unions, spearheaded by Douglas Fraser, leader of the still independent UAW, to establish a wide-ranging, permanent coalition with other "progressive" elements within the Democratic Party. This particular initiative was abandoned, largely because there was no need for it after George Meany retired in 1979. Lane Kirkland took over, promising "steady at the helm," but was, in fact, ready to lead the AFL-CIO in a different direction.

When Meany headed the AFL-CIO, there was constant public grumbling from the likes of Jerry Wurf and the socialist president of the Machinists, William Winpisinger. But the Left was quite happy with Kirkland. He brought back the UAW, which gave the Left more leverage and, then, much later, the Teamsters, under new, more liberal leadership. Moreover, his consensus style of leadership gave the Left unions more influence than when the more confrontational Meany was in charge.

The role that labor played in the 1980 primaries was yet another indicator of its shift to the left. There was widespread dissatisfaction with President Carter within labor's ranks, as there was in the country at large. The AFL-CIO did not support a candidate in the Democratic primaries. But many unions did, and most of them (by a margin of approximately 2:1) supported the Left liberal stalwart Ted Kennedy over President Carter.

In December 1978, "Kennedy used the Democratic Party miniconvention in Memphis to deliver an arm-waving, podium pounding harangue on the need for national health insurance and an end to social welfare budget cuts." It was like throwing red meat at labor chieftains. "By 1979 Kennedy seemed to be taking pokes at Carter every chance he had. . . . when Bella Abzug [the ex-Communist, former congresswoman from New York] was dismissed as Carter's adviser on women's issues" and in April, when he criticized Carter's proposal for a windfall profits tax on oil as 'a transparent fig leaf' over the vast new profits the industry will realize." All these were attacks from the Left. Kennedy did criticize Carter on Iran and Afghanistan. Conversely, he blamed the seizure of hostages on the fact that Carter allowed the shah of Iran entry to the United States to receive medical treatment.[22]

According to William Schneider,

> What Kennedy came to represent in 1980 was a new party consensus, a kind of "deal" between the party regulars and the New Politics liberals who had spent so many years fighting over Vietnam: the liberals would accept the "big government" economic programs and the commitment to organized labor that Democratic party regulars had long stood for, while the regulars would accede to a less interventionist foreign policy and a more progressive stance on social issues.[23]

At the 1980 convention, labor acted as a member of a left-wing coalition that supported adoption of a $12 billion jobs bank over the objection of the Carter forces, who feared it would be labeled as inflationary. (This was part of a general effort to radicalize the platform over the objections of Carter. Planks supported the use of Medicaid funds for abortions and also denied party support to candidates who did not support the ERA.) Yet, polls showed that the undecided voters were concerned about inflation and, therefore, wanted the federal government to reduce, not increase, spending. More than twice as many people that year considered inflation a greater problem than unemployment than vice versa. In other words, they would have rejected the Kennedy, and labor, jobs plank.[24]

After Carter lost in 1980, Kirkland led the federation back into the Democratic Party over the objections of retiring COPE Director Al Barkan, who denounced the "accommodations that Mr. Kirkland and others have made to the party's rules. Mr. Barkan complained that affirmative action for minority groups and the requirement for equal division of men and women on party bodies . . . had brought only trouble for labor and the Democrats."[25] But no one paid attention to this anachronistic opinion.

The New Left

Labor would never have left the party if the New Politics had not gone on the attack. Now, the powers in the party were welcoming labor back with open arms. And the most welcoming arms, by far, were those of the party's left wing.

As the left-wing economist Robert Kuttner put it in 1984, the labor movement was a "radical movement for social change. . . . Labor has been a key constituency for every major piece of decent social legislation since the New Deal. Without a strong labor movement, moderately liberal members of Congress become fatally dependent on business support, and there is no reliable ideological counterpart to business's natural preference for market supremacy regardless of human cost."[26]

In 1981, the Democratic Party established the Hunt Commission, named after its chairman, North Carolina Governor James B. Hunt. Its goal was to ensure that the presidential nomination was clinched sooner rather than later to reduce internal bloodletting and to increase the time available to run against Reagan. As Jack Germond and Jules Witcover put it,

> As a practical matter, this goal was achieved largely because the controlling forces in this commission were—to no one's surprise—Ted Kennedy, Fritz Mondale and the AFL-CIO. The Commission proposed—and the Democratic National Committee finally approved in 1982—a system with several devices from protecting the power of the permanent establishment and nominating a Kennedy or, once he stepped aside, a Mondale.[27]

In 1984, labor decided to increase its input and influence by endorsing a candidate for the first time before the nomination conventions of the parties had been held. AFL-CIO leaders were able to agree on Walter Mondale early on and gave him inestimable help in winning the nomination. The campaign represented actual convergence of the labor and the New Politics movements. Lane Kirkland introduced Mondale at the 1983 AFL-CIO convention as from the same cloth of "our old comrade in arms, Hubert Humphrey and Scoop Jackson."[28] Not quite. Mondale had been a disciple of Hubert Humphrey. But, "during Mondale's twelve years in the Senate, the dovish Americans for Democratic Action (ADA) included 67 foreign policy votes in its annual legislative scorecard. Mondale voted right, in ADA's eyes, 64 times and wrong only twice, missing one vote. Henry Jackson, by comparison, voted right by ADA standards just 12 times, wrong 50 times, and missed five votes."[29] The Mondale of the 1984 campaign was not a conservative or even a moderate. He was a garden-variety left-liberal who gave voice to the views of all the left-wing, special-interest groups that backed him, the AFL-CIO prominent among them.

Following the 1984 debacle, moderates in the party organized a new group called the Democratic Leadership Council. Its purpose was to fight to return the national party to the mainstream. The DLC was to take up the fight against the New Politics that had been initiated by the CDM. But there was one crucial difference. Now that the AFL-CIO was not only part of the effort, it opposed it with more vehemence than any other single element in the party. Twelve years previously, the New Politics had to defeat labor to drive the party to the Left. Now the DLC would have to defeat labor and its new allies to take the party back to the center.

In a 1990 symposium on the 1980s, Jeane Kirkpatrick, another traditional liberal turned conservative, discussed an article in which the political sociologist Seymour Martin Lipset analyzed why "the national Democrats have been more disposed to adhere to a redistributionist, progressive tax, anti-business orientation than most social-democratic parties elsewhere." They returned "to the thesis . . . that for American intellectuals, the attachment [to Marxism] has been inspired and sustained more by a desire to be anti-establishment, to be adversarial toward bourgeois and national patriotic values." In the Democratic Party, Kirkpatrick continued,

> the America depicted is one of debt and depression, of decline, hopelessness, and homelessness, of insecurity and intolerance, of neglected children and neglected aged. Ronald Reagan's America—as they depict it—is a callous, careless society with polluted air and water and drug-ridden, violent cities in which the homeless are left to freeze on winter streets. It is an America of greed and need.[30]

Maybe so. But America was depicted in the same terms by leaders of labor like Kirkland. And the redistributionist ideology of the Democratic Party was much more attributable to the labor movement and its civil rights allies than to any constituency of intellectuals, especially by the late 1980s. At the February 1992 executive council meeting, "5 unions said they were still polling their members, 14 said they supported Senator [Tom] Harkin and 3 (AFSCME, AFT and the Hotel and Restaurant Employees) were for Governor Clinton."[31] Kirkland was one of Harkin's most vigorous advocates. Labor came within a hair's breadth of endorsing the candidate who most closely resembled George McGovern and was the most left-wing of all Democratic contenders. That Harkin was a Left isolationist of the first order did not count against him in the eyes of AFL-CIO leaders. But his positive appeal came from "his rabble-rousing rhetoric and his appeals to economic nationalism."[32] Far more than any other candidate for the nomination, he was the advocate of state control of the economy and state control of trade.

But what now separated Right from Left was a struggle over competitive capitalism. The Right was engaged in an effort to reconcile liberal or progressive politics with the fundamentals of free market economics. The Left rejected them. And, in that struggle, American labor has made it unmistakably clear where and with whom it stood.

10
The Failure of Labor Organizing

As huge trusts rose to dominate the economic landscape of late-nineteenth-century America, Samuel Gompers had voiced the hope and expectation that trade unions would act as the tribune of the people, expressing the general will. The "trust is the voluntary association of the few for their own benefit," whereas "the trade union is the voluntary association of the many for the benefit of all the community."[1] Gompers added, "In every community where trade unions exist, they are recognized as the spokesmen . . . of all except the employing and the idle rich class."[2]

When Gompers died in 1924, craft unions predominated in the federation's membership as they had at the start. Labor leaders blamed this failure to organize all but a small minority of workers on the efforts of capitalists to suppress trade unionism, directly through the use of armed Pinkertons and the like and indirectly through control of the state. This remains true today. Thus Lane Kirkland spoke on the 1920s in America: "This was the time when markets ruled. Whatever business wanted it got. Business had command of the state, for all practical purposes. And it used the state to frustrate and to brutally oppress the organization of working people into unions of their own choosing."[3]

This hardly explains the AFL's early lack of success. The federal government in the early twentieth century was not nearly so hostile to organized labor as union leaders like Kirkland have alleged.

While serving as Harding's secretary of commerce, Herbert

Hoover was largely responsible for getting the steel industry to abandon the twelve-hour day. Coolidge signed into law the Railway Labor Act of 1926. In appreciation of this and other helpful acts, John L. Lewis, soon to lead the AFL's Committee for Industrial Unionism, endorsed Hoover over Democrat Al Smith in the 1928 presidential election. During his own presidency, Hoover signed the milestone Norris-Laguardia Act, which prevented courts from issuing injunctions against most union strikes and boycotts and from enforcing yellow-dog contracts (under which employers required job-seekers to sign away the right to join a union).

The Role of the Courts

If the executive and legislative branches of the federal government cannot be blamed for labor's organizing shortfalls, what of the third branch, the judiciary? It is true that the federal courts in the post–World War I era were notoriously conservative, possibly even reactionary. Yet, they did far less damage to labor's cause than is generally thought. Let us consider, first, the courts' use of antitrust laws against the labor movement during the first three decades of the century. Clearly, these decisions were wrong: the purpose of both the Sherman Anti-Trust Act of 1890 (which banned "conspiracies in restraint of trade") and the Clayton Act of 1914 was to attack business combinations, not labor unions.

But what did these decisions actually prohibit? In *Loewe* v. *Lawler* (1908), better known as the Danbury Hatters case, the Supreme Court set the precedent for using the Sherman Anti-Trust Act against union actions. The plaintiff was one of twelve (of a total of eighty-two) U.S. hatmaking concerns that the United Hatters of America had not yet organized. To force the plaintiff to negotiate, the Hatters Union not only called a strike but also organized a secondary boycott of the wholesalers and retailers with whom the plaintiff did business. While such boycotts were legal at the time (until the Court overreached to ban them), they were later specifically prohibited by the Taft-Hartley Act of 1948, on the ground that they dragged third parties into disputes between labor and management. While the Danbury hatters case was wrongly decided, the union tactics were later determined to be illegitimate.

The 1921 case that set the precedent for use of the Clayton Anti-Trust Act against labor, *Duplex Printing Press Co. v. Deering*, also centered on a secondary boycott and sympathy strikes, all orchestrated to reinforce a direct strike by the International Association of Machinists. The direct strike itself was not at issue. Indeed, the Court's opinion strongly suggested that a strike by employees against their employers was not actionable under the Clayton Act.

These cases and rulings were representative. In time, the Court no longer used the Sherman Act to prohibit all strikes.

> In the course of time . . . the usefulness of the Sherman Act as a strike-breaking weapon was curtailed. . . . If a union made up of employees at a manufacturing establishment called a strike for the purpose of raising their wages or improving their working conditions, the combination did not violate the Sherman Act even though shipments in interstate commerce were halted or reduced. . . . However, if a union which had organized some establishments in an industry were to call an organizational strike or institute a boycott in order to organize non-union factories and protect its members against the competition of cheap, non-union factories and goods, then the strike would be unlawful.[4]

The Success of Capitalism

What hampered labor's efforts to organize the majority of workers in the early decades of the century was not any act of commission or omission by public power but the success of American capitalism itself. In 1900, only 4 percent of the U.S. work force was organized— lagging far behind England and Germany—while U.S. wages (as everyone knew) were the highest in the world, belying Gompers's claim that unions alone protected blue-collar Americans from pauperization. H. G. Wells, Fabian socialist, described New Yorkers in the first decade of the twentieth century: "Even in the congested entrances, the filthy back streets of the East Side, I find myself saying as a thing remarkable: 'These people have money to spend.' "[5]

Contrary to the claims of both Gompers and Marx, wages in America rose (and income inequality declined) as productivity increased. Gompers himself was witness to the most dramatic examples of capitalists raising wages in response to and as a spur to further productivity increases. The fiercely anti-union Henry Ford, for example, raised the wages of auto workers in 1914 by 40 percent overnight, a far greater increase than ever negotiated by even the most effective trade unions. During the Roaring Twenties, higher compensation and better working conditions made things difficult for labor. This increasing affluence diminished the labor movement during the decade.

The credit that business received for its achievements came partly at labor's expense. Workers could see that widespread wage gains had little to do with a labor movement that represented so few of them. Others, too, perceived that the labor movement did not do what it claimed. Supreme Court Justice Oliver Wendell Holmes, in his famous dissent in *Plant v. Woods* (1900), argued in favor of the legality of strikes and boycotts. Yet, in the same dissent, he recognized that "organization and strikes may get a larger share for the members of an organization, but, if they do, they get it at the expense of the less organized and less powerful portion of the laboring mass. They do not create something out of nothing."[6]

Much later, empirical research would confirm Holmes's analysis of the zero-sum character of labor actions. In a widely cited study, economist H. Gregg Lewis concluded that "the effect of unions on the average relative wage is zero."[7] In his classic *The Economics of Trade Unions*, Albert Rees summarized research identically: "No union effect on labor's share [in the distribution of income] can be discovered with any consistency." He suggested that

> the likeliest effect of unions in the distribution of income is to redistribute it among workers . . . in either or both of two ways. First, the money wages of non-union workers may be held down by the reallocation of labor produced by unionism; second, the non-union workers may have to pay more for the products produced by union labor.[8]

Welfare Capitalism. American business did not just raise wages; it was beginning to make basic changes in its treatment of workers. Mistreatment of workers had caused labor unrest and increased interest in trade unionism. It had also contributed to employee turnover, a massive problem at the beginning of the century:

> In the years before World War I, it was not unusual for a tenth of the work force to be absent on a given day. Between 1905 and 1917, the majority of industrial workers changed jobs at least once every three years. And one out of three stayed at his job less than a year——often only for days or weeks. . . . Surveys of textile mills, automobile plants, steel mills, clothing shops, and machine workers showed labor turnover rates at 100 percent and higher. . . . In 1913, when

the Ford Motor Company first introduced the assembly line, it had a staggering turnover rate of 370 percent.[9]

Instances of workers being badly used were publicized, increasing the pressure on business to reform. New labor laws (and the threat of still more) in key industrial states sought to check abuses in wages, hours, and working conditions. Even though the Supreme Court overturned many such laws, business could read the handwriting on the wall and knew that its most odious practices were no longer tolerable.

In response, managers began initiatives for welfare capitalism. On the heels of a victory over the Amalgamated Association of Iron, Steel, and Tin Workers, for instance, U.S. Steel Corporation started first a profit-sharing plan (1902), then an employee-safety plan (1906), an old-age pension system (1910), and so on. Such initiatives multiplied over the next decade. The control of shop foremen was curtailed, for example; personnel offices were instituted to provide some objectivity in employment practices.

Refusing to accede to organized labor's demands, yet needing a way to keep in touch with their workers, many corporations established employee-representation plans (ERPs). Unions decried ERPs as paternalistic, which almost all of them were, at least at the start. Nonetheless, the plans gave workers some say in their working conditions and, in a few cases, in their compensation. As labor historian Milton Derber noted, such plans "marked a profound change from the non-unionized situation where the shop was ruled autocratically, or benevolently, at the discretion of the foremen and the company heads."[10] It is, at least conceivable that, given time, ERPs would have been the seedbeds of independent enterprise unions similar to ones found in Japan today.

Labor Obstructionism

While business was reaping the credit for America's economic progress, unions were stumbling. In a sense, they were their own worst enemies. Gompers staunchly maintained that labor was in no way opposed to progress; he and every other federation leader stood by silently as the craft unions that dominated the AFL emulated as best they could the reactionary guilds of Europe. Consider the circumstances leading up to the famous Homestead Steel strike of 1892, so often cited in union lore as evidence of the brutal way management smashed unions. According to Louis Hacker, the Amalgamated Association of Iron and Steel Workers

> had deported itself like a medieval guild, insisting that its monopoly hold of its jobs at Homestead be respected. . . . When vacancies appeared, the Amalgamated made its own replacements, sending back to Britain for substitute workers. . . . Even more, its work rules in 1892 forbade the training of apprentices, limited the output of its members and even prescribed the quality of pig iron to be used and the proportion of other materials entering into the mix.[11]

In retrospect, it is not surprising that Andrew Carnegie, who had previously expressed his belief in the "right of workingmen to combine and form trades unions," decided to break this one.

Nor was the situation that led up to the strike at Homestead an aberration. In the printing trade, the International Typographical Union (ITU) had arrogated to itself so many managerial functions that the eminent labor historian and theorist Selig Perlman described the state of affairs between labor and management as "practical 'job syndicalism.' "[12] As labor historian Milton Derber wrote, the ITU "exercised unilateral control over . . . hiring, apprenticeship, and discipline."[13] Although the ITU was unusually successful, other unions aspired to such a syndicalist stranglehold in their industries. For a union to gain the upper hand—although only a union like the printers' could do so—"was for the union, without displacing the employer as the owner of his business and risk taker, to become the virtual owner and administrator of the jobs."[14]

In general, labor opposed innovations in organizing work. It long opposed Taylorism, the system of scientific management named after the efficiency expert Frederick W. Taylor. Hailed by Peter Drucker as the man "who defeated Marx and Marxism. . . . [by] increasing workers' wages while at the same time cutting the product's prices and thereby increasing the demand for it. (Taylor actually refused to take a factory as a client unless the owners first substantially raised wages, sometimes tripling them.)"[15] Although Taylorism won the support of progressives like Louis Brandeis, Gompers and his colleagues took a different view. They saw it as a sign of labor's increasing political clout in 1912, it was successful in attaching to an appropriation bill riders that "prohibit[ed] the introduction of scientific management methods into government arsenals." Among labor's concerns with scientific management was "the fear that through [time and motion] studies the employer is enabled to penetrate into the skilled worker's trade secrets and to multiply his competitors at will."[16] Not until the 1920s did Gompers realize that Taylorism was a fact of industrial life and that complaining about it did labor no good.

These were among the reasons why influential Progressives such as Jane Addams and Herbert Croly worried about labor's influence. Both opposed the trusts and championed the right of workers to join unions if they wished, but, according to historian Richard Hofstadter, they were also "troubled about the lengths to which union power might go if labor-unionism became the sole counterpoise to the power of business. The danger of combinations of capital and labor that would squeeze the consuming public and the small businessman was never entirely out of sight."[17] Theodore Roosevelt's even-handed attitude was typical: "At the same time I wished the labor people absolutely to understand that I set my face like flint against violence and lawlessness of any kind on their part, just as much as against arrogant greed by the rich, and that I would be as quick to move against one as the other."[18] Moreover, Roosevelt was concerned that labor could gain too much political influence; he worked to prevent the development of a class-based party like Britain's Labour Party.

Unions also forfeited the support of progressive Americans with their insistence on the closed shop. Business countered with a campaign in favor of the open shop. In the former, workers would be required to join even before starting work; in the latter, individual workers would be free to join or not join a union before and after they were hired. By calling their own proposal the American plan, the proponents of the open shop implied that the closed shop was un-American. The significance of the difference between the two concepts was highlighted at a conference attended by top-level business and union leaders. John D. Rockefeller took part, as did Judge Elbert Gary of U.S. Steel, while the high-ranking union officials present included Samuel Gompers. Gary and Rockefeller supported a resolution that "began with a recognition of the right to organize and a commendation of collective bargaining, but ended with the assertion that this 'must not be understood as limiting the right of any wage earner to refrain from joining any organization or deal directly with his employer if he chooses.' "[19]

What they were proposing was identical in substance to the

right-to-work laws in force in some states today and to the present labor law of Britain. It would have been a giant step forward in the 1920s. But the labor representatives turned the proposal down, casting doubt on their professed commitment to voluntarism. Progressive Herbert Croly criticized them on just this score, complaining that "unionist leaders frequently offer verbal homage to the great American principle of equal rights, but what they really demand is the abandonment of that principle. What they want is an economic and political order which will discriminate in favor of unions and against nonunion labor."[20]

The Opportunity of the Depression

Given the astounding achievements of capitalism and the concerns that a stronger labor movement aroused, no wonder by the late 1920s labor was nearly moribund. Then, the Great Depression gave it a new lease on life. Then, by removing the threat of injunctions in labor-management disputes, the Norris-LaGuardia Act of 1932 put labor and management in the center ring and government in a neutral corner, just as Gompers had always dreamed. Yet labor still had trouble recruiting new members.

At the beginning of the depression, corporations presented themselves in the best light. President Hoover had appealed to business not to engage in wage slashing; corporations, especially the practitioners of welfare capitalism, responded by trying to hold the line. For the first two to three years of the depression, unorganized manufacturing industries such as steel, auto, and rubber did not reduce wages. As the depression worsened, however, companies had no choice but to lay off workers and cut the pay of those who remained, badly tarnishing the image of business, and implicitly of capitalism itself, in the eyes of workers and the public at large.

This was a radical's—and a trade unionist's—dream come true. For both American radicalism and American unionism, class consciousness had ever been the elusive *sine qua non*. Its absence had been debilitating; its presence filled radicals and laborites alike with a new energy. Business played into labor's hands by treating its own work force as a class enemy, a fateful reversal of the enlightened labor relations during the 1920s. The corporate response to understandable and unavoidable labor unrest was to throw fuel on the fire:

Barbed-wire fences and sandbag fortifications began to ring the plants of some of America's industrial giants. Citizens' Law and Order Associations sprang up, liberally financed by employers and were armed. Through the streets of company towns swaggered hoods and thugs sworn in as special deputies to uphold the law. From January 1934 to July 1936, General Motors spent $994,855.68 on an industrial spy system.[21]

Business's ill-advised belligerence assured passage of the new labor laws. First, Congress passed the National Industrial Recovery Act (NIRA) of 1933 with its section 7a, which protected union organizing efforts. When the Supreme Court ruled the NIRA unconstitutional, Congress passed the National Labor Relations Act (NLRA) of 1935, otherwise known as the Wagner Act. The bill, in effect, made federal government a "partisan" of labor and "virtually ordered employers to stop resisting the spread of unionism."[22]

But passage of the Wagner Act represented more a rebuke of business for its blatant and often vicious violation of workers' rights than it did an endorsement of labor. President Franklin Roosevelt, for one, did not believe that the union movement offered a solution to any of the problems facing the country. Like Secretary of Labor Frances Perkins, FDR had little interest in trade unionism per se (his support for the Wagner Act was late and grudging). With his ties to the Progressive tradition, Roosevelt was more inclined to seek progress through laws governing unemployment insurance, wages, and hours.

Union Growth

Even workers' support for trade unionism proved much weaker and short-lived than expected. A spate of successful organizing followed the enactment of the NIRA, but primarily in industries that had been highly unionized. Equally important were legal changes permitting collusion between operators, which allowed for big wage increases even during the depression.

Using the misleading but nonetheless highly effective cry of "The President wants you to join the Union," John L. Lewis reinvigorated the United Mine Workers. While it would be wrong to imply that President Hoover, Roosevelt's predecessor had been hostile to labor, the friendly attitude of the federal government certainly helped. But it is important to keep in mind that miners were a special case: they often lived in isolated company towns and had been highly receptive to trade unionism for decades, not only in the United States but throughout the world.

The garment workers' unions also revived; both the International Ladies' Garment Workers and the Amalgamated Clothing Workers tripled in size during the first year following the enactment of the NIRA. But there were special circumstances here as well. Many workers in these industries were Jewish immigrants, often with Socialist leanings. Also, many employers had been garment workers themselves and, for ideological reasons, preferred that their firms be unionized if it could be done without bankrupting them.

In contrast, industries that had never been unionized, like steel and auto, remained relatively unionfree. Trade union membership hardly increased at all between 1929 and 1935, when the NIRA was declared unconstitutional and the NLRA was passed.

How the Industrial Unions Won. After the NLRA became law, unionization did not proceed at the same pace in all sectors; the manufacturing and construction unions grew much faster than others. Even where unions did succeed, they did not always have the overwhelming support of workers.

The most important victories in manufacturing were in the auto and steel industries. The UAW and the Steelworkers Organizing Committee (SWOC, later to become the United Steelworkers) established trends that spread throughout American mass industry when they won representation rights and later negotiated ground-breaking contracts. How these two unions organized their industries is instructive.

For the UAW, the sit-down strike at General Motors in late 1936 was key. The great advantage of the sit-down strike was precisely that it did not require the support of all or even most workers. Rather, success depended only on winning the support of a strategically located minority of workers who could shut down an entire integrated operation. At the time of the 1936 sit-down strike, the UAW did not have sufficient support to call a proper strike. Even after the strike, the UAW was uncertain of its support, turning down a GM offer to hold an election among workers for fear of losing.

The organization of the steel industry followed a different course, but, again, the support of workers for the union was not nearly so strong as we have been led to believe. The big break-through for the SWOC came on the heels of the sit-down at GM, when industry leader U.S. Steel suddenly agreed—for reasons that have never been fully explained—to recognize and negotiate with the union. It was certainly not because the union had the over-whelming support of workers. CIO counsel Lee Pressman believed that "we could not have won an election for collective bargaining on the basis of our membership or the results of the organizing cam-paign."[23]

U.S. Steel did not want to pick a fight with its workers. The company's head, Myron Taylor, had been a strong exponent of wel-fare capitalism; his liberal tendencies were, undoubtedly, a factor in the corporation's decision. Another consideration was that crucial political leaders, FDR and Governor Amos Pinchot of Pennsylvania included, sympathized with the union's organizing effort. Pinchot indicated where his sympathies lay when he announced that strik-ing steelworkers would be eligible for relief.

A final factor was that prospects for steel, in general, and U.S. Steel, in particular, were looking up as the war loomed ahead. Op-portunities for increased sales might be lost if there were a strike. No matter how they came, the victories in auto and steel certainly inspired workers and unions in other industries. By the end of 1937, membership in CIO-affiliated unions topped 7 million.

The CIO Peaks. Labor historian Walter Galenson ventured that "by October 1937, when the first national conference of CIO national union officers was held . . . the CIO was already past the apogee of its relative strength and influence in the American labor move-ment."[24] This is confirmed by ILGWU leader David Dubinsky: "There were signs that the great momentum of the CIO drive was running out."[25]

David McDonald, then a SWOC organizer and later president of the United Steelworkers, remembered that the campaign to orga-nize the smaller, more "entrepreneurial" steel companies that com-prised Little Steel encountered fierce resistance from management, as well as reluctance on the part of workers. To encourage the latter, workers' committees would stand at factory gates with ax handles and baseball bats, threatening to use them if workers tried to walk past without paying up. The SWOC also used a tactic called dues picketing to sign up members, despite the Supreme Court ruling restricting mass picketing. After a majority of workers signed, Mc-Donald wrote, "we would show the cards to the manager and demand an election or representation without the formality of an election." McDonald estimated that three-fourths of the workers did not care one way or the other whether there was a union, adding: "This is the group we prodded into signing enough cards to give us a majority."[26]

The Benefits of War. Because of the trough that the depression hit in 1937–1938, the unions' ability to negotiate wage increases was severely constrained. In 1939, the UMW, realizing that it could not negotiate higher wages in a depression, demanded and then struck for a union shop. It won that but only because FDR put pressure on the operators to settle. Other unions, such as the United Electrical and Radio Workers (UERW), actually negotiated wage decreases. Philco, which had quickly capitulated in 1936, withstood a four-month strike in 1938 and forced the UERW to capitulate: base pay decreased, the workweek returned to forty-four hours, and the closed shop ended.

Organizing picked up again with the economic recovery stimulated by spending on war preparations. But the initiative had shifted to the AFL, which made big gains a few years before Pearl Harbor, particularly in industries whose revival depended on government contracts. In the building trades, for instance, "the value of federally financed construction . . . increased from $1.478 billion in 1935 to $2.316 billion in 1940, then soared to $5.931 billion the following year. In 1940, more than half of the labor required for on-site construction was being absorbed by public construction work."[27] Contracts for construction on public works required companies to abide by the Davis-Bacon and Wash-Healy laws, both of which strongly favored the use of unionized companies by depriving non-unionized firms of their natural cost advantage.

The fastest growing AFL union during the period was the Teamsters, whose membership increased as the trucking industry grew. Although worker support for the Teamsters was strong, the organizing breakthroughs in trucking involved tactics that would have been actionable under the antitrust laws as restraints of trade, had unions not been specifically exempted. In Minneapolis, the radical Teamster leaders Farrell Dobbs and the Dunne brothers successfully demanded that drivers into Minneapolis terminals hold union membership. Teamster leader Dave Beck (much later the first of a string of top Teamster officials to be convicted on racketeering charges) developed the idea that Teamsters in one area of the country apply pressure on employees in other areas to recognize the union:

> We could tie up the flow of freight by rail and boat, merely by refusing to transport goods to the docks or railroad stations destined for shipment to the South. And we could refuse to move shipments from the South after they arrived at Northern or Western rail or water terminals. . . . the same system was used in organizing Southern California.[28]

As a result, the Teamsters tripled in size from 1936 to 1941. But a union that used such tactics was surely headed for trouble. While sit-downs could circumvent the problem of thin worker support, they cost the unions the support of the general public. Indeed, the strong critical reaction to the 1936 GM sit-down was a sign that neither politicians nor the public at large had unlimited sympathy for union goals, to say nothing of some union tactics. The proof was not long in coming. When the UAW, fresh from its triumph at GM, organized a sit-down strike at Chrysler, that company emphatically rejected the union's demand to be recognized as the sole bargaining agent of Chrysler workers. Frank Murphy, the governor of Michigan, whose refusal to send in troops to clear out strikers at GM was vital, made it clear that he would use force if necessary to remove sit-down strikers at Chrysler plants. The UAW, having badly overplayed its hand, had no choice but to fold.

Declining Public Opinion

The prewar recovery helped the CIO unions back to their feet as well. Once again, contracts called for wage increases, which was the best possible advertisement for trade unionism. Even as the unions made headway, they were losing the public favor that undergirded all their hopes for secure progress. Violent tactics of the sort described by McDonald reduced support for his union. Elected Democrats from FDR on down valued the political support of organized labor but always had to weigh that support against the opposition that an association with labor could arouse. Wildcat and sit-down strikes, violent mass demonstrations—all reduced the popularity of the president and his party.

In the spring of 1937, Roosevelt seized an opportunity to distance himself from the union movement. In late May, as the SWOC
campaigned to organize the workers of Little Steel, police fired on
workers and their supporters as they approached the gates of Republic Steel's Chicago plant, killing or mortally wounding twelve
and injuring eighty-eight more. A Senate committee investigating
the incident blamed the police for what has become known as the
Memorial Day Massacre. But when asked about the episode, FDR
observed that "the majority of the people are saying just one thing,
'A plague on both your houses.' "[29] A furious John L. Lewis denounced the president on nationwide radio: "It ill behooves one who
has supped at labor's table and who has been sheltered in labor's
house," Lewis thundered, "to curse with equal fervor and fine impar-
tiality both labor and its adversaries when they become locked in
deadly embrace."[30] Roosevelt, who clearly knew the political impact
of his stance, remained unmoved.

Roosevelt's judgment was confirmed many times in the years
ahead, as labor's public support continued its downslide. Elected officials who had not distanced themselves from labor suffered at election time. Prolabor candidates fared particularly poorly in the 1938
congressional elections. The lesson was duly learned. In 1943, following a strike by coal miners, Congress passed the Smith-Connally
Act over Roosevelt's veto. This law authorized the president to seize
struck plants, made it a crime to strike against a government plant,
and established general rules restricting the right to strike.

The Failures of the Wages Act

The NLRA, conceived with the idea of reducing industrial strife, had
clearly failed to achieve its stated purpose. There was no reason for
believing that the act could bring labor peace. The incidence of
strikes in the past had borne no discernible relationship with the
passage of labor legislation. But, according to labor economist Robin
Flemming, "the argument that the Wagner Act would reduce industrial strife was framed principally with an eye to the constitutional
hurdle which the Act faced. The draftsmen [had to] justify federal
action on the basis of the federal government's right to control inter-
state commerce."[31]

The act also fell short of its stated goal of strengthening commitment to the country's democratic way of life. "Let men become the

servile pawns of their masters in the factories of the land," Senator Wagner had argued, and "there will be destroyed the bone and sinew of resistance to political dictatorship."[32] But American workers were never wage slaves; they were also remarkably resistant to totalitarian appeals, even during the 1930s and even without the Wagner Act.

Not American workers but American intellectuals were drawn to radicalism. To them, the Wagner Act was a boon. Communists infiltrated and gained influence in (and, in some cases, outright control of) many industrial unions—60 of the SWOC's 100 organizers were Communists. Lewis had virtually invited them in; their talent and fervor were key to the CIO's success. To those who warned of the Communists' ulterior motives, Lewis's retort was, "Who gets the bird, the hunter or the dog?"[33]

The Communists were an even stronger force in the UAW than elsewhere in the CIO. Key leaders were either party members or fellow travelers. During the great organizing campaigns, one of the two principal factions was the so-called Unity Caucus, a coalition of Communists and Socialists. The anti-Communist faction, the Progressive Caucus, was then led by the UAW's first president, Homer Martin, whom David Dubinsky rated as a hopelessly poor organizer. In 1934, Dubinsky sent Jay Lovestone to meet with Unity Caucus leader Walter Reuther and offer him ILGWU support. Reuther turned down the offer when he heard the quid pro quo: open endorsement of "a militant, energetic campaign against the operations of the Communist Party faction in the union."[34] Reuther himself was an anti-Communist by this time, but he appreciated how dependent the union was on Communists. Party members filled key positions at CIO headquarters. General counsel Lee Pressman and Len Le DeCaux, the editor of its newspaper, were both party members, as were lower-ranking officials.

Even after the war, Lewis's successor Philip Murray refused to confront the Communists. Communists and Communist-dominated unions were purged only after their slavish adherence to the party line had made them a total political liability. The final straw came in 1948, when they supported the presidential campaign of Henry Wallace, Roosevelt's eccentric former secretary of agriculture, even though the CIO had endorsed Harry Truman. That same year, the Communists opposed the Marshall Plan, even though the CIO, as most of the labor movement, strongly supported it.

Finally, by encouraging the organization of unions, the Wagner Act was supposed to help increase total purchasing power and thereby lift the economy out of the depression. The economy started reviving, however, before the organizing breakthroughs. Contrary to predictions, the economy then slipped back into recession in 1937 and 1938, just as the unions were gaining strength. Negotiated wages increased again only after the prewar recovery.

Labor Loses Public Favor

Public opinion surveys registered a falloff in labor's support. A 1939 poll showed 71 percent of respondents saying that the unions needed reform; the comparable figures for government and manufacturing industry were 52 and 39 percent, respectively.[35] By 1940, support for amending the Wagner Act to restrict the right to strike was already strong and on the rise. The loss of popularity accelerated in response to Communist-led political strikes during the Hitler-Stalin accord of 1939–1941. It fell, too, in response to strikes called by John L. Lewis, who was fast becoming the most disliked man in America. In 1941, five times as many people disapproved of Lewis as approved of him; two years later, his disapproval-to-approval ratio was nine to one.

The failures of the Wagner Act provoked a public backlash. States across the country enacted laws to curb labor's excesses, particularly in the South and Southwest, which were trying to attract industries that wanted to escape from the unionized and high-wage North. "Texas passed a drastic anti-picketing act in 1941. Colorado and Georgia placed limitations on strikes. California outlawed secondary boycotts or refusals to handle 'hot cargo' [goods produced or handled by an employer whom labor considers unfair]. And Maryland declared sitdown strikes illegal."[36]

The government bought labor peace during World War II with a maintenance-of-membership policy: workers had only fifteen days after the signing of a contract to resign from the negotiating union. As a result, the percentage of workers organized into unions increased rapidly. Indeed, the percentage of workers organized by 1945 was only two percentage points less than the high point registered in the mid-1950s.

After the war, there was a rash of strikes—three times more in 1946 than in 1945, the previous high point. The public blamed the strikers for dislocation of industry and for price increases. Some strikes aroused intense public hostility. The country condemned the coal and railroad strikes of 1946, for instance, for violating the public interest. In the former instance, President Truman seized the mines; he would also have taken over the railroads had the unions not given in at the last moment. A followup coal strike in 1947 was denounced by a judge as an "evil and monstrous thing."[37]

People's reaction to the strikes was the same everywhere. By 1947, all but three of the states with laws similar to the Wagner Act amended them to combat unfair labor practices by both corporations and unions. States prohibited labor practices such as mass picketing, secondary boycotts, sit-down strikes, and coercing workers to join unions.

The growing public antipathy to labor actions contributed to the devastating liberal losses and Republican takeover of Congress in 1946. Few of labor's legislative champions survived the storm of ballots. In 1948, Congress passed the Taft-Hartley Act, denounced by labor as the slave labor law. Philip Murray warned that passage of the act was "the first real step toward the development of fascism in the United States."[38] Given the depth and extent of public hostility, however, labor was lucky to escape with the moderate change in the Wagner Act that Taft-Hartley represented.

Labor tried repeatedly to amend or repeal Taft-Hartley. Every attempt failed, invariably, for lack of public support. (Indeed, even unionized workers proved lukewarm. In his insightful *The Future of American Politics*, Samuel Lubell recounts Ohio workers' intense disapproval of labor's attempt in 1950 to unseat the law's coauthor, Senator Robert Taft, to teach him a political lesson.)[39]

Despite their hyperbole about slave labor when Taft-Hartley was enacted, labor leaders then did not believe that, in and of itself, the bill would defeat their organizing efforts. American unions continued to enjoy far more protection than their counterparts in the rest of the Western world. In a security clause virtually unique to the United States, the law enshrined the union shop, which held workers in unions for generations after an affirmative vote on union representation. The *Monthly Labor Review* reported that in eight West European countries such arrangements were not central. Membership in French and Italian trade unions was voluntary; only members paid dues or (as in the case of agency shops) the cost of negotiating and enforcing collective-bargaining agreements. In

1993, Great Britain adopted a labor reform act that prohibited dues checkoff (whereby management automatically deducts dues from workers' paychecks) for any employee who did not indicate such annually.

A full seven years after the passage of Taft-Hartley, the AFL and CIO merged. The leaders of the new organization confidently predicted that, within a decade, they would double union membership. The forecast was never fulfilled. Without exception, all organizing efforts have been demoralizing failures. If not Taft-Hartley, what has been to blame for these disappointments? For the most part, it has been the changing nature of the American economy.

The Lure of the South

As labor economist Albert Rees has noted, a major reason for "the slow growth of manufacturing unionism from 1956 to 1974" was the "geographical shift of manufacturing employment toward states with a low extent of union organization."[40] Brookings economist Robert W. Crandall observed that

> it is probably no coincidence that in 1970 union membership averaged 38.5 percent of nonagricultural employees in the two Census regions suffering the greatest loss in employment (Middle Atlantic and East North Central), while the three Southern Census regions that gained substantial manufacturing employment (South Atlantic, East South Central and West South Central) had only 20.4 percent of nonagricultural employees in unions.[41]

This geographical shift has continued for forty years. In 1992, the *New York Times* reported that, once again, "Southern states led the nation in the number of new plants built or major plant expansions from 1990 to 1992."[42]

Trade unionists attributed the low union density in the South to the prevalence of right-to-work laws there, as well as to the federal government's failure to enforce provisions of the Wagner Act that protect workers' right to organize. There is truth in these charges, but neither right-to-work legislation nor federal indifference has been a decisive cause of union weakness in the South. Trade unions in Europe and elsewhere have always operated under equivalent legislation. Moreover, American industrial unions like the United

Steelworkers organized and negotiated long before they won union security clauses.

The real, underlying problem that unions faced in the South was the generally negative attitude that workers and the general public bore toward unionization. Southern workers understood that plants were opening in their states to avoid unions. That was a reason in and of itself not to support unionization. Southern workers also saw that economic expansion itself raised their incomes more than unions would have. As the *New York Times* has reported: "In 1960, per capita income in North Carolina (which has one of the lowest percentages of organized workers in the country) was 71 percent of the national average, South Carolina was 62 percent and Georgia was 74 percent. In 1992, the figures were 89 percent, 81 percent and 91 percent."[43] That was due to rapid rates of wage growth in the South and to slowing wage growth in the heavily unionized North. Slower wage growth in the North resulted as unions there had to moderate their wage demands to prevent more manufacturing firms from moving south.

The Declining Significance of Manufacturing

Worse yet from labor's perspective, America's manufacturing sector, the power base of industrial unionism, was shrinking relative to the total size of the national economy. Manufacturing itself was holding its own, but, as George Meany feared, automation and productivity growth were facilitating production of far more with the same or even fewer workers. Other highly unionized industries, such as mining, were suffering similar employment declines. By the mid-1980s, manufacturing's share of U.S employment dropped to about 20 percent from its share exceeding 33 percent in 1947; mining's percentage of total employment fell by about 50 percent.[44]

Moreover, the service sector was growing at a rate that outpaced even the relative shrinkage of the manufacturing sector. Most of the new jobs were white-collar positions, and those who held them had little interest in trade unionism. As of 1988, "the percentage of private sector white-collar workers who are union members is extremely low—below 8 percent—and rapidly dropping."[45]

Whatever their discontent, most service-sector workers were not subjected to anything like conditions within dark satanic mills. As a former machinist wrote, "Sweat running down one's face or an aching back caused by handling castings all day served as constant reminders that one was 'worked' and that someone else was not working." In general, the "demarcation of class lines in service sector workplaces is never as clear as it was in the old factory," which naturally made it harder to organize workers.[46]

The Deadly Effect of Competition

More important still were the increasing levels of competition in the U.S. and then the global economy. From Gompers's time, American unions have recruited workers by promising more—higher wages and better benefits. To do that, they believed that they would have to take wages out of competition. Experience taught labor that the whole, or nearly the whole, of the relevant industry had to be organized.

The building trades solved the problem by organizing all construction firms in an area into employers' associations, with all members agreeing to pay union-scale wages. Industrial unions were faced with a challenge of a different order. For the most part, the industries that they organized were not restricted, or did not have to be restricted, to one locality.

Clearly, the more concentrated the industry, the easier it was to organize. Once a union organized a few or even one corporation in a concentrated industry, it could apply tremendous pressure on the rest to follow suit. But, by 1950, labor had already organized nearly all the concentrated industries; of manufacturing firms with more than 10,000 workers, "fifty-five were between 80 to 100 percent organized and another thirty between 50 to 80 percent organized."[47]

Small firms were tough nuts for labor organizers to crack. Employees in such concerns tended to identify more with their employers than did workers in huge, faceless corporations. Moreover, unions simply could not promise small-firm workers as much, for it was not possible to take wages out of competition in industries with hundreds if not thousands of employers.

Some unions in such industries tried to emulate the building trades, but success was only temporary. In the 1920s, the ILGWU entered into an agreement with jobbers (the dress-manufacturing companies) in the cloak industry whereby the latter would require that contractors (the manufacturers contracted out work to them) pay union wages and maintain union working conditions. "The *quid pro quo* for the employers was the right to 'reorganize' in the interest of efficiency, which meant they could dismiss as much as 10 percent of their work force in the course of a year."[48] In 1942, the union went so far as to establish a Management Engineering Department to advise owners on how to increase efficiency and productivity, this in response to competition from nonunion shops outside the union's area of strength. As ILGWU president David Dubinsky put it,

> you had to be an idiot not to see that the union would be neglecting its duty to its members if it did not see that the contractors had a strong organization of their own to make sure that they got from the jobbers what was needed for the workers and also what was needed for themselves.[49]

Sidney Hillman's Amalgamated Clothing Workers Union also practiced what was then called the new unionism so that unionized firms could compete more effectively.

These efforts, valiant and ingenious though they were, were destined to fail. Competition from the nonunionized sector could be kept at bay only so long. Of firms making men's apparel, for instance, 90 percent were unionized by 1938, but workers saw few improvements.[50] Average wages only just approached the rate of 1924, although workers in the general manufacturing sector had seen great pay increases. The Amalgamated, despite brilliant leadership, continued to fall behind. The plight of the ILGWU was similar, despite its equally talented president. Wages for ladies garment workers have fallen continually in relation to the wages of other workers since the end of World War II. Between 1955 and 1965, wages in the ladies garment industry rose only one-third as much as in the automobile industry, a fact that Dubinsky attributed to the competition in the former and the lack of competition in the latter. "[T]he union," A. H. Raskin wrote in 1977, "is hard-pressed these days to enforce scales twenty or twenty-five cents an hour above the federal minimum wage."[51]

There was absolutely no reason to think that unions in other competitive industries would be any more successful in resisting the natural consequences of competition. On the contrary, they would likely be less successful, if only because the garment-workers' unions had two exceptional leaders, Hillman and Dubinsky. Union density in manufacturing fell from a high of 42.4 percent in 1953 to less than 25 percent overall. In both construction and mining, the comparable figures are at 1930s levels.[52]

Foreign Competition. The effect of increased foreign competition has been similar. In response to it, unionized manufacturing firms have increasingly opted out of the pattern bargaining (whereby all the firms in an industry would agree to essentially the same terms and conditions for unionized workers) that had enabled the industrial unions to take wages out of competition. The same no-strike experimental negotiating agreement (ENA) between the Steelworkers and industry that was "to help the industry stem the foreign steel intrusions into the domestic market" produced "a dire impact . . . on the industry's competitiveness," leading to the end of industrywide bargaining.[53]

Pattern bargaining continues with the Big Three auto companies, but negotiations are now conducted in a radically different environment. Formerly, each of the Big Three companies hoped the UAW would not select it as the strike target with which labor would negotiate the model contract for the other two companies. In 1993, however, "each of the Big Three has declared its willingness to be the target this time. In setting the industry-wide pattern, the target company has the opportunity to negotiate provisions that address its particular concerns."[54] Clearly, pattern bargaining in the automobile industry is on its last legs.

Foreign competition is affecting the UAW as much as the Steelworkers. In 1992, Caterpillar refused to be bound by a settlement that the union had earlier reached with the John Deere Company. Caterpillar contended that it was competing more against its main competitor in the international market, a Japanese firm, than against Deere and, therefore, that the wages and labor costs of the former were more relevant than of the latter. The UAW struck to force Caterpillar to agree to follow the pattern set by Deere, but, after five months, the once-powerful union ordered strikers to return to work when Caterpillar began advertising for replacement workers.

Increasing competition had been forcing unions into concessionary bargaining since the early 1980s. Unions had to make concessions from one industry to another, primarily as wage freezes or cuts. Such competition need not be foreign—the deregulation of the trucking industry in 1980 was followed by the bankruptcy of almost 20 percent of the large unionized carriers. Smaller, independent, and, for the most part, nonunion companies replaced them. As the bargaining strength of the once-great unions declined, so did their appeal to workers. And just as the strength of a UAW had been an advertisement for workers in other industries to join a union, its weakness became an indication that, in the new economic environment, unions, in general, did not and could not have the clout that they once seemed to.

Resisting the Unions

Undeniably, bottom-line considerations have led business in general to resist unionization more than in organized labor's heyday. Some union supporters find this opposition irrational. In their widely acclaimed and cited 1984 study (*What Do Unions Do?*), Richard Freeman and James Medoff claimed that unionized firms are more productive largely because of lower turnover.[55] But this defense is in dispute. Thomas Kochan and his colleagues compared a sample of union and nonunion firms and found "no significant union-nonunion differences" in turnover rates.[56] Moreover, as economist Daniel Benjamin pointed out, to the extent that a union premium discouraged a worker from quitting his job for a more productive one, it discouraged "the reallocation of resources to higher valued uses, implying an opportunity cost that must be deducted to estimate the net benefit of lower quits. Doing so reduces the Freeman and Medoff estimate by about two-thirds."[57]

Freeman and Medoff's claims about the effect of unions on productivity in general are even more debatable. Labor economist Orley Ashenfelter argued in 1985 that "until better evidence is available, it may be more reasonable to conclude that unions have little or no effect on productivity."[58] Economist Barry Hirsch opined initially, in 1985, that the "overall union productivity effects are at best only moderately positive."[59] He found that unionized companies actually invested less in physical capital, noting that "half of this appears to be a direct union effect, while about one half is an indirect effect resulting from significantly lower earnings among unionized companies."[60] By 1994, Hirsch concluded that union effects were nil or negative.[61]

The 1993 McKinsey Global Institute report on the competitiveness of manufacturing industries found that "there are labor agreements in the auto and steel industries in the U.S. that prevent the reduction of employment and the reassignment of workers to new tasks that could increase productivity." Conversely, the report "also found examples where competitive pressure led to substantial changes in labor rules. When unionized plants in the U.S. were faced with the necessity of changing in order to survive [as at Ford and Chrysler], changes to work rules were made."[62]

Significantly, Hirsch discovered that the results from union efforts to increase productivity were greatest when competition was intense.[63] The proximate cause of productivity gains seems to be competition, not the presence or absence of unions. In the end, most unions will agree to changes to prevent unionized firms from going under. But, in almost all instances, such changes were initiated by management and agreed to by unions only after nonunion plants began to use novel methods. These included work team systems, pay for knowledge, and "more direct communication between workers and supervisors," innovations that proved "more efficient than the traditional work practices utilized in unionized plants based on narrow job classifications and detailed regulations of work practices through highly formalized rules" that unions had negotiated and fought to maintain.[64]

Ironically, one of the best-known cases in which labor-management cooperation increased productivity—GM's Saturn experiment—also exemplifies how unions resist productivity-enhancing reorganizations. Unionists frequently cite the Saturn agreement as evidence that unions want to cooperate with management to increase the productivity and competitiveness of American industry. Yet, it is well-known that the current UAW leadership is not nearly so enthusiastic about the Saturn agreement as was past leadership and does not want the experiment repeated anywhere else. Its attitude may even jeopardize the provisions in the current Saturn contract that provide for greater management flexibility in the organization and assignment of work. Yet, in comparison with teams at nonunion firms like Motorola, "Saturn teams are relatively lightweight, with little decision-making power. At Saturn, the role of senior managers is limited, in effect, to that of external team adviser—counterbalanced by an adviser from the United Auto Workers union."[65]

Further, it is an acknowledged fact in the automobile industry that General Motors is far less efficient than its competitors, by one account taking an average of thirty-nine hours to build a car although Ford needs only twenty-two hours.[66] GM produced far more parts in-house than the other Big Three companies. Yet, for years now, the company has suffered through two strikes a month. These strikes protested the company's efforts to reorganize and subcontract work that could be performed elsewhere at lower cost. In other words, the UAW was acting like a public-employee union protesting the privatization of work, even though it was clear to all industry analysts that the proposed contracting out was in the short- and long-term interest of the company.

Union concern about employee-involvement programs is understandable. The hallmark of the new system of organization is an emphasis on the individual employee. Innovative management approaches stress "pushing decision making down," giving workers individual autonomy and even encouraging workers to practice entrepreneurship of a sort.[67]

Indisputably, unionized firms are less profitable. Even if productivity in specific unionized firms is higher, the difference is clearly not great enough to compensate for the higher labor costs associated with unionization. Therefore, in a competitive market, profit-seeking enterprises can be expected to put up stiff resistance to union organizing efforts. But that is not to say that the cause of the decline of trade unionism is a massive violation of workers' rights.

Union leaders have charged that workers are routinely fired for trying to organize unions but have offered little direct proof. The argument about the numbers of workers illegally dismissed for organizing activities now revolves around abstruse arguments about the meaning of the number of National Labor Relations Board (NLRB) reinstatements. According to the most careful and balanced analysis of NLRB statistics, by Robert LaLonde and Bernard Meltzer of the University of Chicago, there were intentional discharges in perhaps 30 percent of all organizing campaigns.[68] But even this number may be misleading. Intentional discharges may increase the chances of a union's winning an election. After all, the far rougher behavior of firms in the 1930s only increased pro-union sentiment. At least one recent study indicates that employer violations of employee rights still have the same effect:

> In none of the regression analyses did unfair labor practices appear to have even the slightest influence upon the percentage of union vote, union vote loss, or election outcome. The only evidence of a statistically significant relationship between the commission of unfair labor practices and voting behavior . . . showed that in close elections, unions actually gained support when employers engaged in unlawful conduct.[69]

The allegations that unions frequently make regarding rights violations are at odds with standard union-avoidance strategy. As early as 1979, labor reporter Abe Raskin wrote: "Gone are the private industrial armies and labor spies of the 1930s. Now suave lawyers and behavioral scientists team up with Madison Avenue communicators to design campaigns aimed at convincing employees that unions can do nothing for them that the company can't do better."[70]

Managing the Work Force

New ways of managing workers that have been pioneered by non-union firms have also lessened, and in some instances eliminated, the perceived need for trade union representation. During their boom, mass industries were organized as hierarchies; the simplistic division of tasks was to promote efficiency. Workers were not viewed as individuals.

Recognizing that this system could be used to its advantage, unionism "developed its own conception of industrial morality, in which the worker's relationship to industry and to the employer is as a group rather than as separate individuals."[71] To maintain that group identity, unions adopted an adversarial stance toward management. Industrial unions and craft unions alike refused to accept any responsibility for management functions, such as increasing productivity. As one labor theorist put it, "In the nature of the case, the union is an organization deliberately created to protect and promote the interests of employees as employees, and not to advance the management's *competing* interest in higher business efficiency."[72]

Productivity was thought to depend greatly on the maintenance of labor peace—hence the rise in the corporate hierarchy of the industrial relations manager, who was to reduce the number of labor disruptions. In 1952, the Bureau of National Affairs surveyed large firms and found that "in roughly 70 percent . . . the personnel/industrial relations function was thought to be as important as production, marketing or finance."[73] A symbiotic relationship arose between industrial relations executives and labor leaders—the role and status of both depending on the status quo. Both often opposed innovations that threatened the industrial relations system on which they depended. In other words, the industrial relations system that developed in response to the rise of the industrial unions discouraged companies from implementing programs to increase the productivity of workers by maximizing their potential as individuals.

While the new methods of organizing work empower individual workers, they are proving devastating to the unions that want to represent them. Firms that instituted innovations focusing on the individuality of the worker, including "autonomous work, . . . pay for knowledge, [and] flexible work hours," reduced the probability of unionization on the average by 17 percent.[74] Such innovations naturally encourage enterprising workers to want to rise on the basis of their own merits, whereas one of the "achievements" of trade unions is to flatten wage differentials to the extent possible. Most workers do not want to be treated as fungible labor and *therefore* have no interest in joining a union. The decline in the demand for unions has been precipitous. According to a Louis Harris survey conducted in 1984 for the AFL-CIO, fully 65 percent of nonunion workers said that they would not vote for a union in a secret-ballot election.[75] Other polls have shown even steeper declines. Only 29 percent of nonunion respondents in a 1977 University of Michigan survey indicated they would vote for a union; only 24 percent indicated so in a poll taken in 1986 by the *Washington Post* and ABC News.[76] Labor economist Henry Farber has attributed all the decline in the demand for union representation among nonunion workers to "the increase in the nonunion workers' [job] satisfaction and decrease in perceptions of union instrumentality."[77]

Will the Public-Sector Unions Save American Labor?

Public-sector bargaining in the United States is now accepted as a matter of course, hardly to be questioned. In that respect, the public-sector unions today are treated as their private-sector counterparts were following World War II. In the long run, however, public-sector unions will not escape the fate of the private-employee unions.

First, public-employee unions and public-sector bargaining are relatively new—and newly legitimate—phenomena. Well into the 1950s, the prevailing view in the United States was that entering into an enforceable collective-bargaining agreement with an organization representing public employees would violate a government's sovereign authority and its public trust. Not even the trade union movement took issue. As late as 1959, George Meany expressed the opinion that "it is impossible to bargain collectively with government."[78] Not until 1960 did the AFL-CIO officially support collective bargaining for public employees; by that time, public-sector bargaining was virtually a fait accompli. Of the multiple reasons for the tardiness of labor's endorsement, ironically one was the Gompersian rationale for private-sector bargaining.

Gompers had argued that the function of unions was to create a fairer balance between the compensation of workers, on the one hand, and the profits of owners, on the other. Since governments were not profit-making bodies, public-employee unions would not serve that purpose. Moreover, the public employee did not need the protection from the employer that Gompers believed the private employee did. Gompers and his successors argued that, in the absence of unions, competition would force private employers to cut costs by slashing wages. But since public employers did not compete over price, they would have no reason to drive down wages.

On the contrary, to attract qualified workers (and because public employees were a potent political constituency), governments, at all levels, paid competitive wages and salaries. Many had, by decree or legislation, adopted what was known as the prevailing wage principle. The Advisory Commission on Intergovernmental Relations determined "that in 1960, on the eve of the public bargaining era, public-employee wages were 93.3 percent of those earned by private-industry employees in comparable jobs."[79] If anything, public employees received better fringe benefits, for example, pensions. Moreover, employment in the public sector was more secure, with less chance of temporary or permanent layoffs. By this time, too, civil service systems almost everywhere gave public employees strong protection against arbitrary discipline, up to and including dismissal from service.

On top of all this, public-sector unions lacked a public-interest rationale. Gompers had argued that the private-sector unions served the public interest in that the wage increases they negotiated enabled workers to buy back the product of manufacturers and, thereby, prevented recessions and depressions. But wage increases negotiated by public-sector unions were financed by private-sector employees, whether directly in the form of income and sales taxes or indirectly in the form of taxes on employers. What economic gain was to be realized by transferring money from one worker's wallet to another's?

Gompers and his successors had also argued that, by raising wages, unions forced employers to invest in labor-saving capital and, thereby, increase labor productivity. Since public employers were not profit-making institutions, there was no reason for believing that higher wages and better working conditions in the public sector would do anything but raise labor costs. There was no good Gompersian rationale for public-employee unionism. In the event, however, no rationale was needed. Political considerations proved entirely sufficient.

The years just after World War II saw an increasing number of public-employee strikes. Legislation banning such strikes passed in a number of states, but when such laws made it onto the books in the most liberal, heavily unionized areas of the country, they went unenforced. By 1950, many local governments and unions worked out bargaining arrangements. Public officials responded to public dismay over labor unrest, even as they refused to levy penalties on unions for strikes. Some public officials, including New York City's Mayor Robert F. Wagner, Jr. (the son of the author of the National Labor Relations Act), attempted to woo public-employee unions and their members by giving in to their demands. By 1958, Wagner had issued directives for recognizing unions and dealing with collective bargaining.

In 1960, political considerations also convinced Democratic presidential candidate John F. Kennedy to promise the powerful postal workers' union (which had acted as an employee association) that, if elected, he would negotiate with it and other federal unions. This promise had little public support; lack of congressional support forced Kennedy to issue executive order 10988 in January 1962, establishing a labor-management relations program for executive branch employees. This move set an important precedent for state and local governments, which found themselves hard-pressed to explain why they should deny their employees what the president of the United States had granted his.

The Impact of Public-Sector Bargaining

Some predicted that public-employee unions would be more successful than private-sector unions in raising wages and improving benefits of workers. The argument was that public employers would not be constrained by bottom-line considerations but would be responsive to the politically powerful unions and to the general public, which would hold long, inconvenient strikes against them.

At first, those predictions seemed to be borne out. In the 1960s and through the mid-1970s, public-employee wages soared in cities where they had collective-bargaining rights. Yet, appearances were deceiving. The wages of public employees in cities such as Chicago, where there was no collective bargaining in the public sector, also rose quickly during the period. So did wages of federal employees, whose unions were never given the right to bargain over compensation. Most gains of state and local employees during this period came because their governments had more money to spend in a period of rising real incomes and general prosperity. Also, intergovernmental transfers from the federal to lower levels of government increased rapidly during the period.

Still, these were halcyon days for the public-employee unions. According to labor economist David Lewin: "During that period [1960–1975] the average relative compensation (not just pay) effect of public employee unions was on the order of 20–25 percent. . . . The effects were . . . larger for unions of uniformed service employees (police, fire, and sanitation employees)" and weakest for the teachers' unions, which raised wages by less than 10 percent.[80] The average would be close to the union differential in the private sector during the 1970s.

But this success did not last. Pay hikes for public employees helped to push spending so high that cities across the country were threatened by fiscal crisis. With their backs up against the wall, city officials started resisting public-employee unions' demands; the public backed the officials. Indeed, public opinion came near to a 180-degree turn on the question of public employees. When he was assassinated in Memphis, Tennessee, in 1968, Martin Luther King, Jr., was there to support a strike by the city's sanitation workers. Less than a decade later, Maynard Jackson, mayor of Atlanta, with the full support of public figures including the Rev. Martin Luther King, Sr., stood up to sanitation workers, vowing that "before I take this city into a deficit financial position, elephants will roost in trees."[81] Jackson fired all strikers and immediately began to hire permanent replacements.

Whereas once the public had thought that public employees

were underpaid, by the mid-1970s it had come to believe that they were overpaid. In California, public discontent with the high taxes that the public-employee unions fed on led directly to the passage in 1978 of proposition 13, a tax-cutting referendum that started a spate of similar measures that spread across the country. Public-employee unions, at first, did not recognize the sea change in public attitudes. There was a flurry of public-sector strikes in the late 1970s, but officials in most instances stood their ground.

The public-employee unions suffered their worst defeat in 1981, when President Reagan dismissed air traffic controllers who had struck in violation of federal law. Reagan did what big-city mayors had been afraid to do in the 1950s—and received great public acclaim. More than any other single event, this action signified that the public would no longer tolerate public officials buying labor peace with tax dollars. For the next decade, salary increases negotiated by public-employee unions were exceedingly modest. By 1992, economist Richard Kearney reported that "the best estimate of an overall union effect is 5–6 percent, which is well below the 20–25 percent union compensation advantage in the private sector."[82]

The Quality of Public Service

The officials who established the structures for collective bargaining in the public sector justified their decisions on the ground that public-sector bargaining would increase the quality of public services. But this was wishful thinking. There never was any good reason to believe that unionization would, in any way, improve the quality of public service. Such improvement was certainly not a concern of most public-employee union leaders. A reader will search in vain for any mention of the productivity issue in Joseph Goulden's authorized biography of Jerry Wurf, the former president of the American Federation of State County and Municipal Employees who built the union into the powerhouse it is today. Goulden quoted Wurf's argument that "sound labor relations . . . are needed to boost employee efficiency and morale, without which the best of programs will suffer." Efficiency and morale clearly matter, but Wurf cited no evidence that the gains unions could make through collective bargaining would, in any way, improve either. He admitted as much in the 1970s, when his response to the growing public anger over the high cost and low quality of public services was that "productivity in the public sector depends on good management."[83]

The precipitous decline in the quality of public services that coincided with the rise of public-employee unions extended into all reaches of public employment. There was a strong correlation, for example, between the rise of teachers' unions and the decline in collegeaptitude test scores. Scores fell first and most rapidly where teacher unionism took hold first and strongest. Some of the decline was due to the negotiation of rigid work rules that "give big-city governments their reputation for Third World efficiency."[84] In Philadelphia, for example, AFSCME negotiated new work rules in 1962 that resulted in gross inefficiencies and featherbedding on a grand scale. Three decades later, "sludge [that] . . . came out of the city's water pipes was shoveled into trucks, then dumped on the ground and once again shoveled into another truck. . . . all this to employ ten persons."[85]

In 1992, Philadelphia voters chose as their new mayor Democrat Ed Rendell, who had campaigned on a pledge to renegotiate such work rules. The public-employee unions—with national AFL-CIO support—responded to Rendell's demands for change with a citywide strike. But because of the public's support of Rendell, the unions returned to work almost immediately, after agreeing to new and more efficient work rules.

Rendell's tough stance contrasts with the accommodation of New York City Mayor David Dinkins in negotiations that same year with New York City public-employee unions. Campaign support by those unions explained why, "despite Mr. Dinkins' long term pledge to grant increases only if the unions paid for them in better productivity, the agreement does not impose even one reform. . . . Real reforms can last generations. . . . That's why unions fight them so fiercely."[86]

Almost without exception, the politically influential unions endorsed the mayor against his Republican opponent Rudolph Giuliani. Guiliani won despite minuscule support by the unions. This victory, in turn, allowed him to announce an economic program that featured a plan to reduce the number of public employees and to privatize municipal hospitals, some sanitation services, and the like.

And so it goes. Public-employee unions cannot wall themselves off from the competitive forces that have already wreaked havoc on their private-sector counterparts. It will take longer, but in the end, privatization—even the threat of privatization—will have the same impact on the public-employee unions that competition from non-union sources had on the private-sector unions and with the same devastating consequences.

The Impact of the New Leadership

T he new leadership of the AFL-CIO has promised to stem and reverse the decline of the labor movement. For starters, the leaders are reinvigorating and increasing the funding of the organizing apparatus of the federation. But we know from past experience that this exercise alone will not turn things around. At its formation, the AFL-CIO launched a campaign to recruit millions of new members. Fifteen years later, Walter Reuther established a new labor federation, the American Labor Alliance, whose highest priority was organizing. In the intervening quarter of a century, the AFL-CIO sporadically undertook major new organizing initiatives. Without exception, these efforts failed, as will the new initiative, unless the time is now ripe for organizing as it was in the 1930s. This explains why the new leadership has been consciously applying the lessons of the 1930s, as it understands them, and at every turn drawing comparisons between that era and our own. In the 1930s, a combination of factors gave rise to the industrial unions:

- energized union leaders who had the general support of the Left and who specifically involved radical activists in organizing campaigns
- a severe economic situation for which the Republican Hoover administration was blamed
- callous and stupid treatment of workers by major corporations
- public sympathy for trade unionism and substantial antipathy toward business

The new leadership is apparently willing to do whatever it takes to win the active support of the Left. To wit, Sweeney and the core constituency that elected him intend to remove the only ideological barrier between labor and the Left at the end of the Kirkland reign: the CIO's reputation for supporting defense and foreign policites that advance the national interest. That reputation will not survive the Sweeney regime. For the most part, Sweeney and the core constituency that elected him opposed the anti-Communist efforts of the United States (and then AFL-CIO leadership) in Nicaragua and El Salvador, and they also publicly opposed sending U.S. troops to the Persian Gulf in 1991. As far as defense policy is concerned, during the Cold War they opposed the SDI and supported a nuclear freeze and they passed a resolution at the 1995 AFL-CIO convention that called for yet more cuts in the defense budget.

To make the import of these moves unmistakably clear, Sweeney himself joined the now far-Left Democratic Socialists of America in the runup to the convention where he was elected president of the AFL-CIO. This was a virtual invitation to the Left to join forces with labor.

And the Left has accepted. Since Sweeney's election there has been a rapprochement between labor and the Left, armchair intellectuals and activists alike. These moves have successfully effectuated a rapprochement between labor and the Left, armchair intellectuals and activists alike. For instance, Nelson Lichtenstein, a labor historian who has criticized Walter Reuther for not drawing on talents of radicals in the late 1940s and 1960s, writes (with co-author Steven Fraser) that "in an era when elite opinion makes a fetish of the free market, the unions—with their old-fashioned ideas about solidarity, equality and collective bargaining are just the kind of subversive institutions this country needs. . . . The new leadership of the AFL-CIO is not without its faults, but we are ready to reenlist in its cause."[87]

Veterans of past radical campaigns are also on board. As just one example, the director of the summer 1996 union organizing campaign, Andy Levin, boasts of his participation in a myriad of left-wing causes including "apartheid, anti-nuclear, environment, civil rights, community organizing, student protest."[88] In the long run, association with radicals of this sort will come to haunt labor, but for the time being it is a big advantage, bringing as it does fresh blood to a nearly moribund movement. But while fervor and talent are necessary, they are not sufficient. Labor must also make the case that conditions now are ripe for organizing as they were in the depression.

To this end, Sweeney and others have been making the case that the workers and the country need unions now more than at any time since the rise of the CIO in the 1930s. According to Sweeney, workers are, in fact, "suffering as they haven't since the Great Depression."[89]

Confronted with the increased competition since the early 1970s, Sweeney and others charge that "corporate America," with crucial support from the U.S. government, has declared "war" on American workers.[90] The arsenal at the disposal of the government includes but is not limited to "downsizing, right-sizing and contracting-out that workers now know are code words for laid off and out-of-luck." Workers lucky enough to have a job are being forced by corporations to work for lower real wages and fewer and less-generous fringe benefits. To make ends meet, the workers must work longer hours and hold down multiple jobs. Even at that, working families are falling ever deeper into debt. The problem, though, goes beyond economics. It is also that workers are now "without a voice in their lives and their livelihoods."[91] How can workers regain their voice and fight back? By joining unions, answers labor.

Nightmare scenarios of the sort that Sweeney and other labor leaders conjure up will easily attract support from the Left, which is always on the lookout for new faults with America. But ordinary workers, who by all indications have moved right with the rest of the country over past decades, will not be won over unless there is a significant correspondence between the dark Dickensian portrait Sweeney draws of contemporary America and the reality they experience and perceive. The difference, though, is almost as stark as that between night and day.

Though no one would ever know from reading Sweeney's new book, *America Needs a Wage Raise,* in the spring of 1996 the United States was not in a depression. Rather, it was in the midst of one of the longest periods of economic expansion since World War II. Jobs were being eliminated, of course, as they always are in a dynamic economy. But there was no basis for the fear-mongering about downsizing and the like. As James Glassman noted in the *Washington Post,* "A recent study found that in 1991 (the most recent statistics), men aged 45 to 54 had been in their current jobs an average of 12.2

years. That's up from 11.0 years in 1978 and 8.8 years in 1966 [about the same time that George Meany was bemoaning the baleful effects of automation]. Tenure for women in this age group has increased as well."[92]

Moreover, new jobs were being created at a far faster rate than jobs were being eliminated. In contrast to the European economies, which had created hardly any new private-sector jobs for decades, the U.S. economy had created 60 million in a decade and a half, millions of new jobs each year—so many that the economy was running about as close as possible to full employment without producing inflationary pressures.

Furthermore, the jobs being created were good jobs. President Clinton's Council of Economic Advisers reported that the majority of new jobs paid above the national average. Many of these jobs went to laid-off workers: "27 percent got wages at least 20 percent higher than at their previous jobs; 26 percent got wages up to 20 percent higher; 16 percent suffered a pay loss no greater than 20 percent; and 31 percent suffered pay losses more than 20 percent."[93] So half gained, and half lost, initially. Later, some of the latter made up the ground they had lost, and then some. So, while there is no denying the trauma that sometimes accompanied layoffs due to down sizing, the fact is that more laid-off employees come out ahead in the end.

Moreover, in contradiction to Sweeney's claims, pay levels had also risen, once nonwage compensation (an increasing percentage of total compensation, with tax advantages) was factored in.[94] And when accurate cost-of-living adjustments were factored in, wages increased even faster.[95] And after accurate cost-of-living adjustments were factored into the equation, wages had increased even faster. This accounts, in large part, for the fact that adjusted per capita income rose by more than 50 percent in only one generation, even though (once again contra Sweeney) there had been no percentage increase in the number of workers taking on multiple jobs. According to a member of the Council of Economic Advisers, the percentage of workers holding more than one job had not increased in the least since 1970.[96]

Sweeney's charge that America's workers are now powerless and voiceless was also untrue. As he was certainly aware (and as has been detailed in earlier pages of this book), American corporations have increased, not decreased, the responsibility (that is, "the voice") of workers in the production of goods and the delivery of services, quite often over the objection of unions that wanted to define and therefore limit the role of workers in contracts. Workers also have more, not less control ("power"), over their lives. Millions have won promotions as they gained experience and education. Millions more have voluntarily left their jobs as better ones became available to them. America today is more than ever an equal opportunity society, where individuals can rise on their merits, a condition that makes unions irrelevant.

This is not a propitious time for organizing: one can hardly imagine a worse time. The new leadership will not make an appreciable difference. The decline of American labor is destined to continue.

Notes

CHAPTER 1: INTRODUCTION

1. Seymour Martin Lipset, *The Third Century* (Chicago: University of Chicago Press, 1980), p. 190.

CHAPTER 2: THE PHILOSOPHY OF THE AMERICAN LABOR MOVEMENT

1. Senate testimony, Sixty-second Congress, 3rd sess., Senate Reports N1326 (Washington, 1913), vol. 11, p. 1728ff, reprinted in Richard Hofstadter, ed., *The Progressive Movement* (Englewood Cliffs, N.J.: Prentice Hall, 1963), p. 102.

2. Quoted in Stan Kaufman and Peter Albert, eds., *The Samuel Gompers Papers* (Urbana: University of Illinois Press, 1986), p. 531, from *North American Review*, July 8, 1894.

3. The hyperbole is George Meany's (he was prone to hyperbole throughout his career), but the idea is common to most trade union leaders, past and present.

4. Quoted in Kaufman and Albert, *The Samuel Gompers Papers*, p. 237, from *National Labor Tribune*, 1892.

5. Samuel Gompers, *Seventy Years, Samuel Gompers Papers*, v. 63, *Unrest and Depression* 1891–94.

6. Michael Novak, *The Spirit of Capitalism* (New York: Simon and Schuster, 1982), p. 43.

7. Gompers and Murray are no exceptions; no past or present leader of American labor would agree that labor is or should be a commodity.

8. Selig Perlman, *A Theory of the Labor Movement* (New York: A. M. Kelley, 1949), p. 200.

9. Samuel Gompers, Hayes Robbins ed., *Labor and the Common Welfare* (New York: Arno Press, 1969), from *American Federationist*, November 1907, p. 15.

10. Matthew Woll, *Current History*, May 1930, p. 247.

11. William Green, *Labor and Democracy* (Princeton: Princeton University Press, 1939), p. 147.

12. Arthur Schlesinger, Jr., *The Coming of the New Deal* (Boston: Houghton Mifflin, 1959), p. 403.

13. Ibid., p. 419.

14. Joseph C. Goulden, *Meany: The Unchallenged Strong Man of American Labor* (New York: Atheneum, 1972), p. 53.

15. Ronald Schatz, "Philip Murray and the Subordination of Industrial Unions to the U.S. Government", in Melvyn Dubofsky and Warren Van Tine, eds., *Labor Leaders in America* (Urbana: University of Illinois, 1986).

16. Irving Howe and B. J. Widdick, *The UAW and Walter Reuther* (New York: Random House, 1949), quoting 1946 pamphlet.

17. Ibid.

18. David Brody, *Workers in Industrial America* (New York: Oxford University Press, 1980), p. 192.

CHAPTER 3: THE RADICALIZATION OF LABOR'S ECONOMIC POLICY

1. AFL-CIO, *Labor Looks at Automation* (Washington, D.C.: AFL-CIO, 1966), p. 16; George Meany, testimony before the Platform Committee of the Democratic Party on July 8, 1960, reprinted in *FTU News,* July 1960, vol. 15, no. 7, p. 1. "There are actually 2 million *less* jobs in manufacturing, mining and the railroad industry than there were in 1953. And there is only the same number of jobs in construction, communications, and utilities, such as the gas and electric companies."

2. Herbert Stein, *Presidential Economics: Reagan and Beyond* (New York: Simon and Schuster, 1985), pp. 96–97.

3. See Milton Friedman, *Capitalism and Freedom* (Chicago: University of Chicago Press, 1962), p. 122.

4. Ibid., p. 123.

5. One of the main thrusts of Drucker's work is that no corporation, no matter how large, is immune from competition.

6. Joseph Schumpeter, *Capitalism, Socialism and Democracy,* 3d ed. (New York: Harper Torchbooks, 1950), p. 93.

7. From *AEI Memorandum,* 1978, p. 2.

8. White, *America in Search of Itself* (New York: Harper & Row, 1982), pp. 149–50.

9. Report of the executive council to the 1957 convention, from convention proceedings, p. 117, *National Economy.*

10. Irving Kristol, *Two Cheers for Capitalism* (New York: Basic Books, 1978), p. 180.

11. "Congress and the Nation," *Congressional Quarterly,* 1969–1972, p. 708.

12. Stein, *Presidential Economics,* pp. 217–18.

13. Alan S. Blinder, *Hard Heads, Soft Hearts, Tough-Minded Economics for a Just Society* (Reading, Penn.: Addison-Wesley, 1987), pp. HB171, B535.

14. Report of the executive council to the 1977 convention, p. 81.

15. Report of the executive council to the 1975 convention, p. 94.

16. "The National Economy 1957," *Proceedings of the Executive Council*, p. 21.

17. AFL-CIO, *Economic Program and Policies for the 60s*, p. 2.

18. Leon Keyserling, "Key Policies for Full Employment," *Conference on Economic Progress*, Washington, D.C., 1962, p. 49.

19. George Meany, "Progress or Stagnation Is the Choice before Us," in AFL-CIO, *Economic Programs and Policies for the 60s*.

20. Report of the executive council to the tenth constitutional convention, Bal Harbor, Florida, October 18–23, 1973, vol. 2, p. 87.

21. Report of the executive council to the 1975 convention, p. 106.

22. Kristol, *Two Cheers for Capitalism*, p. 212.

23. Lane Kirkland, address to October 1983 convention, reprinted as *Together in Solidarity*, publication 161, pp. 2–3.

24. Lane Kirkland, testimony before the House Committee on Ways and Means, February 5, 1992; AFL-CIO reprint, p. 2.

25. Heywood T. Sanders, "What Infrastructure Crisis?" *The Public Interest*, no. 110 (winter 1993), p. 6.

26. Ibid., p. 8.

27. *New York Times*, February 7, 1993, p. F5.

28. Ibid.

29. "American Survey," *Economist*, October 10, 1992, p. 25.

30. Report of the executive council to the 1975 convention, p. 120.

31. Report of the executive council to the ninth constitutional convention, vol. 2, Bal Harbour, Florida, November 18–22, 1971, p. 102.

32. Blinder, *Hard Heads*, pp. 146–47.

33. Ibid., p. 153.

34. Albert Nichols and Richard Zeckhauser, "Government Comes to the Workplace: An Assessment of OSHA," *The Public Interest*, fall 1977, pp. 55–56.

35. *New York Times*, March 24, 1993, p. A16.

36. "European Worker Benefits," *AFL-CIO Reviews the Issues*, Report 55 (September 1991), p. 3.

37. Ibid., p. 4.

38. *New York Times*, quoting C. Fred Bergsten, director of the Institute for International Economics, "Rewriting the Contract for Germany's Vaunted Workers," February 13, 1994, p. F5.

39. "Mercedes Workers Practice: 'Howdy, Hans; Guten Tag, Bubba,'" *Washington Post*, February 14, 1994, p. A21; "Germany's Economic 'Miracle'

Turns into Worst Slump since the War," *Washington Post*, November 16, 1993, p. A32.

40. "Mercedes Workers Practice," p. A21.

41. Policy resolutions adopted November 1963, by the fifth constitutional convention, pub. 3–6, February 1964, *The National Economy*, p. 3, also *Proceedings of 1963 Convention*, p. 364.

42. Executive council report to the 1977 AFL-CIO convention.

43. Peter Schuck, "National Economic Planning: A Slogan without Substance," *The Public Interest*, February 1976, p. 72.

44. Policy resolutions adopted November 1981 by the fourteenth constitutional convention, AFL-CIO, pub. January 3, 1982, p. 5.

45. AFL-CIO policy resolutions adopted November 1989 by the eighteenth constitutional convention, p. 31.

46. Lane Kirkland, "Industrial Policy: An Answer to Economic Chaos," *Stanford Law and Policy Review*, vol. 5, no. 1 (fall 1993), p. 75.

47. Lane Kirkland, address to the convention of the International Alliance of Theatrical, Stage Employees and Motion Pictures Operators, August 30, 1978.

48. Report of the executive council to the 1981 constitutional convention, p. 85.

49. Lane Kirkland, address at UAW educational conference, Chicago, September 23, 1982, quoting with approval chancellor of CUNY at commencement.

50. Lane Kirkland, speech to AFL-CIO regional conference, Nashville, Tennessee, June 7, 1985.

51. Lane Kirkland, speech to Industrial Union Department, September 19, 1979.

52. Leo Troy, *The New Unionism in the New Society: Public Sector Unions in the Redistributive State.* (Fairfax, Va.: George Mason University Press, 1994), p. 11.

53. "Breaking the Federal Budget Straightjacket," Resolution passed at 1991 Public Employee Department convention, Atlantic City, N.J., October 3–4, 1991, p. 10, in *Adopted Resolutions*.

54. Ibid., p. 15.

55. *The Right Choice for New York 1992* (Albany: Fiscal Policy Institute, March 1992), p. 20.

56. "Public Services and Economic Competitiveness," Resolution passed at the 1991 Public Employee Department convention, Atlantic City, N.J., October 3–4, 1991.

57. *Passing the Bucks* (Washington, D.C.: AFSCME, 1983), p. 14.

58. "Government for Sale," in *Passing the Bucks*, p. 15.

59. See James Q. Wilson, *Bureaucracy: What Government Agencies Do and Why They Do It* (New York: Basic Books, 1989), p. 50.

60. Chester E. Finn, Jr., Letters column, *Commentary*, vol. 88, no. 4 (October 1989), p. 10.

61. Sandra Feldman, "Children in Crisis: The Tragedy of Underfunded Schools and the Students They Serve," *American Educator*, vol. 16, no. 1 (spring 1992), p. 10.

62. Albert Shanker, "Where We Stand," *New York Times*, February 14, 1993, p. E7.

63. *Washington Post*, February 19, 1993.

64. Albert Shanker, testimony before Committee on Education and Labor, Subcommittee on Elementary, Secondary, and Vocational Education, July 11, 1991.

65. August 3, 1993, conversation with Alan Ginsberg, Department of Education.

66. Feldman, p. 10.

67. "Record Low Dropout Rate Is Met with Skepticism," *New York Times*, June 11, 1993, p. B3.

68. *New York Times*, June 30, 1993, p. B2.

69. *New York Times*, June 18, 1993, p. B1.

70. Memorandum for the Center for Educational Innovation, from Raymond J. Domanico, June 28, 1993.

71. Eric Hanushel, "The Economics of Schooling," *Journal of Economic Literature*, vol. 24 (September 1986).

72. American Federation of Teachers, *Convention Report, 1992* (Pittsburgh: AFT, 1992), p. 66.

73. Albert Shanker, "Where We Stand," *New York Times*, July 22, 1990.

74. Wilson, *Bureaucracy*, p. 363.

CHAPTER 4: THE FOREIGN POLICY OF AMERICAN LABOR

1. Samuel Gompers, editorial, *American Federationist*, July 1894, pp. 99–100.

2. Samuel Gompers, address at Chicago Jubilee, October 18, 1898, reprinted in the *American Federationist*, November 18, 1898, and in Gerald Emmanuel Stern, ed., *Gompers* (Englewood Cliffs, N.J.: Prentice Hall, 1971).

3. Simon Larson, *Gompers, the AFL and the First World War, 1914–1918* (Rutherford, N.J.: Dickenson Press, 1975), p. 21.

4. Hayes Robbins, *Labor and the Common Welfare*, ed. (New York: E. P. Dutton), p. 196.

5. Lewis L. Lorwin, *American Federation of Labor, History, Policies, and Prospects* (Washington, D.C.: Brookings Institution, 1933), p. 142.

6. Gompers, *Seventy Years of Life and Labor*, Augustus Kelly, ed. (New York: E. P. Dutton, 1925), p. 336.

7. Ibid., p. 397.

8. Ibid., p. 400.

9. Lorwin, *Labor and Internationalism*, p. 124.

10. Robbins, *Labor and the Common Welfare*, p. 210.

11. David Dubinsky and A. H. Raskin, *David Dubinsky: A Life with Labor* (New York: Simon and Schuster, 1977).

12. Philip Taft, *Defending Freedom: American Labor and Foreign Affairs* (Los Angeles: Nash, 1973), p. 49.

13. Ibid., p. 50.

14. Stephen Fraser, *Labor Will Rule: Sidney Hillmann and the Rise of American Labor* (Toronto: Free Press, 1991), p. 434.

15. Dubinsky and Raskin, *David Dubinsky*, p. 245.

17. John Windmuller, *American Labor and the International Labor Movement 1940–1953* (Ithaca, N.Y.: Institute of International Industrial and Labor Relations, Cornell University, 1954), p. 173.

18. George C. Lodge, *Spearheads of Democracy: Labor in the Developing Countries* (New York: Harper and Row, 1962), p. 198.

19. Carl Gershman, *The Foreign Policy of American Labor* (Beverly Hills, Calif.: Sage, 1975), p. 29.

20. Lodge, *Spearheads of Democracy*, p. 99.

21. Ibid., Dubinsky and Raskin, *David Dubinsky*, p. 259.

22. Walter Laqueur, *Europe in Our Time: A History, 1945–1992* (New York: Viking, 1992), p. 72.

23. Taft, *Defending Freedom*, p. 85.

24. Ibid, p. 92.

25. Sidney Lens, "American Labor Abroad, Lovestone Diplomacy," *Nation*, July 5, 1965, p. 14.

26. Ibid.

27. Laqueur, *Europe in Our Time*, p. 81.

28. Roy Godson, *American Labor and European Politics, The AFL as a Transnational Force* (New York: Crane, Russak, and Company, 1976), p. 68.

29. See Val Lorwin, *The French Labor Movement* (Cambridge, Mass.: Harvard University Press, 1954), p. 124.

30. Ibid., p. 129.

31. Irving Brown, "Stalin's Hold on French Labor," *New Leader*, January 28, 1952, p. 18.

32. Arnold Beichman, "George Meany," *Policy Review*, winter 1992, p. 49.

33. Tom Braden, *Saturday Evening Post*, May 20, 1967; Peter Coleman, who interviewed Brown, *The Liberal Conspiracy, The Congress for Cultural Freedom and the Struggle for the Mind of Postwar Europe* (New York: Free Press, 1989), p. 35.

34. Hugh Seton-Watson, *From Lenin to Malenkov: The History of World Communism* (New York: Praeger, 1953), p. 299.

35. Ronald Filippelli, *American Labor and Post War Italy, 1943–1953: A Study of Cold War Politics* (Stanford, Calif.: Stanford University Press, 1989), p. 115.

36. Daniel Horowitz, *The Italian Labor Movement* (Cambridge, Mass.: Harvard University Press, 1963), p. 236.

37. Conversation with Daniel Horowitz, whose tome on the Italian Labor movement includes no mention of Brown or of the AFL.

38. Joshua Muravchik, *Exporting Democracy: Fulfilling America's Destiny* (Washington, D.C.: AEI Press, 1991), pp. 97, 100.

39. Richard Deyerall, "Two Labor Conventions in Japan," *American Federationist*, vol. 62, no. 16 (October 1955), pp. 10–11.

40. Robert A. Scalapino, "Japan," in Walter Galenson, ed., *Labor and Economic Development*, (New York: John Wiley and Sons, 1959), p. 139.

41. "American Labor's Cold War in Occupied Japan," *Diplomatic History*, p. 260, from NSC statement.

42. Richard Pipes, *Survival Is Not Enough: Soviet Realities and America's Future* (New York: Simon and Schuster, 1984), p. 104.

43. Paul Johnson, *Modern Times: The World from the Twenties to the Eighties* (New York: Harper and Row, 1983), p. 505.

44. Wogu Ananaba, *The Trade Union Movement in Africa: Promise and Performance* (New York: St. Martin's Press, 1979), p. 76.

45. Lodge, *Spearheads of Democracy*, p. 33.

46. Ibid., p. 32.

47. Quoted in Martin Meredith, *The First Dance of Freedom: Black Africa in the Post-War Era* (New York: Harper and Row, 1984), p. 192.

48. Serafino Romualdi, *Presidents and Peons: Recollections of a Labor Ambassador in Latin America* (New York: Funk and Wagnalls, 1963), p. 240.

49. Lodge, *Spearheads of Democracy*, p. 104.

50. Arthur M. Schlesinger, Jr., *A Thousand Days: John F. Kennedy in the White House* (Boston: Houghton Mifflin, 1965), p. 778.

51. Ibid.

52. *Labor Profile: Guyana: Foreign Economic Trends*, American Embassy, Georgetown, 1982, p. 2.

53. Ibid.

54. Romualdi, *Presidents and Peons*, p. 210.

55. Ibid., pp. 401–2.

56. Lens, "American Labor Abroad," p. 27.

57. Romualdi, *Presidents and Peons*, p. 291, quoting from December 1965 San Francisco convention.

58. N. G. Ranga, "A Look at Unionism in India," *American Federationist*, vol. 63, no. 4 (April 1955), p. 25.

59. Norman Podhoretz, *Why We Were in Vietnam* (New York: Simon and Schuster, 1982), p. 172.

60. William Hyland, *The Cold War Is Over* (New York: Time Books/Random House, 1996), pp. 145, 149.

61. Gene Klar, "The Labor Movement of South Vietnam," *American Federationist*, vol. 76, no. 12 (December 1968), p. 16.

62. Adam Ulam, *The Rivals: America and Russia since World War II* (New York: Viking, 1971), p. 349.

CHAPTER 5: THE DEFEAT OF COMMUNISM

1. AIFLD Briefs, "The Captured Documents, Guerrilla Penetration of Salvadoran Trade Unions," AIFLD, Freedom House, April 30, 1986, p. 4.

2. David Asman, "El Salvador Still Digging Its Way Out of the Aid Trap," *Wall Street Journal*, p. A11.

3. Ibid., p. C128.

4. Jeane Kirkpatrick, "U.S. Security and Latin America," *Commentary*, January 1981, pp. 39, 40.

5. Report of the AFL-CIO Executive Council, 1987, AFL convention, October 26, 1987, p. 254.

6. AIFLD briefs, September 28, 1989.

7. Romualdi, *Presidents and Peons*, pp. 19, 20.

8. Mark Falcoff, "Nicaraguan Harvest," in Howard J. Wiarda and Mark Falcoff, eds., *The Communist Challenge in the Caribbean and Central America*(Washington, D.C.: AEI Press, 1987), p. 229.

9. Ibid., pp. 227–28.

10. From William A. Douglas and Roy Godson, "Labor and Defense Spending," *International Labor Program Papers*, no. 4 (spring 1980), quoting 1979 executive council statement.

11. See executive committee reports in AFL-CIO of convention proceedings, p. 195.

12. Interim report of the AFL-CIO Committee on Defense to the AFL-CIO Executive Council, 1987, p. 17.

13. From February 19, 1985, executive council press conference.

14. 1985 executive council, February 19, 1984, Bal Harbor.

15. Executive council, August 1979, quoted in Lane Kirkland, address to National Strategy Information Center, Washington, D.C., January 25, 1983.

16. David Moberg, *In These Times*, March 24–30, 1982.

17. Don Oberdorfer, *The Turn from the Cold War to a New Era: The United States and the Soviet Union, 1983–1990* (New York: Poseiden Press, 1991), p. 29.

18. *Washington Post*, February 26, 1993.

19. *The Report of AFL-CIO Committee on Defense on the Strategic Defense Initiative*, August 19, 1987, p. 9.

20. Ibid., p. 10.

21. *AFL-CIO Executive Council Statement on the Strategic Defense Initiative*, p. vi.

22. Lane Kirkland, remarks to the Conference on Economic Transition in Post-Communist States, Warsaw, November 16, 1992.

23. Samuel Huntington, "Religion and the Third Wave," *The National Interest*, no. 24 (Summer 1991), p. 31.

24. Lech Walesa, *The Struggle and the Triumph: An Autobiography* (New York: Arcade Publishing, 1991).

25. Leslek Kolakowski, quoted in Vladimire Tismaneanu, *Reinventing Politics: Eastern Europe from Stalin to Havel* (New York: Free Press, 1992), p. 124.

26. Theodore Draper, "A New History of the Velvet Revolution," *New York Review of Books*, January 14, 1993, vol. 40, nos. 1&2, p. 15.

27. Tismaneuanu, *Reinventing Politics*, p. 69.

28. Ibid., p. 232.

29. Charles Fairbanks, "The Nature of the Beast," *The National Interest*, no. 31 (spring 1993), p. 53.

30. Lane Kirkland, remarks before the Socialist International, New York City, October 9, 1990, p. 2.

CHAPTER 6: LABOR AND ECONOMIC DEVELOPMENT ABROAD

1. Irving Brown, "Europe Hopes for a 'New Deal' as ECA Reconstructs Economy," *New Leader*, vol. 32, no. 17 (1949).

2. Denis MacShane, *International Labor and the Origins of the Cold War* (Oxford: Clarendon Press, 1992), p. 93.

3. Report of proceedings of 1949 convention, p. 314.

4. Paul Johnson, *Modern Times: The World from the Twenties to the Eighties* (New York: Harper and Row, 1983), p. 581.

5. Ibid., p. 583.

6. Laqueur, *Europe in Our Time*, p. 82.

7. Irving Brown, "New Trends in European Labor," *New Leader*, December 6, 1954, p. 12.

8. Michael Balfour, *West Germany* (New York: Praeger, 1968), p. 177.

9. Irving Brown, "Europe 1952," *New Leader*, October 13, 1952, p. 7.

10. Paul G. Buchanan, "The Impact of U.S. Labor," in Abraham F. Lowenthal, ed., *Exporting Democracy: The United States and Latin America* (Baltimore: Johns Hopkins University Press, 1991), p. 309.

11. Walter Galenson, ed., *Labor and Economic Development* (New York: John Wiley and Sons, 1959), p. 8.

12. AFL-CIO, Clay Committee, "U.S. Labor Dissents, Free Trade Union," *Reports*, vol. 18 (Washington, D.C., April 1983).

13. Anne O. Krueger, *Economic Policy Reform in Developing Countries* (Cambridge: MIT Press, 1993).

14. Ibid., p. 25

15. Schlesinger, *A Thousand Days*, p. 610.

16. "Survey Asia: A Billion Consumers," *Economist*, October 30, 1993, p. 12.

17. Ezra F. Vogel, *The Four Little Dragons: The Spread of Industrialization in East Asia* (Cambridge: Harvard University Press, 1991), pp. 56–57.

18. See "Taiwan Survey," *Economist*, March 5, 1988, p. 14.

19. See "Survey South Korea," *Economist*, May 21, 1988, p. 20.

20. Harry Harding, *The American Enterprise*, May/June 1992; *China Labor Notes*, vol. 3, no. 7 (July 1992), p. 1, quoting *Far Eastern Economic Review*.

21. Kenneth Hutchinson, *China Labor Notes*, October 10, 1993.

22. See Walter Galenson, *Labor and Economic Growth in Five Asian Countries* (New York: Praeger, 1992), p. 53.

23. Ibid., p. 58.

24. Ibid., p. 59.

25. "Survey of Thailand," *Economist*, October 31, 1987, p. 6.

26. "Survey Indonesia," *Economist*, April 17, 1993, p. 3.

27. "Asia Survey," *Economist*, October 30, 1993, p. 14.

28. Mark Falcoff, *Modern Chile, 1970–1989: A Critical History* (New Brunswick: Transaction Publishers, 1989), pp. 20, 21.

29. David Gallagher, *The Chilean Experience in Development and Democracy* (Johannesburg: Urban Foundation, 1992), p. 8.

30. Ibid., pp. 10–11.

31. Elliott Abrams, "How to Avoid the Return of Latin Populism," *Wall Street Journal*, May 21, 1993, p. A3.

32. Kenneth Hatchinson and Garland Howell, "Asian Democracy," *Bulletin of the Department of International Affairs*, March 1993.

33. See Mark Falcoff, "Chile Is the Next Necessary Step in the Enterprise for the Americas Initiative," *Latin American Outlook*, August 1992, p. 2.

34. "Privatization: Cure-All or Swindle," *Bulletin of the International Affairs Department*, vol. 5, no. 9 (September 1990), p. 4.

35. Falcoff, "Chile Is the Next Necessary Step," p. 2.

36. "Privatization," p. 4.

37. Ibid., p. 5.

38. Ibid., p. 4.

39. Ibid.

40. Rudolph Oswald and William C. Doherty, "Executive Summary," *Latin American Labor and Structural Adjustments in the 90s: A Union View of Open Markets and a Worker Ownership Response* (1991), p. 29.

41. "A Survey of the World Economy," *Economist*, September 19, 1992, p. 18.

42. AFL-CIO statement at ICFTU Conference, San Jose, Costa Rica, October 31–November 1991, quoted in *Bulletin of the Department of International Affairs*, vol. 6, no. 12 (December 1991), p. 5.

43. William Doherty, testimony to the Committee on Foreign Affairs of U.S. House of Representatives, February 28, 1989, pp. 3–4.

44. Speech to Social Democrats U.S.A., reprinted in part as "Privatization: For the People or for the Capitalists?" *Bulletin of the Department of International Affairs*, March 1990.

45. Peter Drucker, "Trade Lessons from the World Economy," *Foreign Affairs*, January/February 1994.

46. Doherty, testimony, p. 3 in the Bulletin of the Department of International Affairs, February 28, 1989.

47. Conference on Labor Rights.

CHAPTER 7: THE STRUGGLE AGAINST FREE TRADE

1. George Meany, "American Trade Policy in the Free World," *International Free Trade Union News*, vol. 9, no. 1 (January 1954), p. 1.

2. David McDonald, "What American Steel Wants," *International Free Trade Union News*, May 1959, p. 1.

3. "Get America Back to Work," AFL-CIO, 1962.

4. Ibid.

5. For example, see *International Free Trade Union News*, November 1959, p. 6.

6. AFL-CIO, Department of Research, *AFL-CIO Looks at Foreign Trade: A Policy in the Sixties* (1961).

7. See executive council statement of August 13, 1963, reprinted in the *International Free Trade Union News*, September 1963.

8. AFL-CIO, Industrial Union Department, *The Developing Crisis in International Trade* (1970).

9. *American Federationist*, July 1972, p. 5.

10. Lane Kirkland, address to the Thirty-third Constitutional Convention of Bakery Workers, Toronto, July 12, 1990.

11. Lane Kirkland, address to 1985 convention, reprinted as *Meeting the Challenge of the Future*.

12. Memo from COPE, April 30, 1973, p. 1.

13. Michael Porter, *The Competitive Advantage of Nations* (New York: Free Press, 1990), p. 302.

14. Peter Drucker, *The Age of Discontinuity* (New York: Harper and Row, 1968), pp. 98–99.

15. William Lewis, "The Secret to Competitiveness," *Wall Street Journal*, October 22, 1993.

16. The United Automobile Workers is represented in only three foreign-owned assembly plants in the country; efforts to organize other plants have most often resulted in humiliating failure.

17. Peter Drucker, *Managing for the Future* (New York: Truman Talley Books/Plume, 1993), p. 31.

18. Ibid., p. 39.

19. See "How to Keep Exports on a Roll," *Fortune*, October 19, 1992, p. 68.

20. Ibid.

21. Lane Kirkland, *U.S. News and World Report*, August 8, 1977.

22. Anne Krueger, *Economic Policies at Cross Purposes* (Washington, D.C.: Brookings Institution, 1993), p. 107.

23. Jagdish Bhagwati, *Protectionism* (Cambridge: MIT Press, 1989), p. 3.

24. Ibid., p. 35.

25. AFL-CIO, "Foreign Trade and U.S. Jobs" (1971), pp. 1, 2.

26. Bhagwati, *Protectionism*, p. 51.

27. From James Bovard, *New York Times*, July 12, 1992, based on study by Donaldson, Lufkin, and Jenrette.

28. *Washington Post*, July 5, 1992.

29. *International Trade, Where We Stand*, AFL-CIO, 1992, pp. 11–12.

30. AFL-CIO, Task Force on Trade, "Labor Rights and Standards and NAFTA," February 14, 1993.

31. Jagdish Bhagwati, *World Trading System at Risk* (Princeton: Princeton University Press, 1991), p. 22.

32. Lane Kirkland, testimony on goals of U.S. trade policy before Senate Finance Committee, January 20, 1987.

33. Editorial, "For NAFTA," *New Republic*, vol. 209, no. 15 (October 11, 1993), p. 7.

34. *Exploiting Both Sides: U.S.-Mexico Free Trade*, AFL-CIO, February 1991, p. 1.

35. Ibid.

36. Lane Kirkland, "US-Mexico Trade Pact: A Disaster Worthy of Stalin's Worst," *Wall Street Journal*, April 18, 1991, p. A17.

37. "Mexican Workers Defend Border Jobs Targeted by NAFTA Critics," *Washington Post*, October 13, 1993, p. A24.

38. Lane Kirkland, press conference, August 3, 1993, p. 2.

39. Hufbauer, "NAFTA: Friend or Foe?" *New York Times*, November 15, 1993, p. A17.

40. Lane Kirkland, "A Backward Looking Deal," *Washington Post*, November 12, 1993, p. A25.

CHAPTER 8: LABOR AND AMERICAN VALUES

1. Samuel Gompers, *Seventy Years of Life and Labor*, p. 489.

2. Samuel Gompers, "Federationist," February 1914, in Marc Karson,

Labor Unions and Politics, 1900–1918 (Carbondale: Southern Illinois University Press, 1958).

3. Samuel Gompers, "Workers and the Eight Hour Day," in Louis Reed, *The Labor Philosophy of Samuel Gompers* (New York: Columbia University Press, 1930).

4. See Philip Taft, address to the Second Congress of the Pan-American Federation of Labor, 1921, in *The A.F. of L. in the Time of Gompers* (New York: Harper and Brothers, 1957), p. 326.

5. Harold Livesay, *Samuel Gompers and Organized Labor in America* (Boston: Little, Brown, 1970), p. 92.

6. Samuel Gompers, "Federationist 4/01," reprinted in Marc Karson, *American Labor Unions and Politics* (Carbondale: South Illinois University Press, 1958), pp. 138–39.

7. From Mark Karson and Ronald Radosh, *The American Federation of Labor and the Negro Worker, 1894–1949*, p. 159. All trades would have been more integrated had it not been for the trade unions. Unions contributed to the exclusion of blacks from trades merely by insisting that all workers receive the same wages. Since blacks, as a whole, were not as skilled workers and since employers operated in a racist environment, "for the same wages employers usually preferred white workers."

Also, by excluding blacks from membership and then signing closed-shop agreements with employers, unions prevented black workers from practicing their trade. Thus, "Negro craftsmen apparently fared better in the South than in the North after emancipation" and that was due in large measure to the A.F. of L. unions. In 1905, John R. Commons concluded that the plasterers, carpenters, masons, and painters unions admitted Negroes freely in the South but that few Northern plasterers unions and almost none of the other crafts accepted Negroes. The practice of racial exclusion then spread from the Northern to the Southern unions.

Gompers and other trade union leaders realized that discrimination against black workers contradicted their claim to represent the interests of the entire working class. But given the clear self-interest of white workers in preventing competition from blacks, the AFL craft unions that represented them resisted integration for as long as they could.

8. Karson, *Labor Unions and Politics*, p. 8.

9. Hayes Robbins, ed., *Labor and the Common Welfare* (New York: E. P. Dutton and Co., 1905) pp. 30–31.

10. Gompers, *Seventy Years*, p. 161.

11. Robbins, reprint of address to National Civic Federation, New York City, December 1905.

12. See Taft, *The A.F. of L. in the Time of Gompers*, p. 326.

13. See address to 1894 convention of the A.F. of L. in Taft, *The A.F. of L. in the Time of Gompers*, p. 303.

14. See Karson, p. 138, from *Proceedings of 1914 Convention of A.F. of L.*

15. Gompers, *Seventy Years*, p. 130.

16. See David A. Shannon, *The Socialist Party of America, A History* (New York: Macmillan, 1955).

17. From Bayard Rustin, *Down the Line, The Collected Writings of Bayard Rustin* (Chicago: Quandrangle Books, 1971), p. 341.

18. George Meany, 1959 AFL-CIO convention, San Francisco, September 1959, quoted in Jervis Anderson, *A. Philip Randolph, A Biographical Portrait* (New York: Harcourt Brace), p. 299.

19. Alan Draper, *Rope of Sand: The AFL-CIO Committee of Political Education 1959–67* (Westport, Conn.: Praeger, 1989), p. 78.

20. Ibid.

21. Lane Kirkland, address to labor luncheon of NAACP, July 1, 1980.

22. Rustin, *Down the Line*, p. 149.

23. Lane Kirkland, address to National Urban League, July 24, 1979.

24. Lane Kirkland, address to NAACP convention, Washington D.C., July 2, 1988.

25. Norman Hill, quoted in Social Democrats USA, *SD Notes*, Washington, D.C., September 1992, vol. 23, no. 8, p. 1.

26. "Congress and the Nation," *Congressional Quarterly*, 1969–1972, p. 11.

27. John Corry, "The Many Sided Mr. Meany," *Harpers*, March 1970, p. 56.

28. Donald Slaiman, debate with Herbert Hill, reprinted in *Congressional Record*, July 15, 1971, by Hon. James G. O'Hara.

29. United Steel Workers of America v. Weber, 443 U.S. 193 (1979).

30. 1984 AFL-CIO platform proposals to the Democratic and Republican conventions.

31. *The AFL-CIO and Civil Rights* (1992), p. 2.

32. Nathan Glazer, *Affirmative Discrimination, Ethnic Inequality and Public Policy* (New York: Basic Books, 1975), p. 52.

33. Ibid.

34. Joseph Epstein, *Blue-Collar Cicero: The World of the Blue-Collar Worker* (New York: Quadrangle Books, 1972), pp. 91–104, based on *Dissent*, winter 1972.

35. Jonathan Rieder, *Canarsie, The Jews and Italians of Brooklyn against Liberalism* (Cambridge: Harvard University Press, 1985).

36. See Thomas Byrnes Edsall with Mary D. Edsall, *The Impact of Race, Rights and Taxes on American Politics* (New York: W. W. Norton and Co., 1984), p. 21.

37. "Congress and the Nation," p. 517.

38. See Theodore H. White, *America in Search of Itself: The Making of the President 1956–80* (New York: Harper and Row, 1982), p. 121.

39. Jack Germond and Jules Witcover, "Who Cares What Lane Kirkland Thinks?" *Washingtonian*, June 1982, p. 98.

40. Rustin, *Down the Line*, p. 140.

41. George Will, *The Pursuit of Happiness and Other Sobering Thoughts* (New York: Harper and Row, 1978), p. 212.

42. Archie Robinson, *George Meany and His Times, A Biography* (New York: Simon and Schuster, 1981), p. 249.

43. Ibid.

44. *Executive Council Statement on Turmoil in Los Angeles*, adopted at meeting in Washington, D.C., May 5–6, 1992.

45. Lane Kirkland, New Media Labor Day Roundtables, September 1, 1992.

46. Lane Kirkland, statement on Los Angeles police jury verdict, April 30, 1992.

47. "The Untold Story of the LA Riot," *U.S. News and World Report*, May 31, 1993, p. 38.

48. Hugh Graham Davis, *The Civil Rights Era, Origins and Development of National Policy 1960–1972* (Cambridge: Oxford University Press, 1990), p. 211.

49. Rustin, *Down the Line*, p. 148.

50. Glazer, *Affirmative Discrimination*, p. 42.

51. Ibid., p. 41.

52. Lane Kirkland, remarks to the AFL-CIO 1992 General Board Meeting, Washington, D.C., September 3, 1992, p. 3.

53. 1968 AFL-CIO platform proposals to Republican and Democratic Party conventions.

54. Memo from COPE, "Welfare: Everybody's Whipping-Boy," February 5, 1973.

55. Report of the executive council to the 1985 convention, pp. 228, 229.

56. Charles Murray, *Losing Ground, American Social Policy 1950–1980* (New York: Basic Books, 1984), p. 207.

57. Gertrude Himmelfarb, *Marriage and Morals among the Victorians* (New York: Vintage Books, 1987), p. 37.

58. "Making Government Work," Public Employee Department, based on 1990 PED Conference, p. 3.

59. p. 5. Also note that Wurf was opposed to Carter's welfare reform, putting CETA workers on the public payroll at minimum wages, with no benefits, etc. See Goulden, p. 265.

60. "Unions Fear Job Losses in Welfare Reform," *Washington Post*, January 6, 1994, p. A25.

61. Douglas Besharov, "The End of Welfare as We Know It?" *The Public Interest*, spring 1993, pp. 104–5.

62. "Mr. Bush and New Jersey's Welfare," *New York Times*, February 3, 1992, p. A14.

63. *PED Forum*, vol. 8, no. 1 (winter 1992), p. 3.

64. See AFL-CIO, Public Employee Department, *Welfare Reform: Strategies for Successful Programs* (1989).

65. Ibid.

66. Urban Institute, "The Washington State Family Independence Program," October 1992.

67. Thomas B. Edsall with Mary B. Edsall, *Chain Reaction* (New York: Norton, 1991), p. 131.

68. Draper, *Rope of Sand,*

69. *Wall Street Journal*, July 17, 1967.

70. From Richard M. Scammon and Ben J. Wattenberg, *The Real Majority* (New York: Coward, McCann & Geooghegann, Inc., 1970), p. 195.

71. Al Barkan, "What the Unions Are Doing to Elect Their Friends," *U.S. News and World Report*, October 27, 1966, quoted in Alan Draper, *Rope of Sand*, p. 112.

72. Alan Draper, "Labor and the 1966 Elections," *Labor History*, vol. 13, no. 1 (winter 1989), p. 86.

73. Glazer, *Affirmative Discrimination*, p. 194.

74. From Corry, "The Many Sided Mr. Meany," p. 54.

75. Robinson, *George Meany*, pp. 322–23.

76. Theodore H. White, *The Making of the President 1972* (New York: Atheneum Publishers, 1973), p. 178.

77. *Washington Post*, September 9, 1982.

78. Charles Krauthammer, *Cutting Edges: Making Sense of the Eighties* (New York: Random House, 1985), p. 134.

79. Evelyn Dubrow, "Equal Rights Amendment Endangers U.S. Women's Gains," *International Free Trade Union News*, September 1970, p. 3.

80. *AFL-CIO Executive Council Statement on Reproductive Issues and Access to Medical Information*, adopted at meeting in Detroit, Michigan, November 9 and November 14, 1991.

81. Women's Leadership Committee for Workplace Fairness, *Justice for Women Workers: Achieving the American Dream* (1992).

82. *AFL-CIO and Civil Rights*, 1990, pp. 2, 7.

83. Will, *The Pursuit of Happiness*, pp. 55–56.

84. Lane Kirkland, address to AFL-CIO General Board Meeting, September 14, 1980.

CHAPTER 9: UNIONS AND THE POLITICAL ORDER

1. Archie Robinson, *George Meany and His Times* (New York: Simon and Schuster, 1981), p. 154.

2. Ibid., p. 91.

3. Daniel Bell, "Labor's New Men of Power," *Fortune*, June, 1953, p. 151.

4. Theodore H. White, *The Making of the President 1964* (New York: Atheneum, 1965), p. 287.

5. AFL-CIO convention proceedings, 1965, quoted in Alan Draper, *A Rope of Sand.*

6. Theodore H. White, *America in Search of Itself: The Making of the President 1956–80*, pp. 125, 126.

7. Robert H. Bork, *The Tempting of America: The Political Seduction of Law* (New York: Free Press, 1990), p. 348.

8. White, *America in Search of Itself*, p. 122.

9. see James Wooten, *Dasher.*

10. "Humphrey in Apology to McGovern in Debate," *New York Times*, p. 28.

11. Robinson, *George Meany*, p. 323.

12. George Meany, press conference, July 19, 1972.

13. Joshua Muravchik, "Why the Democrats Lost," *Commentary*, January 1985, p. 16.

14. *Report of the AFL-CIO Executive Council*, October 2, 1975.

15. Penn Kemble, "Who Needs the Liberals," *Commentary*, October 1970, pp. 64, 58.

16. David Broder, *Changing of the Guard: Power and Leadership in America* (New York: Simon and Schuster, 1980), p. 75.

17. Gary Hart, *The Good Fight, The Education of an American Reformer* (New York: Random House, 1993), p. 123.

18. George Will, *The Pursuit of Happiness*, p. 175.

19. William Schneider, "The November 4 Vote for President," in Austin Ranney, ed., *The American Elections of 1980* (Washington, D.C.: American Enterprise Institute, 1981), p. 227.

20. *Wall Street Journal*, March 8, 1979.

21. A. N. Raskin, "Reporter at Large: After Meany," *New Yorker*, August 25, 1980, p. 55.

22. Jack W. Germond and Jules Witcover, *Blue Smoke and Mirrors: How Reagan Won and Why Carter Lost the Election of 1980* (New York: Viking Press, 1981), pp. 49, 51, 147.

23. Schneider, "The November 4 Vote," p. 261.

24. See Michael J. Malbin, "The Conventions, Platforms and Issue Activists," in Austin Ranney, ed., *The American Elections of 1980* (Washington, D.C.: American Enterprise Institute, 1981), p. 137.

25. "Labor and the Democrats," *New York Times*, November 20, 1981.

26. Robert Kuttner, "Can Labor Lead?" *New Republic*, March 12, 1984, pp. 19, 25.

27. Jack W. Germond and Jules Witcover, *Wake Up When It's Over, Presidential Politics of 1984* (New York: Macmillan, 1985), pp. 42–43.

28. Joshua Muravchik, "Why the Democrats Lost," p. 17.

29. Ibid.

30. Jeane J. Kirkpatrick, "The American 80's: Disaster or Triumph," *Commentary*, vol. 90, no. 3 (September 1990), pp. 14–15.

31. *New York Times*, February 20, 1992.

32. Lawrence Mead, "The Democrats' Dilemma," *Commentary*, January 1992, p. 45.

CHAPTER 10: THE FAILURE OF LABOR ORGANIZING

1. Gompers from Hayes Robbins, *American Federationist*, November 1907, p. 15.

2. Samuel Gompers, address before the Chicago Conference on Trusts, *American Federationist*, October 1907, p. 882.

3. Lane Kirkland, remarks to the Conference on Economic Transition in Post-Communist States, Warsaw, Poland, November 16, 1992.

4. Derek Bok and John Dunlop, *Labor and the American Community* (New York: Simon and Schuster), pp. 57–58.

5. Walter Galenson, "The Historical Role of American Trade Unionism," in Seymour Martin Lipset, ed., *Unions in Transition* (San Francisco: Institute for Contemporary Studies, 1986), p. 43.

6. Holmes, Plant v. Holmes.

7. H. Gregg Lewis, "Wage Impact of Unions, 1929–1958," in Clark Kerr and Paul D. Staudohar, eds., *Economics of Labor in Industrial Society* (San Francisco: Jossey-Bass, 1986), p. 259.

8. Albert Rees, *The Economics of Trade Unions* (Chicago: University of Chicago Press, 1962), pp. 94, 96.

9. *Harvard Business Review*, September 1979, p. 39.

15. Herbert Croly, "Unionism and the National Interest," p. 98.

10. Milton Derber, "The Idea of Industrial Democracy in America: 1915–1935," *Labor History*, vol. 8, no. 1 (winter 1967), p. 21.

11. Louis M. Hacker, *The World of Andrew Carnegie 1865–1901* (Philadelphia: J. B. Lippincot, 1968), pp. 378–79.

12. Quoted in Mark Perlman, *A Theory of the Labor Movement*, p. 264.

13. Milton Derber, "The Idea of Industrial Democracy in America," pp. 14, 15.

14. Mark Perlman, *A Theory of the Labor Movement*, quoted in *Labor Union Theories in America* (Evanston, Ill.: Row Peterson, 1958), p. 197.

15. Peter F. Drucker, *The New Realities* (New York: Harper and Row, 1989), p. 189.

16. Selig Perlman and Philip Taft, *History of Labor in the United States* (New York: Macmillan, 1935), p. 159.

17. Richard Hofstadter, *The Age of Reform* (New York: Vintage Books, 1955), p. 241.

18. Ibid., p. 235.

19. Perlman and Taft, *History of Labor in the United States*, p. 490.

20. Rees, *The Economics of Trade Unions*, p. 96.

21. Thomas R. Brooks, *Toil and Trouble* (New York: Dell, 1964), p. 164.

22. Herbert Northrup and Gordon Bloom, *Government and Labor: The Role of Government in Union-Management Relations* (Homewood, Ill.: R. D. Irwin, 1963), p. 44.

23. Brody, *Workers in Industrial America*, p. 106.

24. Galenson, *The CIO Challenge*, p. 31.

25. David Dubinsky and A. H. Raskin, *David Dubinsky: A Life with Labor* (New York: Simon and Schuster, 1977), p. 234.

26. David Macdonald, *Union Man* (New York: Dutton, 1969), p. 146.

27. Galenson, *The CIO Challenge*, p. 519.

28. Ibid., p. 474.

29. Robert H. Zeigler, *John L. Lewis, Labor Leader* (Boston: Twayne), p. 105.

30. Ibid., p. 106.

31. R. W. Flemming, "The Significance of the Wagner Act," in Milton Derber and Edwin Young, *Labor and the New Deal* (Madison: University of Wisconsin Press, 1957), p. 133.

32. From Flemming, "Wagner," *New York Times*, Sunday, May 9, 1937.

33. Zeigler, *Lewis*, p. 101.

34. Dubinsky and Raskin, *Dubinsky*, quoting Jay Lovestone, p. 242.

35. C. Wright Mills, *The New Men of Power, America's Labor Leaders* (New York: Harcourt, Brace and Company, 1948), p. 41.

36. Joel Seidman, *American Labor from Defense to Reconversion* (Chicago: University of Chicago Press, 1953), pp. 69–70.

37. Seidman, *American Labor from Defense to Reconversion*, p. 243.

38. Ibid., p. 268.

39. See Samuel Lubell, *The Future of American Politics* (Garden City, N.J.: Doubleday, 1956).

40. Albert Rees, "The Size of Union Membership in Manufacturing in the 1980s," in Hervey A. Jervis and Myron Roomkin, eds., *The Shrinking Perimeter* (Lexington, Mass.: Lexington Books, 1980), p. 47.

41. Robert W. Crandall, "The Transformation of U.S. Manufacturing," *Industrial Relations*, vol. 25, no. 2 (spring 1986), p. 127.

42. "In Race to Outrun Recession, Southeast Sets Dazzling Pace," *New York Times*, November 27, 1992, p. A1.

43. "States Raise Stakes in Fight for Jobs," *New York Times*, October 4, 1993.

44. Robert W. Crandall, "Transformation of U.S. Manufacturing," p. 121.

45. Charles Heckscher, *The New Unionism: Employee Involvement in the Changing Corporation* (New York: Basic Books, 1988), p. 64.

46. *Harvard Business Review*, September 1979, p. 44–45.

47. Bell, citing *Fortune* survey showing most of concentrated industries organized.

48. Dubinsky and Raskin, *David Dubinsky*, pp. 66–67.

49. Ibid., p. 123.

50. Galenson, *The CIO Challenge*, p. 292.

51. Raskin, in Dubinsky and Raskin, *David Dubinsky*, p. 13.

52. Leo Troy, "The Rise and Fall of American Trade Unions: The Labor Movement from FDR to RR," in Seymour Martin Lipset, ed., *Unions in Transition* (ICS), p. 88.

53. David Brody, "Labor Crisis in Perspective," in George Strauss, Daniel G. Gallager, and Jack Fiorito, eds., *The State of the Unions* (Madison, Wis.: Industrial Relations Research Association, 1991), p. 302.

54. *New York Times*, August 2, 1993, p. D2.

55. Richard B. Friedman and James L. Medoff, *What Do Unions Do?* (New York: Basic Books, 1984), pp. 21–22.

56. Thomas A. Kochan, Harry C. Katz, and Robert B. McKensie, *Transformation of American Industrial Relations* (New York: Basic Books, 1986), p. 104.

57. Daniel K. Benjamin, "Combinations of Workmen," in Lipset, ed., *Unions in Transition*, p. 216.

58. *Industrial and Labor Relations Review*, review symposium, vol. 38, no. 2 (January 1985).

59. Barry Hirsch, *Labor Unions and the Economic Performance of Firms* (Kalamazoo: UpJohn Institute, 1991), p. 88.

60. According to the author, a fair interpretation of his work to date.

61. Conversation, March 16, 1994.

62. Barry Hisch and John Addison, *The Economic Analysis of Unions: New Approaches and Evidence* (Boston: Allen and Unwin, 1986).

63. Ibid.

64. Katz, *Labor Relations in the Auto and Other U.S. Industries*, p. 187.

65. "The Team Dream," *Economist*, September 5, 1992, p. 69.

66. "3,000 on Strike at G.M. Plant; 2d Labor Dispute in a Month," *New York Times*, September 24, 1992, quoting Maryann Keller.

67. From Charles C. Heckscher, *The New Unionism, Employee Involvement in the Changing Corporation* (New York: Basic Books, 1988), p. 92.

68. Robert J. LaLonde and Bernard Meltzer, "Hard Times for Unions: Another Look at the Significance of Employer Illegalities," *University of Chicago Law Review*, vol. 58 (1991), p. 1014.

69. Seymour Martin Lipset, "North American Labor Management: Perspectives," in Lipset, ed., *Unions in Transition*, quoting study by Laura Cooper, "Authorization Card and Union Representation Outcomes: An Empirical Assessment Underlying the Supreme Court's Gissel Decision," *Northwestern University Law Review*, vol. 79 (March 1984), pp. 139–140.

70. A. H. Raskin, "The Big Squeeze on Labor Unions," *Atlantic*, 1979 pp. 43–44.

71. Perlman and Taft, *History of Labor in the United States*, p. 159.

72. McKinsey Global Institute, *Manufacturing Productivity* (Washington, D.C. , 1993).

73. Kochan et al., *Transformation of American Industrial Relations*.

74. Ibid., chap. 3.

75. From Leo Troy, *Harvard Journal*, p. 596.

76. From Lipset, *Labor Pains*.

77. From Troy, *Harvard Journal*, p. 598; Henry Farber, "Trends in Worker Demand for Union Representation," National Bureau of Economic Research Working Paper 2857, February 1989; also see Samuel Estreicher, "Employee Voice in Competitive Markets," *American Prospect*, summer 1993, p. 49, citing Henry Farber and Alan Krueger on decline of union density from 1977 to 1991.

78. Leo Kramer, *Labor's Paradox: The State, County, and Municipal Employees, AFL-CIO* (New York: John Wiley, 1962), p. 340.

79. "Talking Tough to Public Workers," *Business Week*, April 27, 1981, p. 103.

80. David Lewin, "Public Employee Unionism, and Labor Relations in the 1980s: An Analysis of Transformation," in Seymour Martin Lipset, ed., *Unions in Transition, Entering the Second Century* (San Francisco: Institute for Contemporary Studies, 1986), p. 261.

81. "The Public Sector Strikes Back," *Newsweek*, September 18, 1978, p. 127.

82. Richard C. Kearney, *Labor Relations in the Public Sector*, 2nd ed. (New York: Marcel Dekker, Inc., 1992), p. 189.

83. Joseph C. Goulden, *Jerry Wurf, Labor's Last Angry Man* (New York: Atheneum, 1982), pp. 122, 234.

84. Paul Glastris, "On Politics: A Democrat's Tough-Love Lessons," *U.S. News and World Report*, October 5, 1990, p. 46.

85. Robert Lenzner "The Philadelphia Story," *Forbes*, 1992, p. 54.

86. Editorial, "A Missed Opportunity on City Labor," *New York Times*, November 9, 1992.

87. John Sweeney, remarks to the Association for a Better New York, December 6, 1995.

88. John Sweeney, *America Needs a Raise: Fighting for Economic Security and Social Justice* (New York: Houghten Mifflin Co., 1996), p. 80.

89. Ibid., p. 3.

90. Nelson Lichtenstein and Steven Fraser, "New Life for the Labor Movement," *Washington Post*, December 31, 1995.

91. Andy Levin, "Aiming to Make '96 the 'The Summer of Labor,' " *Foward*, June 7, 1996.

92. James K. Glassman, "Jobs: The (Woe Is) Me Generation," *Washington Post*, March 19, 1996.

93. Robert Samuelson, "News Cut to Fashion," *Washington Post*, March 13, 1996.

94. Amity Shlaes, "A National Case of the Jitters," *Wall Street Journal*.

95. See Amity Shlaes, "Doom, Gloom, and the Middle Class," *Commentary*, February 1996, p. 22.

96. Ibid.

Index

Abel, I. W., 126
Abortion, 117–19
Abrams, Elliot, 86
Addams, Jane, 141
Affirmative action, 106–7, 131
AFL-CIO
  A. Philip Randolph Institute, 105
  actions in El Salvador, 68–69
  anticommunism of, 7, 67
  Asian-American Free Labor Institute, 85–86
  backing of trade union movement in El Salvador, 68–69
  Central America, 67–70
  civil rights position, 10
  concern related to imports (1960s), 91
  Defense Committee positions, 71–73
  drift to the left, 3
  endorsement of Mondale (1984), 132
  Industrial Union Department, 26, 90–91
  International Affairs Department, 88
  lack of support for cold war foreign policy, 73
  as member of ICFTU, 50–51
  merger, 4–5, 122, 152
  opposition to privatization, 87–88
  position on abortion, 118–19
  position on economic reform in Latin America, 86–87
  postmerger growth, 20
  post–World War II support for free trade, 90–91, 94
  Public Employee Department, 37–38, 114
  role in Guatemalan coup (1954), 61–62
  role in Polish workers' struggle, 74
  shift in position on defense spending, 70–73
  Vietnam, 65–66
  See also American Federation of Labor (AFL); Congress of Industrial Organizations (CIO)
AFSCME. *See* American Federation of State, County, and Municipal Employees (AFSCME)
Allende, Salvador, 85, 86
American Federation of Labor (AFL)
  anticommunism of, 7, 50, 54–55
  concern related to the environment, 29–31
  discrimination policies, 9–10
  exclusionary practices, 101–3
  Force Ouvière in France, 54
  influence of New Deal policies on, 16
  merger with CIO (1955), 4–5, 122, 152
  objectives of founders, 3
  position on abortion, 118
  position on independence for Algeria, 59

About the Author

MAX GREEN was the executive director of the Young Peoples Socialist League for three years and the special representative for the United Federation of Teachers in New York City. He was the assistant staff director at the U.S. Commission on Civil Rights from 1983 to 1985 and the associate director of the White House Office of Public Liaison from 1985 to 1988.

Mr. Green was a consultant on international issues and is a financial and investment adviser. His articles on labor-related issues have appeared in *Policy Review* and in the *Wall Street Journal*.

The author earned a law degree from Brooklyn College and an M.A. from the New School for Social Research.

A NOTE ON THE BOOK

This book was edited by Ann Petty
of the publications staff
of the American Enterprise Institute.
The index was prepared by Shirley Kessel.
The text was set in New Century Schoolbook.
Coghill Composition Company,
of Richmond, Virginia, set the type,
and Edwards Brothers Incorporated,
of Lillington, North Carolina,
printed and bound the book,
using permanent acid-free paper.

The AEI Press is the publisher for the American Enterprise Institute for Public Policy Research, 1150 Seventeenth Street, N.W., Washington, D.C., 20036; *Christopher C. DeMuth,* publisher; *Dana Lane,* director; *Ann Petty,* editor; *Leigh Tripoli,* editor; *Cheryl Weissman,* editor; *Jennifer Lesiak,* editorial assistant.